D1602726

SUSPECT COMMUNITIES

SUSPECT COMMUNITIES

Anti-Muslim Racism and the Domestic War on Terror

NICOLE NGUYEN

 University of Minnesota Press | Minneapolis | London

Published by the University of Minnesota Press
111 Third Avenue South, Suite 290
Minneapolis, MN 55401-2520
http://www.upress.umn.edu

The University of Minnesota is an equal-opportunity educator and employer.

Library of Congress Cataloging-in-Publication Data
Names: Nguyen, Nicole, author.
Title: Suspect communities : anti-Muslim racism and the domestic war on terror / Nicole Nguyen.
Description: Minneapolis : University of Minnesota Press, [2019] | Includes bibliographical references and index. |
Identifiers: LCCN 2018061113 (print) | ISBN 978-1-5179-0639-9 (hc) | ISBN 978-1-5179-0640-5 (pb)
Subjects: LCSH: Terrorism—Prevention—United States. | Islamophobia—United States. | Islamic fundamentalism—United States. | Muslims—Civil rights—United States.
Classification: LCC HV6432 .N555 2019 (print) | DDC 363.325/170973—dc23
LC record available at https://lccn.loc.gov/2018061113

CONTENTS

ACKNOWLEDGMENTS

Like all projects, this book would not have been possible without the labor and love of so many people. I am humbled by all those who contributed to, supported, and sustained this work. Of course, any shortcomings remain my own, although I hope I have done some justice by those who gave their time, ideas, and love.

I am indebted to the national security policymakers, practitioners, and scholars who provided insight into their daily work. Though they cannot be named here, I learned so much from our time together and their perspectives continue to shape my thinking, in and through our discussions, disagreements, and deliberations. I am grateful for the time they gave, the debates they inspired, and the stories they shared about the possibilities and limitations of contemporary security regimes.

Although this project began as an exploration into the lifeworlds of national security workers, I quickly encountered thriving organizing communities working to end the criminalization of Muslim youth. I appreciated the opportunity to learn from and contribute to these efforts. The nuanced perspectives, critiques, and organizing of activists enhanced this book's analysis and my research's role in the movement to end targeted criminalization. I hope I did this work ethically and with humility.

Local coconspirators offered intellectual engagement and encouragement through the UIC Race and U.S. Empire Working Group, Teachers for Social Justice, Communities against Surveillance, and other incubators of critical praxis in Chicago. I especially thank Iván Arenas, Andy Clarno, Rod Ferguson, Rico Gutstein, Kim Lawless,

Patrisia Macías-Rojas, Nadine Naber, Akemi Nishida, Marlynne Nishimura, and Atef Said. Pauline Lipman and David Stovall offered support, clarity, and reprieve from the constant assault on critical scholarship that continues to define the neoliberal academy. Stacey Krueger contributed immensely to this research project by conducting interviews, providing sharp analyses, and pushing me to think and act more critically. Erik Love and Lisa Stampnitzky provided important critiques that strengthened my analyses. Sari Knopp Biklen taught me to think like an ethnographer and remains ever-present in my work.

I also thank my students whose scholarship has enhanced my own: L. Boyd Bellinger, Nico Darcangelo, Chris Emerling, Glenance Green, Cecily Relucio Hensler, Aja Reynolds, Hafsa Siddiqui, Jessica Suarez, Gia Super, and Asif Wilson. Each year, graduate students in my Criminalization of Youth in Urban Schools class deepen, challenge, and enliven my thinking. Thank you.

Further afield, community organizers and scholar-activists challenged me and held me accountable: Fatema Ahmad, Shannon Al-Wakeel, Mike German, Gerald Hankerson, Bri Hanny, August Hastings, Arifa Ibrahim, Zareen Kamal, Nesreen Hasan, Faiza Patel, Sangeetha Ravichandran, Muhammad Sankari, Debbie Southorn, Sue Udry, Yusuf Vidal, Lesley Williams, Mary Zerkel, and so many others from the #StopCVE coalition. News reporters Aaron Leibowitz and Alex Ruppenthal filed Freedom of Information Act requests and provided additional data vital to this project.

I wrote this book at the same time I began running and I owe a debt of gratitude to Chandni Desai, Alison Mountz, Jackie Orr, and all those who taught me how to find time for health, healing, and happiness within academic life. Many thanks to R. Tina Catania, Dan Cohen, Sol Gamsu, Alice Huff, Emily Kaufman, Amrit Kaur, Elizabeth Kubis, Yasmin Ortiga, Megan Scanlon, and Julia Snider, whose constant friendship helped sustain this work.

At the University of Minnesota Press, I thank editorial director Jason Weidemann, editorial assistant Gabriel Levin, assistant managing editor Mike Stoffel, and the many others who worked hard to finish this book. I also thank Doug Easton, who developed the index.

I am grateful for the administrative staff at University of Illinois–Chicago, especially Alejandra Cantero, Karen Dop, Sharon Earthely, and Adrienne Gilg, whose invisible labor and hallway chats supported the development of this book.

And finally, many thanks to my parents, Eric, and Kristin—and to Eleanor, who has brought so much joy to our lives.

INTRODUCTION
Defining the Enemy Within

In September 2015, ninth-grade student Ahmed Mohamed brought a homemade clock to his U.S. public high school. As a robotics enthusiast, Ahmed proudly showed his engineering teacher his latest invention, complete with a circuit board and digital display. Ahmed's English teacher, however, later confiscated the clock and reported him to school administration. The principal escorted Ahmed to his office, where five police officers questioned him for ninety minutes. Believing the clock was a "hoax bomb," the police arrested Ahmed and transported him to a juvenile detention facility for fingerprinting and additional questioning (Selk 2015). Ahmed's story illustrates how anti-Muslim racism affixes the "terrorist" label to students perceived to be Muslim. Governing national security policies and discourses infused with anti-Muslim racism shaped how school staff responded to Ahmed as a potential terrorist.[1]

Ahmed's experience fits into broader national security fears, anxieties, and practices that position youth as incipient terrorists. The U.S. Federal Bureau of Investigation (FBI) (2016d), for example, warns that "high school students are ideal targets for recruitment by violent extremists seeking support for their radical ideologies, foreign fighter networks, or conducting acts of targeted violence within our borders" (1). Given this framing of students, the FBI cautions that "high schools must remain vigilant in educating their students about catalysts that drive violent extremism and the potential consequences of embracing extremist beliefs" (1). Moreover, the FBI calls on teachers, guidance counselors, and other social service providers to "observ[e] and assess[] concerning behaviors and communications" indicative of "students embracing extremist ideologies and progressing on a trajectory toward violence" (3). Much like the growth of high school homeland security programs, the FBI's call places teachers on the frontlines of the global war on terror.

Just a few months before Ahmed's arrest, President Obama convened a global summit where he formally introduced a new "countering violent extremism" (CVE) initiative to facilitate "community-oriented approaches to counter hateful extremist ideologies that radicalize, recruit, or incite to violence" (Office of the Press Secretary 2015, para. 1). Increasingly concerned about "homegrown terrorists," the Obama administration promoted CVE as a new national security strategy to deter young people from joining "violent extremist" groups like the Islamic State of Iraq and Syria (ISIS) without abrogating their constitutional rights. The Obama administration designed CVE with the understanding that communities "are best placed to recognize and confront the threat" and therefore should serve as critical partners in "efforts to combat violent extremist ideologies and organizations that seek to weaken our society" (White House 2011, 3). In this new national security model, community members act as key national security operatives tasked with countering terrorist propaganda as well as identifying, reporting, and working with individuals perceived to be at risk of or in the process of radicalizing.

The CVE model has mobilized social service providers like Ahmed's teachers as coproducers of national security in the domestic war on terror. In addition, local, state, and federal officials have called on "American Muslims," "Somali-Americans," "U.S. minorities," "refugees and immigrants," and "cities with significant Muslim Diasporas" to protect their children from terrorist radicalization by contributing to CVE programming.[2] Working from the premise that Muslim, immigrant, and other nondominant youth are uniquely susceptible to terrorist radicalization, CVE actors have argued that this coproduction of national security offers a progressive alternative to conventional counterterrorism methods like FBI stings, preemptive prosecutions, and indefinite detention.

To develop this model, U.S. security experts used the United Kingdom's comprehensive antiterrorism portfolio, CONTEST, as a blueprint for countering violent extremism in the United States

(Thomas 2010). Launched in 2003, CONTEST relies on a four-pronged approach to combat terrorism: Pursue, Prevent, Protect, and Prepare. The Pursue, Protect, and Prepare initiatives work to prosecute terrorists, increase hard security measures like border enforcement, and mitigate the impact of a terrorist attack, respectively.[3] To support these counterterrorism measures, Prevent strives to win the "hearts and minds" of British Muslims who "share core British values" and "stand up to terrorists and their extremist supporters" (U.K. Department for Communities and Local Government 2007). To stymie violent extremism, Prevent seeks to counter terrorist recruitment, persuade British Muslims to reject violence, identify and support individuals vulnerable to radicalization, and gather intelligence on Muslim communities.

To carry out Prevent, the United Kingdom has called on social service providers to detect and report individuals vulnerable to, or in the process of, radicalizing. Prevent's Duty Guidance, for example, requires teachers and childcare providers to refer students to the government's deradicalization program, Channel, if students express "vocal or active opposition to fundamental British values, including democracy, the rule of law, and mutual respect and tolerance for those with different faiths and beliefs" (Her Majesty's Government 2015, 19). Legal scholars, civil rights advocates, and community members have contested Prevent, especially after teachers began reporting Muslim youth for benign discussions, behaviors, and political debates in the classroom. In a shocking but familiar incident, nursery staff referred a four-year-old Muslim child to Channel after he mispronounced the word *cucumber* as "cucker bum." Nursery staff interpreted this mispronunciation as "cooker bomb" and therefore completed a government "Early Help Assessment" form, writing that the child's drawings "have previously had violent tendencies" (Prevent Watch 2016). The child's mother, however, explained that her son enjoyed watching *Power Rangers* and other popular media featuring superheroes, which informed his artwork (Prevent Watch 2016). Despite growing opposition to these referrals that disproportionately have targeted Muslim children, the Prevent program informed the design of the U.S. countering violent extremism policy framework. Like Prevent, CVE has served as one component of a multipronged approach to combatting terrorism.[4]

Informed by Prevent, CVE initiatives intend to (1) counter online extremist propaganda, (2) identify individuals vulnerable to terrorist radicalization, (3) intervene in a "person's pathway to radicalization before the line of criminal activity is crossed," (4) rehabilitate and reintegrate individuals convicted of terrorism-related crimes or returning from combat with a violent extremist organization, and (5) prevent or "build resilience to" violent extremism through the provision of social services like culturally relevant counseling, soccer leagues, and religious training (Department of Homeland Security 2015, 2). Like Prevent, CVE has mobilized social service providers and community members as the "eyes and ears" and "foot soldiers" on the frontlines of the domestic war on terror (participant observation, October 27, 2017).

This national security approach has involved both "prevention" and "intervention" lines of effort. In the CVE policy environment, "prevention" refers to the proactive measures that "seek, as much as possible, to stop extremism and a pathway toward violence from arising in the first place" (Muslim Public Affairs Council 2014, 35). At the time of my fieldwork, these proactive community-wide measures included counter-messaging campaigns to thwart terrorist propaganda, after-school activities like youth soccer leagues to reduce feelings of disaffection and alienation, family programs to increase "parental involvement and supportive adult mentorship for youth," and civic participation initiatives to "tap into that youthful energy" and "channel [it] in a positive direction" rather than toward an extremist group (Muslim Public Affairs Council 2014, 42; Susan Bailey, participant observation, May 16, 2017). These preemptive programs have worked to prevent youth from radicalizing.

To support this mission, the FBI (2016b) developed Don't Be a Puppet: Pull Back the Curtain on Violent Extremism, a preventative online learning module to "keep young people . . . from embracing violent extremist ideologies." The FBI describes Don't Be a Puppet as "an interactive website designed to educate teenagers on the destructive and deceptive reality of violent extremism and to strengthen their resistance to self-radicalization and possible recruitment." Through Don't Be a Puppet, young people learn to define violent extremism, recognize extremist propaganda, and identify "where to get help" if they know someone "in trouble." These efforts have sought to prevent radicalization before extreme ideas take root.

Unlike prevention programs, intervention efforts have focused on individuals identified as already "'at the edge' of going down a path of violence, or moving dangerously close to it" (Muslim Public Affairs Council 2014, 56). The Muslim Public Affairs Council (2014), for example, encouraged communities to develop "crisis inquiry teams" to reach "troubled individuals" (62). Composed of imams, social workers, mental health professionals, teachers, law enforcement officials, and lawyers, these crisis inquiry teams identify individuals perceived to be vulnerable to or in the process of radicalizing and then conduct interventions like mental health treatment to "off-ramp" individuals from the pathway toward violent extremism. These teams intervene in the lives of young people when they exhibit the perceived indicators, risk factors, or early warning signs of violent extremism.

In addition to Don't Be a Puppet, the federal government has allocated millions of dollars to support local CVE programs. Across the United States, city officials have used these funds to develop their own programs, often in partnership with other federal, state, and local entities like community organizations, school districts, and law enforcement agencies. Despite shared goals, cities have created and implemented different types of programs, depending on local understandings of CVE, available resources, level of community trust and participation, and demographics.

In Minneapolis, the U.S. Attorney led the development of CVE initiatives to "build resilience to violent extremism" through Somali community organizations and public schools while Rochester Institute of Technology students focused more broadly on Muslim communities in upstate New York through social media messaging that countered extremist propaganda (United States Attorney's Office of Minneapolis 2015; Rochester Institute of Technology 2016).[5] In Chicago, CVE actors mobilized mental health professionals to identify and work with individuals "who exhibit warning signs of radicalization," while Los Angeles officials developed more robust community policing practices to prevent homegrown terrorism (Illinois Criminal Justice Information Authority 2016, 2; Los Angeles Interagency Coordination Group in collaboration with community stakeholders 2015). Local conditions, therefore, have shaped the types of programming each city has developed, creating an uneven but connected geography of CVE initiatives that articulate with context-specific racial hierarchies, social histories, and institutional arrangements.

Despite the rapid proliferation of CVE programs across the United States, military experts, legal scholars, social scientists, and global leaders disagree on the benefits, harms, and effects of CVE programs. Like the FBI, some contend that CVE is the most effective strategy to combat the perceived rise of "homegrown terrorism" while safeguarding constitutional rights. Amnesty International's Naureen Shah (2014b), however, warns that although the CVE approach "may sound innocuous," it "sets American Muslim teenagers apart, stigmatizes them as potential terrorists, and drives a dividing line between them and their non-Muslim peers" (para. 5). In a statement endorsing CVE, United Nations Secretary-General Ban Ki-moon (2016) expressed similar concerns, cautioning against "mindless policy" that "turn[s] people against each other, alienate[s] already marginalized groups, and play[s] into the hands of the enemy" (para. 11). By accelerating stigmatization, some worry that CVE programs both harm Muslim communities in the United States and fuel the very drivers of extremism they aim to combat.[6]

Despite these concerns, some Muslim leaders have welcomed CVE as an alternative to more coercive antiterrorism programs typically deployed without community input or oversight. Others have cautioned that such collaborations have used Muslim leaders to intensify anti-Muslim policing, surveillance, and monitoring while appearing attentive to the civil liberties of targeted communities. These conflicting interpretations of CVE's impetuses and implications have generated distrust, hostility, and resistance within communities, a defining feature that CVE actors have negotiated in their everyday work.

Toward a Critical Analysis of CVE

Given these competing narratives about the benefits and harms of CVE programming, I embarked on a two-year interpretive qualitative study to learn how CVE actors negotiated these contentious debates, responded to community concerns, and justified their controversial work. I traveled across the United States to participate in CVE trainings, workshops, and conferences; observe anti-CVE events; interview policymakers, practitioners, and community leaders; conduct a document analysis of CVE texts like formal policies and informal white papers; and contribute to a coalition of organizers working to end the criminalization of Muslim communities. Through this fieldwork, I came to understand CVE from the perspectives of those most closely affected by this new national security approach.

As a critical policy studies scholar conducting qualitative research, I understand the policy field to be "a socially structured and discursively constituted space, marked by institutional heterogeneity and contending forces" (Peck and Theodore 2012, 23). I also view policy actors and actions as historically embedded, politically mediated, and sociologically complex. Given these understandings, I locate CVE within the broader social, political, cultural, and economic contexts that have organized national security norms, practices, and effects.

Informed by this methodological orientation and corresponding fieldwork, this book examines how CVE actors have worked to increase community control over domestic antiterrorism programs while advancing a framework that has criminalized anyone perceived to be Muslim. By exploring how CVE actors made sense of and justified this contradiction, I investigate how the struggle to make domestic security regimes more liberal—"participatory," "community-driven," and "democratic"—has intensified racialized surveillance, policing, and confinement (Melamed 2011; Khalili 2013). More specifically, I examine how the U.S. security state's mobilization of community leaders and social service providers as proxy national security agents charged with identifying, reporting, and working with individuals vulnerable to violent extremism has increased, not mitigated, racial profiling, coercive policing, and political exclusion.

Through this exploration, I argue that, to gain support for this racialized state project that casts Muslims as both terrorist threats and coproducers of public safety, the U.S. security state has incorporated Muslim leaders into the domestic war on terror. By offering political representation and cultural recognition through CVE collaborations, the U.S. security state has bolstered support for the very institutions that historically have criminalized Muslim communities. This pursuit of increasing Muslim participation in the domestic war on terror to attenuate racial and religious profiling, by design, has distracted from an "active politics of transformation" (Melamed 2011, 93). "Multicultural agendas focused on recognition and representation," after all, "obscure the everyday forms of domination and exploitation internal to the normal politics of cultural pluralism that stabilize racialized capitalist democracy" (123). Through CVE programming, the U.S. security state has managed community objections to the domestic war on terror while enhancing its capacity to criminalize Muslims as incipient terrorists.

These tactics draw from the state management of other political dissidents seeking to dismantle, rather than reform, systems of oppression. During the mid-twentieth century Black freedom struggle, for example, some Black organizers "tempered" their political goals in response to the federal government's unrelenting Counterintelligence Program (COINTELPRO) and assassinations of Malcolm X and Martin Luther King Jr. (K.-Y. Taylor 2016, 83). Facilitated by the coercive pressure exerted on Black political organizers, this shift represented a "pragmatic turn" toward guaranteeing Black civil rights as a "'realistic' alternative to the grassroots freedom struggle" (83, 102). The persistence of anti-Black poverty, police brutality, food insecurity, and educational inequities, however, demonstrates the limitations of political inclusion and cultural recognition as viable paths toward Black liberation.

Since the late 1960s, Canadian political leaders similarly have shifted from a "more or less unconcealed structure of domination" that sought the dispossession and eventual elimination of Indigenous peoples to a "form of governance that works through the medium of state recognition and accommodation" (Coulthard 2014, 25). Affirming the value of Indigenous life, cultures, and limited self-governance, however, "remains structured by a hegemonic framework that treats the relationship between settlers and Indigenous peoples as nation-to-subaltern culture, and thus committed to attenuating—preventing—the renewed nation-to-nation status" (Shaw and Coburn 2017, para. 2). Through these arrangements, "the rusty cage [of colonialism] may be broken, but a new chain has been strung around the Indigenous neck; it offers more room to move, but it still ties our people to white men pulling on the strong end" (Alfred 2008, xiii).

Political recognition has reformulated, rather than addressed, the dispossession of Indigenous peoples and maintained state power. As these examples illustrate, North American states have developed both liberal and illiberal methods to temper political dissent while reaffirming their power and domination over dispossessed populations. Despite these lessons, liberal struggles from gay marriage to land treaties "all too often agitate for recognition, thus inviting additive responses that are not of capable of transforming systems of power and oppression" (Meiners 2016, 97). Recognition, however, "is not an insignificant demand" as "to be seen, to be valued, and to be recognized are powerful affectively and, potentially, politically" (97). Yet organizing to "be understood and recognized by institutions and structures that have historically harmed, erased, or ignored these communities" does not lead to the reconstitution of power, the end of targeted criminalization, or freedom and justice (97). This means that the drive for Muslim recognition by, and integration into, the U.S. political establishment reinforces rather than disrupts contemporary racial hierarchies and national security regimes that harm Muslim communities and articulate with anti-Black, anti-Brown, and anti-immigrant policing.

Furthermore, I argue that by posing as a community-driven alternative to coercive counterterrorism practices like FBI stings, CVE has functioned as a "reformist reform" that maintains state power while appearing to solve the problems of governmental overreaching, spying, and intelligence gathering. A reformist reform like gay marriage leaves intact institutions of state violence by "reject[ing] those objectives and demands—however deep the need for them—which are incompatible with the system" (Gorz 1967, 7). Although the recognition conferred by the state through gay marriage provides important rights and protections, it does not contest the violences imposed by institutionalized heteropatriarchy, including the police killings of transgender women of color (Ritchie 2017). Similarly, "building a jail for transgender people is a form of recognition, but this difference strengthens and builds systems that continue to harm communities" (Meiners 2016, 99). Non-reformist reforms like the deinstitutionalization of marriage and prison abolition, however, "reduce the power of an oppressive system while illuminating the system's inability to solve the crises it creates" (Berger, Kaba, and Stein 2017, para. 3).

Non-reformist reforms strive to eradicate, not improve, institutions of state violence, without appealing to the state to adjudicate justice. Conforming to reformist reforms, CVE actors sought liberal solutions to anti-Muslim national security policies like promoting Muslim advocates to political office, collaborating on national security initiatives, and policing more radical forms of political dissent. As former DHS senior policy advisor Sahar Aziz (2015) explains, "In allying with the government, these leaders believe they can restrain government overreaching through established relationships that over time educate government officials that the overwhelming majority of Muslims in America do not support terrorism." To rein in the domestic war on terror, some Muslims willingly "comply with the very structures of law enforcement that demonize and devastate their constituencies" and "act according to the archetype of the palatable Muslim American, practicing its faith within the contours of US respectability" (Kazi 2017, paras. 15–17). These institutional arrangements, however, "produce[] an unspoken quid pro quo" whereby the protection of civil liberties and the provision of social services depends on Muslim cooperation with the security state "beyond what is expected of any other communities within America" (Aziz 2015). Although these transactional agreements affirm Muslim cultural identities and facilitate their greater inclusion into U.S. society, they do not redistribute power or dismantle the institutions, discourses, and logics that criminalize Muslim communities.

Because these political contexts are not overdetermining, this book also explores how CVE actors negotiated dominant discourses and institutional arrangements forged in the name of national security. Sociologist Avery Gordon (1997) reminds us that "even those who live in the most dire circumstances possess a complex and oftentimes contradictory humanity and subjectivity that is never adequately glimpsed by viewing them as victims or, on the other hand, as superhuman agents" (4). This analysis thus offers a mediation on the intentions, effects, and contradictions of CVE policies and practitioners, taking seriously the complex and often fraught contexts that organize national security work.

Given these arguments, I ultimately contend that studying CVE provides insight into how the drive to bring liberal reforms to contemporary security regimes through "community-driven" and "ideologically ecumenical" programming has further institutionalized anti-Muslim racism in the United States. More specifically, I argue that the U.S. security state has designed CVE to legitimize and shore up support for the very institutions that historically have criminalized, demonized, and dehumanized communities of color, while appearing to learn from and attenuate past practices of coercive policing, racial profiling, and political exclusion. CVE therefore has functioned as an additive reform incapable of transforming oppressive systems and invested in maintaining state power. By undertaking this analysis, this book offers a window into the inner workings of the U.S. security state and provides new understandings of anti-Muslim racism, documenting openings ripe for political contestation and reimaginations.

Reframing Islamophobia as Anti-Muslim Racism

On September 20, 2001, President George W. Bush addressed Congress in the aftermath of the September 11 attacks. In his remarks, Bush (2001a) declared that "the enemy of America is not our many Muslim friends. It is not our many Arab friends. Our enemy is a radical network of terrorists and every government that supports them." Under the direction of President Bush, however, the Department of Justice (DOJ) issued a 2003 fact sheet that ordered a ban on racial profiling, except for the purposes of "terrorist identification" (5). If, for example, "U.S. intelligence sources report that Middle Eastern terrorists are planning to use commercial jetliners as weapons by hijacking them at an airport in California during the next week," DOJ guidelines permitted security personnel to subject "men appearing to be of Middle Eastern origin" to "heightened scrutiny" (Department of Justice 2003, 6). President Bush authorized racial profiling for the purposes of national security simultaneous to his affirmation that "the enemy of America is not our many Muslim friends."

Echoing Bush's 2001 remarks fifteen years later, the U.S. Department of Homeland Security (DHS) called for the rejection of any language that "promotes an 'us and them' narrative of division," including "jihad," "sharia," and "Muslim world" (Homeland Security Advisory Council 2016, 13). Under the Obama administration, DHS suggested that these shifts in vocabulary militated against terrorist recruitment fueled by the charge that the West is at war with Islam (12–13). At the same time, the FBI's (2016a) racial profiling guidance referred to "the reality of common ethnicity, race, religion, or national origin among criminal and terrorist groups" (4–12). This reality permitted the use of racial profiling if such consideration was "relevant to an identified criminal incident, scheme, or organization" (4–13).[7] One law enforcement official, for example, expressed the need for a "well-balanced all-hazards approach" to national security while noting his agency's "bias right now" with "the Muslim kind of concept" (personal communication, November 8, 2016). Like Bush, Obama affirmed Muslim communities while authorizing racial profiling in the name of national security.

The 2016 U.S. presidential election ruptured the thin veil masking the nation's deeply entrenched anti-Muslim sentiments, policies, and practices. In March 2016, for example, presidential candidate Donald Trump stated, "I think Islam hates us. There's something there that—there's tremendous hatred there." A few days later, Trump responded to three suicide bombings in Belgium by commenting, "We're having problems with the Muslims, and we're having problems with Muslims coming into the country" (as quoted in Johnson and Hauslohner 2017). These narratives strategically conflated Islam with terrorism and revivified the racist clash of civilizations thesis that naturalizes the "Muslim world" as an existential threat to the West (Huntington 1996).

This charged anti-Muslim rhetoric has been institutionalized through President Trump's policies, including his two *Protecting the Nation from Foreign Terrorist Entry into the United States* executive orders and *Enhancing Vetting Capabilities and Processes for Detecting Attempted Entry into the United States by Terrorists or Other Public-Safety Threats* presidential proclamation (colloquially known as Muslim Bans 1.0, 2.0, and 3.0).[8] By temporarily suspending the entry of immigrants from predominately Muslim countries in the name of national security, President Trump reinforced racist fears that Muslim immigrants posed a unique and imminent terrorist threat, despite continued mass shootings carried out by white, U.S.-born young men. As these policies illustrate, "the projection of danger onto what is already recognizable as different—as different from the familiar space of home and homeland—allows violence to take place:

INTRODUCTION 13

it becomes a mechanism for the enforcement of boundary lines that almost secure the home-nation as safe haven" (S. Ahmed 2000, 36). Whether under the Bush, Obama, or Trump administrations, racism drives anti-Muslim fears, giving rise to national security policies and discriminatory legislation that criminalize Muslim and "Muslim-looking" communities in the United States (Love 2017).

Given this context, Steven Salaita (2006) calls for the reframing of Islamophobia as anti-Arab racism, noting that the "dislike" of Arabs "is actually based on more than religious acrimony" (11). Reducing discussions to "distortions about Islam" misses the structural forces that historically have marked Muslims and Arabs as civilizational threats. Islamophobia, therefore, "is best understood as a racist ideology that requires a structural analysis" rather than as a series of individual prejudices or hatred (11). In fact, the focus on individual prejudices oftentimes obfuscates a structural analysis of Islamophobia and its historical antecedents that shape commonsense understandings of terrorism.

Although Salaita (2006) views *Islamophobia* as a "valuable word," he prefers *anti-Arab racism* because the term "contextualizes misrepresentations of Islam within a wider culture of prejudice, hatred, and oppression that continually capitulates a modernized form of the traditional American metanarrative of racism" (11). This means that "the word *racism* needs to be part of our vocabulary if we are to successfully juxtapose Arabs with other victims of that metanarrative" (11). Anthropologist Nadine Naber (2008) similarly uses the term *anti-Arab racism* to "locate Arab American marginalization within the context of U.S. histories of immigrant exclusion (e.g., the history of Asian exclusion, anti-Mexican racism, and Japanese internment) in which the racialization of particular immigrants as different than and inferior to whites has relied upon culturalist and nationalist logics that assume that 'they' are intrinsically unassimilable and threatening to national security" (31). Rather than frame these oppressive processes as a byproduct of the September 11 attacks, these scholars tie anti-Arab racism to a "longer, global history of U.S. imperial policies in West and South Asia" and situated "in relation to other, domestic processes of criminalization, regulation, and elimination of racialized peoples by the U.S. state" (Maira 2016, 5).[9]

These racial logics bear on the present, evident in how President

Trump has intensified palpable fears of Muslims by declaring "radical Islamic terrorism" a civilizational threat. For example, when a federal judge's temporary restraining order halted the first "Muslim ban," Trump tweeted, "The judge opens up our country to potential terrorists and others that do not have our best interests at heart. Bad people are very happy!" In a speech three weeks later, Trump (2017) defended the ban, arguing that the "obligation is to serve, protect, and defend the citizens of the United States" by "taking strong measures to protect our nation from radical Islamic terrorism." Falsely citing Department of Justice data, Trump insisted that "the vast majority of individuals convicted of terrorism and terrorism-related offenses since 9/11 came here from outside of our country. We have seen the attacks at home, from Boston to San Bernardino to the Pentagon and, yes, even the World Trade Center."[10] Trump warned that, without the "extreme vetting" of Muslim immigrants, a "beachhead of terrorism" could "form inside America." To prevent the United States from becoming a "sanctuary for extremists," Trump reaffirmed his commitment to "improved vetting procedures" to "keep out those who will do us harm." Trump's rhetoric and subsequent nativist policies have further institutionalized anti-Muslim and anti-immigrant racisms in the name of national security.

These renewed forms of anti-Muslim racism "represent[] a recurring process of the construction of the Other within U.S. liberal politics in which long-term trends of racial exclusion become intensified within moments of crisis in the body politic, as in the contexts of World War II and the aftermath of September 11, 2001" (Naber 2008, 31). Anti-Muslim legislation pulsates through ever-present nativist histories of immigrant exclusion enacted and enhanced through narratives of the unassimilable and threatening outsider. I therefore consider CVE to be tied to these longer racial histories and generative of new social imaginaries, logics, and practices that reproduce dynamic regimes of power on both domestic and global fronts.

To account for the various bodies racialized as Muslim, I use the term *anti-Muslim racism* rather than *anti-Arab racism* or *Islamophobia*. Anti-Muslim racism seeks to capture the heterogeneity of U.S.-based Muslims as well as those (mis)racialized as Muslim, such as Sikhs and Christian Arabs. As a conceptual frame, anti-Muslim racism denotes the public policies, institutional practices, and cultural discourses that maintain racial hierarchies and subject anyone who "looks Muslim" to state and vigilante violence (Love 2017). Given its emphasis on structural inequality rooted in a longer history of U.S. empire, the term *anti-Muslim racism* also draws counter-topographical connections between anti-Muslim surveillance, histories of immigrant exclusion, hyperincarceration, and global counterterrorism operations.[11]

Like Cainkar and Selod (2018), who acknowledge the "complexities of naming the wide group of people caught in the war on terror racial project," I recognize that the term *anti-Muslim racism* risks reifying the state's racial logics by erasing "multiple subjectivities, positionalities, and sites of belonging," including Black Muslims, who are "surveilled both as Blacks and as Muslims," as well as non-Muslims like Sikhs misidentified as Muslim (173). Somali college students, for example, noted that they lived at the intersections of anti-Black and anti-Muslim racisms, pointing to how CVE uniquely criminalized them as Black Muslim refugees. Unfortunately, the U.S. security state indiscriminately uses the "Muslim" marker as a blunt instrument to racialize and criminalize targeted groups as terrorist threats. Profiling, after all, "does not work through accuracy but through its broad racial effects that are terroristic," ultimately catching a "broad group identified by religious, gendered, and racial characteristics produced by histories of racialized imperialism" (Grewal 2017, 12). These linguistic limitations mirror the racializing technologies used by the U.S. security state to advance its agenda. In this way, "there is no single racial naming of this made-up group of people, except that they are understood by the state and the public to be threats: terrorists and potential terrorists" (Cainkar and Selod 2018, 166). By acknowledging the dangerous limitations of the term *anti-Muslim racism*, I invite readers to consider how social phenomena are often more complex than, and sometimes defy, the names we give them.

Rather than treat anti-Muslim racism as a byproduct of the global war on terror, I center these dynamic racial formations within a longer genealogy of colonial warfare, state repression, and coercive policies. This racial project is rooted in the politics of empire, as the diasporic dislocations produced by colonial warfare facilitate imperial regimes within the United States. As Deepa Kumar (2012) explains,

"When the United States goes to war against a foreign enemy, it inevitably makes war on the perceived enemy within" to "win consent for an imperial agenda through a process that orchestrates fear of the enemy within and preempts criticisms of empire-building" (Kumar 2012, 158). U.S. empire therefore articulates "not just through military or global policing but also through 'soft power,' exercised transnationally by particular sets of subjects and processes that gain traction because of histories of white racial, masculinized sovereignty" (Grewal 2017, 17).

The assumption that anti-Muslim racism emerged out of or consolidated through the September 11 attacks also misses the longer history of anti-Muslim racism in the United States. This history includes the forced arrival of enslaved African Muslims, the 1978–1979 Iranian revolution and subsequent mediated panics about Islamist politics in the United States, the rise of the Nation of Islam when "the figure of the Muslim became racialized," and the turn to "differentialist racism" whose "dominant theme is not biological heredity but the insurmountability of cultural differences" (Balibar 1991, 21), thereby "sweeping Arabs and Muslims (along with South Asians, Iranians, and many more nonparallel categories) together into one ill-defined group of Others" and deeming them a threat to U.S. public safety (Abu El-Haj 2015, 12). Given these enduring histories, September 11 is a "turning point, as opposed to the starting point" in anti-Muslim racism in the United States (Naber 2008, 4). Organized by enduring social, cultural, and political histories of U.S. empire, the CVE policy framework reproduces, consolidates, and remakes the racial formations that have enabled and justified the daily operations of the U.S. security state, from targeted criminalization to indefinite detention to military invasions.

Today's most urgent issues "are features of our current global landscape whose etiologies are steeped in the colonial histories of which they have been, and in some cases continue to be, a part" (Stoler 2016, 3). "Security," for example, "has long been the conceptual and political nexus of the expulsions and containments in which imperial formations invest. They are decidedly not the same as—but they are embedded in—the consolidated and honed technologies of security that thrive today" (31). In this way, the colonial past "is imagined to be over but persists, reactivates, and recurs in transfigured forms" (32–33). Given these historical connectivities, this book locates the logics, norms, and discourses CVE actors used to make sense of their work within the dynamic genealogies of imperial formations, racial hierarchies, and freedom struggles. These genealogies haunt contemporary security regimes.

Gendering Anti-Muslim Racism

Anti-Muslim racism articulates with heteropatriarchy, particularly in the social construction of the Muslim male terrorist. U.S. security debates focus on "the dark-skinned, bearded, Muslim male as representative of the primary threat to national security," a stereotype that "consume[s] the (predominately male) government's anxious attempts to prevent the next terrorist attack" (Aziz 2012, 194–95). As a part of this social construction, the U.S. public indicts Muslim men's sexual deviancies as drivers of their terroristic aggression. For example, "We often hear the idea that sexually frustrated Muslim men are promised the heavenly reward of sixty, sixty-seven, or sometimes even seventy virgins if they are martyred in jihad," a corrective to their otherwise failed heterosexuality (Puar and Rai 2002, 124). These racist constructions of deviant Muslim masculinities (re)activate aggressive heterosexual patriotism among white men, noted in the dramatic calls for war after the September 11 attacks and the popular anti-queer poster depicting the Empire State Building anally penetrating, and emasculating, a "turbaned caricature" of 9/11 mastermind and al-Qaeda founder Osama bin Laden (126). The U.S. security state thus pursues, profiles, and prosecutes Muslim men as sexually deviant, inherently barbaric, and, ultimately, incipient terrorists, even though white men and boys have committed more acts of mass murder in the United States (Shane 2015; Craven 2015b; D. A. Graham 2015).

Although U.S. media historically have portrayed Muslim women as victims in need of saving from oppressive Muslim men, new narratives construct hijabi women as "representatives of the suspicious, inherently violent, and forever foreign 'terrorist other' in our midst" (Aziz 2012, 192). As a presumed marker of religiosity and thus political ideology, the hijab marks Muslim women as the dangerous enemy who threatens U.S. national security. More specifically, contemporary images and prosecutions frame Muslim women as the daughters, sisters, or wives—supporters and enablers—of terrorists. Despite shifting perceptions of Muslim women's capacity to commit acts of mass violence, U.S. media still portray Muslim woman as "incapable of developing their own beliefs and protestations" and, instead, as guilty by association through their marriages to presumed terrorist husbands (Aziz 2012, 193). Noor Salman, for example, faced prosecution for knowingly aiding and abetting a designated foreign terrorist organization and obstructing justice (Mazzei 2018). The state pursued these charges on the presumption that Salman had helped her husband, Omar Mateen, commit his 2016 Pulse nightclub attack in Florida. Although a jury acquitted Salman, the state's prosecution of Salman in the absence of any credible evidence sought to scapegoat her and hold her accountable for her husband's actions.

Given the role of gender in the making of the U.S. security state, this book explores how these heteropatriarchal processes of responsibilization have conscripted Muslim women into local CVE programming. The nonprofit organization Futures Without Violence, for example, views Muslim women as possible "supportive wives and mothers to the next generation of extremists," "propogandists, fundraisers, and suicide bombers," and/or "integral stakeholders within the field of countering violent extremism" since they are "uniquely skilled in building trust with local communities and networks, leading to a more collaborative environment between locals and officials" (A. Alexander 2017, 2–3). The call for women's inclusion in the CVE policy environment has depended on gendered assumptions about women's roles, capacities, and "unique skills" as patient, collaborative, and trustworthy women, despite their propensity to aid their terrorist husbands or sons. In this context, women's empowerment has functioned as a critical security concern rather than an issue of gender justice. As we will see, CVE has relied on racialized and gendered images of the terroristic Muslim man and the aiding and abetting Muslim woman who can be reprogrammed and empowered to prevent violent extremism in the home.

Defining a Terrorist: A Technology of
Gendered Anti-Muslim Racism

On June 17, 2015, twenty-year-old Dylann Roof opened fire in a Black church in Charleston, South Carolina, killing nine parishioners in the name of white supremacy. Police apprehended Roof at a traffic stop some 245 miles from the murder site after a nightlong search. Roof sustained no injuries during the police pursuit, capture, and arrest. In fact, Roof enjoyed the protection of a police-issued bulletproof vest immediately following his arrest and, after expressing hunger, on a brief trip to Burger King. In January 2017, Roof was convicted of thirty-three federal hate-crime charges, including nine counts of murder, three counts of attempted murder, and one count of possessing a firearm during the commission of a felony. Convicted on all counts, Roof was sentenced to death.

Although Roof faced federal prosecution for hate crimes, he was not charged with terrorism. FBI director James Comey defended the exclusion of terrorism charges in the federal indictment of Roof, arguing that the murders did not qualify "as a political act," despite Roof's declaration that he sought to provoke a "race war" (McCormack 2016). Roof's racial privilege protected him from wholesale disposability as a "terrorist."

The failure to charge Roof with terrorism informs, and is informed by, legal and public framings of what counts as terrorism. Referencing recent massacres carried out by white men in the United States, legal scholar Glenn Greenwald (2013) observes that "the word 'terrorism' was almost never used to describe that indiscriminate slaughter of innocent people, and none of the perpetrators of those attacks was charged with terrorism-related crimes" (para. 2).[12] Both U.S. courts and public media reserve the "terrorist" label for perpetrators of color. Despite increasing research concluding that white supremacists commit more acts of mass murder in the United States than ISIS (Craven 2015b), the U.S. public insists that white shooters are "good kids" from "good communities" rather than products of a violent white supremacist culture (Anderson 2013; Mason and Zucchino 2013; Wise 2001). These justificatory narratives of the wayward or troubled white shooter persist simultaneous to the continued pathologizing of youth of color as inherently violent.[13]

Legal scholar Leti Volpp (2002) notes that white shooters do not "produce a discourse about good whites and bad whites" because we come to know them as "individual deviants" or "bad actors" (1585). Insulated by "the privilege of individual culpability," this response stands in sharp contrast to the "collective punishment" of all Muslims for the September 11 attacks, "irrespective of the fact that they did not perpetrate them" (Cainkar 2008, 52). This collective punishment divides targeted communities into "good" and "bad" Muslims, differentially deserving of constitutionally protected civil liberties and civil rights. In this racial context, "unless proved to be 'good,' every Muslim [is] presumed to be 'bad,'" thereby obliging Muslims to "prove their credentials by joining in a war against 'bad Muslims'" (Mamdani 2004, 15). Racial privilege, however, shields white communities from such collective blame and subsequent demands to cooperate with the government in the domestic war on terror. In this context, "the political act of labeling certain forms of violence as terrorism is also usually a racialized act" (Kundnani 2014, 22).

Following historical precedent, Roof's act of white supremacist violence did not qualify as "terrorism," according to both the U.S. public and its legal system, nor did it generate an "examination of the roots of these actions in cultivated racial hatreds and essentialized, civilizational discourses" (Cainkar 2008, 52). Instead, U.S. media and politicians framed Roof's violence as an aberration, an individualizing interpretation that "exceptionalizes racism" as the behavior of "one particular racist rather than the problem of an embedded societal racism" (Sian 2012, 295). Framing Roof as an individual racist ignores the persistence of institutional racism that produces anti-Black structural, symbolic, and subjective violence in and through the United States.

Despite the centrality of white supremacy in Roof's actions, many discussions have sidestepped a racial analysis of his targets (Black parishioners), his intent (instigating a race war), and his own racial (white) and gender (male) privilege. The devaluation of criminalized populations, like Roof's victims, means that some acts of violence and their perpetrators are considered less criminal than others. What counts as terrorism is necessarily defined by who enacts this violence and who the subject of such violence is. Under this rubric, anti-Black violence committed by white actors does not qualify as terrorism.

As a part of these discussions, news outlets reported that Roof was "radicalized" online, "absorbing violent white supremacist beliefs from the internet" (Berman 2016). Legal scholars, national security experts, and academics scrutinized Roof's written manifesto to better understand his path toward radicalization. In his manifesto, Roof described his Google search of "black-on-white crime" as pivotal to his own understanding of U.S. race relations and a key motivating factor for his massacre.

Given Roof's declaration, the Southern Poverty Law Center (SPLC) pressured Google to alter its algorithms to limit the influence of white supremacist propaganda. SPLC security expert Hannah Martin argued that changing Google's algorithms could stymie the circulation of white supremacist propaganda by burying racist websites. For Martin, conducting a Google search "was how Dylann Roof came to the conclusion that he needed to get a weapon, he needed to arm himself, and he needed to shoot Black people. He believed essentially he was protecting the white population from out of control violence" (participant observation, October 7, 2016). In this framing, Roof's violence stemmed from his immersion in online white supremacist propaganda rather than from a white supremacist society that has normalized anti-Blackness and encouraged anti-Black violence through its institutions of education, police procedures, popular culture, and national security policies.

These analyses treat Roof's white supremacist violence as an abhorrent anomaly rather than a symptom of "embedded societal racism." In fact, SPLC's advocacy framed Roof as a victim of online radicalization, targeted by sophisticated white supremacists who drew the young man into their propaganda and, eventually, violent cause. This type of "collective denial of ongoing racism" allows the United States "to classify the deaths of nine people killed in a church as the alleged victims of a mentally ill individual rather than a racist terrorist" (Thrasher 2015, para. 5). Mental health often is used as an alibi to justify massacres waged by white shooters, eschewing more complex discussions about the primacy of white supremacy as an organizing frame for violence while criminalizing individuals with psychiatric disability labels. Positioning Roof as a self-radicalized, lone actor ignores the centrality of white supremacy in violent U.S. racial formations, from its settler colonial origins, to the transatlantic slave trade enforced by vigilante violence, to President Trump's "Muslim ban." Symbolic, structural, and subjective violence was, and continues to be, a key tool in the maintenance of racial hierarchies in the United States.

Just two years before Roof's massacre, police captured and arrested Dzhokhar Tsarnaev, who hid in a boat following his participation in the 2013 bombing of the Boston Marathon, alongside his brother, Tamerlan, who was killed in the subsequent police pursuit. While in hiding, Tsarnaev etched a manifesto onto the boat's wall with a pencil. In his manifesto, partially obscured by bullet holes, Tsarnaev declared:

> The US government is killing our innocent civilians but most of you already know that. As a M [bullet hole] I can't stand to see such evil go unpunished, we Muslims are one body, you hurt one you hurt us all, well at least that's how Muhammad (pbuh)[14] wanted it to be [bullet hole] ever, the ummah is beginning to rise/awa [bullet hole] has awoken the mujahideen, know you are fighting men who look into the barrel of your gun and see heaven, now how can you compete with that. We are promised victory and we will surely get it. Now I don't like killing innocent people it is forbidden in Islam but due to said [bullet hole] it is allowed. (Bever 2015)

Although Tsarnaev's manifesto offered a window into the political context that fueled his participation in the Boston bombings, it only received cursory media coverage. Unlike Roof's own writing, I never observed news outlets, conference presentations, or security experts publicly scrutinize Tsarnaev's manifesto. A sustained evaluation of Tsarnaev's near-death declaration would have necessitated an analysis of U.S. foreign policy decisions that informed how Tsarnaev and his brother came to view violence as a valid strategy to arrest U.S.-sanctioned war. This approach would compel the U.S. public to confront the Boston bombings as a form of political violence organized around clear grievances and goals rather than as an inexplicable act of evil waged by evildoers. Despite the intense scrutiny of Roof's manifesto to understand what drove him to violence, the U.S. public quickly applied the "terrorist" label to the Tsarnaev brothers, a conclusion that required no additional analysis.

Although U.S. media debated whether Roof's actions constituted terrorism, prosecutors quickly charged Tsarnaev with thirty federal counts, including unlawfully using and conspiring to use a weapon of mass destruction, a criminal code classified as terrorism. Like Roof, Tsarnaev was convicted and sentenced to death. Recognizing the uneven application of the terrorist label evident in the differential prosecutions of Roof and Tsarnaev, Julia Craven (2015a) concludes that "Dylann Roof wasn't charged with terrorism because he's white." Given the racialization of human value, the criminal-legal system makes it difficult to recognize young white men as terrorists and racially motivated violence as terrorism. The failure to indict Roof on terrorism charges demonstrates that "terrorism is increasingly being defined by the cultural and religious affiliations of the people committing the acts and not necessarily by the acts themselves. In other words, the labeling of an individual as 'Muslim' determines if such acts fall under the definition of terrorism or just random acts of violence" (Bakali 2016). This racial contract exempts Roof's anti-Black violence from the terrorist label and reaffirms the conflation of Islam with terrorism. Unfortunately, broadening the scope of what counts as "terrorism" to include white shooters like Roof merely reinforces, rather than questions, the term and the carceral solutions it authorizes.

These racialized interpretations of the terrorist threat have organized national security policies and programs targeting Muslim, Arab, Somali, and other immigrant populations. The Denver Police Department (DPD), for example, applied for a 2016 Countering Violent Extremism grant funded by the Department of Homeland Security. In its application, the DPD proposed a "CVE-mentoring program" in school districts with "a large number of refugee students," despite referencing three "instances of high profile violent extremism" involving white, U.S.-born actors.[15] Although the DPD (2016) suggested that "Colorado has been the site of recruitment efforts made by foreign terror groups including ISIS," it only referenced the investigation of "five *potential* incidences of homegrown violent extremism" as evidence (2, emphasis added).[16] Even though white, U.S.-born young men committed the most recent acts of mass violence in Colorado, the DPD's proposal defined the "most at-risk population" as individuals who are "disenfranchised and not integrated into their communities" like immigrants (2). DPD also broadened its "target communities" to include "faith communities, Black Lives Matter, diverse communities, refugee communities, and LGBTQ communities, among others, facing disenfranchisement by society" (3). This approach assumes that disenfranchised communities are more susceptible to violence than other groups like white, U.S.-born young men.

As a specifically anti-Muslim policy framework, CVE articulates with and enhances anti-Black, anti-immigrant, and anti-queer policing, evident in the DPD's broad targeting. Contemporary security regimes develop new forms of racialized criminalization, surveillance, and monitoring, which can be (re)directed toward other populations. Social media monitoring tools to identify and report possible gang-involved youth, for example, have been utilized by CVE actors who cull social media accounts to detect potential terrorists. Although these technologies of control activate different racial logics and outcomes, their crossover provides entry points to develop cross-racial social movements that take seriously these racial formations as distinct but co-constitutive ordering systems.

Informed by these differential responses to perceived national security threats, Congressman Keith Ellison—the first Black Muslim congressperson—warned that CVE's laser-focus on, and criminalization of, Muslim communities missed the "Dylann Roofs of America." Ellison argued that the preoccupation with Muslims dangerously diverted attention away from the violence committed by white supremacists and police officers, which occurs at substantially higher rates than "ISIS-inspired" attacks. Citing Roof's guns and white supremacist memorabilia, Ellison incisively asked, "Are we going to do countering violent extremism in *his* community?" (participant observation, August 18, 2016). Guided by Ellison's caution, this book examines how the racialized assignment of social value has organized CVE policies and programs, thereby marking certain bodies as potentially terroristic, "disposable and violable," and "legitimate targets of state and vigilante violence," from Muslim youth to Black organizers (Cacho 2012, 40).

Despite its narrow focus on "disenfranchised communities," the Denver Police Department never justified its targeting, primarily because scientific studies routinely demonstrate that there is no single profile of a terrorist and no proven indicators of violent extremism.[17] Given these scientific shortcomings, I argue against "equal opportunity" CVE inclusive of all populations like the "Dylann Roofs of America." As we will see throughout this book, the scientific limitations of, and discriminatory impetus driving, CVE programs render this approach both ineffective in addressing the perceived problem of violent extremism and harmful to Muslims continually treated as suspect communities. Recognizing how enduring racial hierarchies organize contemporary definitions of the terrorist, this book explores how CVE actors interfaced with these governing logics and managed community concerns related to the flawed and discriminatory science of CVE.

From Terrorism Studies to Radicalization Theories: The Global War on Terror Comes Home

Today, political pundits, academics, think tanks, and politicians publicly debate and discuss the definition, drivers, and roots causes of terrorism. Yet, the field of terrorism studies only began emerging in the 1970s, evident in the gradual rise in publications, conferences, and journals on this political topic. The massacre at the 1972 Munich Olympics has been "inscribed in popular and expert histories of the problem alike as *the* spectacular event that inaugurated the era of modern terrorism," ushering in new ways of understanding political violence (Stampnitzky 2013, 21). During this event, a group of Palestinians kidnapped Israeli Olympians, demanding the release of 230 Arab political prisoners before killing all eleven hostages. Hundreds of journalists contributed to the first televised crisis broadcast across the globe and described as an act of terrorism. Following the televised events at Munich, "terrorism began to take shape as a problem in the public sphere and as an object of expert knowledge" (Stampnitzky 2013, 23). The U.S. government contributed to the field's development by funding terrorism-related research, organizing conferences, and sponsoring emerging experts.

Prior to the formation of terrorism studies, experts conceptualized the type of violence waged at the Munich Olympics as political violence with clear motives, objectives, and underlying grievances. The new discourse on terrorism, however, "tended to characterize terrorists as evil, pathological, and irrational actors, fundamentally different from 'us'" (Stampnitzky 2013, 50). In fact, in 1979, "an entire conference was devoted to the notion of terrorism as psychopathology" (66). The rise of terrorism studies facilitated the reframing of political violence as irrational and immoral acts that defied explanation.

President George W. Bush strategically etched this conceptualization of terrorism into U.S. popular imagination by describing terrorists as "evildoers" throughout his two presidential terms. After the September 11 attacks, for example, Bush (2001c) effused, "Make no mistake about it. This is good versus evil. These are evildoers. They have no justification for their actions. There's no religious justification, there's no political justification. The only motivation is evil." In a meeting with Muslim leaders the following day, one guest asked President Bush if bin Laden maintained any political goals. President Bush (2001b) abruptly responded, "He has got evil goals." This charged rhetoric reduced the horrific September 11 attacks to irrational acts of violence waged by evildoers with no moral or political compass.

Defining terrorism as illegitimate acts of violence carried out by evildoers with "no justification" for their actions marshalled a post–September 11 "politics of *anti-knowledge*" (Stampnitzky 2013, 187). The "root of the politics of anti-knowledge" is that if "terrorists are evil and irrational, then one cannot—and indeed, *should not*—know them" (183). In this explanatory framework, terrorists use violence because of their inherently evil nature. As an act of evil, such violence defies logic and thus cannot be studied or rationalized.

Through "highly exaggerated stereotyping" that blames Islam for terrorism, U.S. media facilitate these interpretations as "much of what one reads and sees in the media about Islam represents the aggression coming from Islam because that is what 'Islam' is" (Said 1997, xi, xxii). This means that media "obliterate" the "local and concrete circumstances" that drive political violence (xxii). "Covering Islam" therefore is a "one-sided activity that obscures what 'we' *do*, and highlights instead what Muslims and Arabs by their very flawed nature *are*" (xxii). By conflating terrorism with Islam, the U.S. public need not pursue more complex understandings of political violence. Islam-as-evil furnishes a politically expedient understanding of terrorism that requires no additional explanation or analysis.

Despite the primacy of these interpretations, nonstate perpetrators of political violence cannot be reduced to evildoers or religious fanatics; they must be recognized as strategic political actors, particularly by "understanding the social forces driving them, the worldly goals they pursue, and the antagonisms they face" in the pursuit of "capturing state power" (Li 2015, paras. 23–24). Rather than demonize violent extremists or reduce terrorism to an irrational response to foreign policy, the United States must "take[] radicalism seriously as a political orientation, whether its idiom is Islamic, communist, or anarchist" (Li 2015, para. 14). In the aftermath of September 11, however, the image of the evil terrorist gained prominence, silencing all efforts to pursue a more complex rendering of the violence waged against the United States. As an epistemic project, the politics of anti-knowledge both refuses any critical inquiry into terrorism and depicts the struggle to understand this problem as itself an evil and traitorous act.

Draped in a sense of "absolute morality," these accounts render those who wage attacks against the United States as "terrorist monsters" who "must be destroyed" (Puar and Rai 2002, 118). As President Bush declared on September 20, 2001, the United States would use "every necessary weapon of war . . . to the destruction and to the defeat of the global terror network." President Bush (2001c) promised "a lengthy campaign unlike any other we have ever seen" using "dramatic strikes visible on TV and covert operations secret even in success." Perceived "acts of evil" justified the use of "every necessary weapon of war."

Given the evil nature of terrorists, the U.S. response to September 11 need not address the underlying political orientation, goals, and grievances that organized the attacks. Instead, the United States deployed decisive military action to eliminate the "global terror network." By reaffirming the constant threat of a terrorist attack conducted by irrational evildoers, Bush justified aggressive "kill or capture" military operations.

Beginning in 2004, however, policymakers, academics, and military strategists questioned this account of terrorism and the general strategy to kill or capture terrorists. The U.S. security state therefore needed a new framework to guide its changing global war on terror strategy and to respond to new domestic terrorist threats. During this time, the concept of "radicalization" emerged, offering new methods to "explore the process by which a terrorist is made" and to "provide an analytical grounding for preventative strategies that [go] beyond the use of state violence" (Kundnani 2014, 116). Presented as "the wiser, more liberal alternative to simple accounts of terrorism offered immediately after 9/11," radicalization research has examined how and why individuals become terrorists and facilitated the development of new tactics to disrupt this process (116–17).

Departing from culturalists who understand Islam as inherently opposed to Western values, radicalization scholars have approached terrorism as a perversion, not a product, of Islam. Rather than dismiss terrorists as evildoers, these scholars have examined the culture, psychology, and theology of known terrorists to "understand the radicalization process and devise strategies to prevent its reaching the point of violence" (Sageman 2008, 71). The rise of radicalization studies germinated from both a rejection of culturalist thinking and the "evolution of the threat to the West," which "comes from the inside, from 'homegrown' terrorists, most of whom have never traveled abroad for training or indoctrination" (71). Because the perceived terrorist threat now "comes from the inside," the United States could no longer rely only on hardening its borders and warfighting to prevent terrorism. In this context, explorations of the radicalization process now dominate terrorism studies and guide new national security strategies like CVE to fight "homegrown terrorism."

Unfortunately, as the radicalization turn in terrorism studies gained prominence, these new theories often have reduced political violence to individual pathologies, religious fanaticism, and cultural deficits. In this framework, "individual psychological or theological journeys, largely removed from social and political circumstances, are claimed to be the root cause of the radicalization process" (Kundnani 2014, 117). The rise of radicalization studies has shifted the scale of analysis to the individual, meaning law enforcement officials, social service providers, and community members could learn to identify and work with individuals vulnerable to, or in the process of, radicalizing. This scalar shift, therefore, has ushered in new ways of addressing the problem of terrorism and new roles for the U.S. public to perform.

Citizens as Police: Coproducing National Security

In his 2002 State of the Union address, President Bush affirmed that, to "better secure our homeland," "America will continue to depend on the eyes and ears of alert citizens." Bush (2002) argued that these actions would "make America not only stronger, but, in many ways, better" as security advancements could improve public health, create safer neighborhoods, and combat illicit drug use. Given the mediated panics about domestic terrorist threats, Bush mobilized the U.S. public as exceptional citizens who take responsibility for maintaining the U.S. security state, ultimately making the nation "stronger" and "better." Echoing President Bush, CVE policymakers have called on Muslims to serve as "our eyes and ears on our frontlines" in the domestic war on terror (Clinton 2016).

As risk and insecurity continue to define the meaning of citizenship, the "good citizen is a citizen who *suspects rather than is suspect,* who watches out for departures from ordinary life in the imagined space of the neighborhood" (S. Ahmed 2000, 28, emphasis in original). The U.S. security state conscripts its subjects as "good citizens" who take on the work of preventing terrorism by "watching out for" suspicious individuals. The Department of Homeland Security, for example, runs a trademarked campaign, "If you see something, say something." Urging the U.S. public to participate in domestic security operations, DHS (n.d.) insists that "if you see something you know shouldn't be there—or someone's behavior that doesn't seem quite right—say something. Because only you know what's supposed to be in your everyday" (para. 1). Framed by a securitized definition of the "good citizen," these demands deputize community members as proxy national security agents tasked with looking for, and reporting, potential threats. As DHS concludes, "Informed, alert communities play a critical role in keeping our nation safe" (para. 1). For some Muslims "cast out" of U.S. citizenship through their racialization, participation in these domestic security operations has offered an opening for their conditional inclusion as "good citizens" (Razack 2008).

Despite continued calls to protect the nation, "the good citizen is not given any information about how to tell what or who is suspicious in the first place" (S. Ahmed 2000, 29). The "see something, say something" campaign, for example, assumes the good citizen already knows when a person's behavior "doesn't seem quite right." A behavioral threat assessment trainer similarly argued that the "uh-oh feeling" a "suspicious" person may arouse serves as an important national security technology that protects good citizens from danger. This trainer asserted that suspicion, experienced as an "uh-oh feeling," is an objective yet instinctual reaction that ensures survival (participant observation, February 7, 2017).

The activation of the "uh-oh feeling," however, depends on the good citizen already knowing a person is suspicious. Our "uh-oh feeling" is "shaped by cultural histories and memories" that calibrate the "eyes and ears of alert citizens" to certain racialized cues that signal an imminent threat and arouse fear (S. Ahmed 2004a, 7). Rather than treat suspicion as an instinctual reaction, this book recognizes how racial formations, cultural histories, and social memories inform who and what are considered suspicious and trigger our "uh-oh feeling." Given the protean nature of racism and the sociality of emotions, this book explores the continued and shifting social construction of the suspect and subsequent cultivation of the "uh-oh feeling" through security initiatives like CVE.

"Follow the CVE Trail": Mapping the CVE Policy World

Given the urgent call to "better secure our homeland" using our "uh-oh feeling" and other available community resources, one practitioner encouraged me to "continue following the CVE trail" to learn from those most involved in, and affected by, this emerging national security approach. Drawing from my experiences on this trail, I explore how the concept of countering violent extremism, and its attendant national security vocabularies and logics, came to be institutionalized and operationalized through the everyday work of CVE actors, from high-level national security workers to local community members. Rather than document an exhaustive or evaluative study of CVE policies, I investigate the often fraught and contradictory policy environment that CVE actors, community members, and protesters negotiated in a concerted effort to keep their children safe. Such an analysis can inform public understandings of new security regimes and community responses to shifting domestic war on terror tactics.

This book stages this exploration through four lines of inquiry: (1) how terrorism studies scholars developed radicalization models that have enabled and constrained how CVE actors conceptualized national security; (2) how CVE actors applied these radicalization models to their daily work; (3) how these models furnished understandings of youth as a "generational threat" in need of psychosocial programming to protect them from terrorist recruitment; and (4) how CVE actors managed public objections to their work. These inquiries provide insight into the epistemic struggle to taxonomize terrorists, the racial hierarchies CVE reconfigured and reinforced, and the processes by which Muslim leaders advanced these national security projects as "good citizens."

Rather than use this analysis to arbitrate what political strategies Muslim leaders should undertake—that is not for me to say—this book examines what the U.S. security state has sought to accomplish through its engagement with Muslim communities. Facing mounting resistance to racial profiling, coercive policing, and political exclusion, the U.S. security state has offered CVE as a "community-driven" and "ideologically ecumenical" alternative to its conventional counterterrorism practices, thereby legitimizing and shoring up support for the very institutions that treat communities of color as the enemy within—internal threats to U.S. national security. The introduction of CVE programs strategically has strengthened, not mitigated, the surveillance, monitoring, and policing of Muslims across the United States while appearing attentive to the civil liberties and civil rights of targeted groups. Such insight offers new ways of understanding the institutionalization of anti-Muslim racism through liberal initiatives that grant Muslim communities cultural and political recognition without redistributing power.

To develop this analysis, chapter 1 introduces readers to the organizing research questions and creative methods I employed to investigate CVE by studying powerful actors within the U.S. security state. I examine the ethical issues I encountered when I interviewed CVE actors, some of whom were Muslim, Arab, Somali, and/or South Asian. Their elite status in, or associations with, the U.S. security state could not insulate them from everyday anti-Muslim racism, generating ethical, methodological, and analytical questions I needed to consider reflexively throughout the research process. In addition, powerful actors contribute to "huge bureaucracies" whose policies and perspectives may conflict with the diverse views of those who work there (Ron Stuart, interview, February 17, 2017). This chapter explores these methodological provocations, paying particular attention to the complex power relations that shaped this research study. Rather than gloss over these issues, I directly address how power and authority organized the research encounter. This analysis contributes to methodological debates about the politics and ethics of studying powerful institutions and their workers.

Chapter 2 examines how policy documents, practitioners, and community members defined CVE in opposition to previous antiterrorism practices. To make sense of these understandings, I excavate the rich genealogies of counterterrorism, counterinsurgency, and community policing paradigms that have informed contemporary countering violent extremism policies. In addition, chapter 3 explores the radicalization theories that have guided the making of CVE and the associated methods used to "inoculate young people from the ideology of violence" (Tanvir Rahman, interview, November 10, 2016). Lastly, I locate these radicalization models in prior practices of identifying, classifying, and correcting "abnormals" or social deviants who purportedly posed an imminent security threat. By approaching radicalization scholarship as a reformulation of previous ways of knowing "abnormals," I invite readers to question how they might think differently about terrorism, agitating against enduring imperial taxonomies that organize contemporary security regimes (Foucault 1999).

Chapter 4 investigates how CVE actors negotiated competing national security approaches, contentious community critiques, and conflicting radicalization scholarship. I document how CVE actors interrogated their own understandings of their work, shifted local programming in response to new information, and/or dismissed, responded to, and critiqued community concerns. Through this exploration, I analyze the narrative strategies CVE actors used to manage public objections to their work and maintain the viability of this national security approach in their communities.

After examining these negotiations, chapter 5 documents how the CVE policy framework has defined Muslim youth as the "generational threat." More specifically, I explore how CVE actors viewed Muslim youth as "searching for belonging, navigating their identity, and looking for emotional connectivity," all "fertile soil" for terrorist recruitment (Homeland Security Advisory Council 2016). I investigate how these urgent narratives have marshalled a series of educational initiatives to protect children from terrorist influences.

Next, I examine how CVE programs like global citizenship education have encouraged Muslim youth to subordinate their racial, cultural, and religious differences to an identification with the global (Bartlett and Lutz 1998). I also investigate other educational initiatives that have conscripted students into the CVE industry, like training youth to identify peers at risk of terrorist radicalization and developing youth-led social media campaigns that counter terrorist propaganda. This chapter thus addresses the national security narratives that have organized prevailing understandings of the generational threat and the educational practices these narratives have authorized.

In the concluding chapter, I revisit this book's central arguments to theorize the relationship between anti-Black, anti-Muslim, and anti-immigrant racisms and their everyday expressions and manifestations. I examine how anti-Muslim national security narratives that authorize the blanket surveillance of "Muslim-looking" populations enhance the U.S. security state implicated in the killing of unarmed Black people, the ongoing detention and deportation of immigrants, and the hyperincarceration of racialized populations. Studying CVE helps conceptualize anti-Black, anti-Muslim, and anti-immigrant racisms as distinct yet co-constitutive state projects that generate different but interrelated forms of violence on local populations. Rather than evaluate one form of violence as deadlier than another, this concluding chapter thinks through the relationship between these forms of racialized state violence to imagine the possibilities for cross-racial solidarity in ways that eschew "deceptive solutions" (A. Y. Davis 2016, 90).

By examining the fraught tensions CVE actors negotiated in their daily work, this book identifies pressure points ripe with political possibility to contest these national security practices in ways that do not concede radical imaginations for liberal reforms. More specifically, I consider how the U.S. security state strategically has used CVE to offer Muslim communities political representation and cultural recognition through their participation in local initiatives. By shoring up support for the very institutions that historically have criminalized Muslim communities, the U.S. security state has enhanced its domestic war on terror operations while appearing to rein in racial profiling, coercive policing, and political exclusion. As college student Hodan Hassan concluded, "There is no middle ground between CVE and nah. There is no reform for something that says your humanity is subpar" (participant observation, April 21, 2017).[18] By centering the perspectives of CVE actors and targeted communities, this book examines how CVE "says your humanity is subpar" and considers alternative solutions that refuse the "middle ground between CVE and nah."

Through this exploration, I document how CVE has been forged through interwoven epistemic, political, and cultural projects that cultivate particular ways of knowing and being that service the U.S. security state and restrict radical resistance. As imperial logics articulate through new national security policies, we must ask: What kind of national security projects do we want to pursue? How do we determine who and what is dangerous? How do we respond to these formulations of danger? What new ways of knowing might generate less violent futures for racialized populations, too often integrated into the political establishment to advance, rather than arrest, abusive systems of power? What role do Muslim communities play in maintaining, negotiating, and/or contesting these systems? How might CVE practitioners from targeted communities excavate histories of radical activism, continuously suppressed but never destroyed, to demand new forms of national security and public safety independent of oppressive institutions? How do we develop, fund, and deliver resources that build healthy communities, without an antiterrorism lens and without police involvement? By studying the conditions that shape, and have been shaped by, CVE, this book seeks to imagine new political possibilities informed by radical struggles that have sustained criminalized communities across history.

CHAPTER 1

ETHNOGRAPHIC DILEMMAS
Rethinking Power Relations When Studying Up

On Tuesday, November 8, 2016, the U.S. public elected Donald J. Trump as the nation's forty-fifth president. Still processing the election two days later, I attended a public roundtable at the Central City Islamic Center, a quarterly event hosted by the Department of Homeland Security's Office for Civil Rights and Civil Liberties. Since 2002, DHS has sought to improve community relations through these forums, particularly in Muslim and Arab communities, across the United States. To do so, these DHS roundtables "bring together American Arab, Muslim, South Asian, Middle Eastern, Somali, Sikh, Latino, Jewish, and Asian/Asian Pacific Islander communities with government representatives" (Department of Homeland Security 2016). Wanting me to better understand how the local community approached countering violent extremism efforts, behavioral threat assessment trainer Elliot Adams invited me to observe the November 2016 DHS roundtable on CVE programming.

Having eagerly accepted Adams's invitation, on November 10, I walked into a room buzzing with conversations among three dozen community leaders, federal national security representatives, and state law enforcement personnel. Looking for an open seat, I weaved my way through community members wearing kufis and hijabs as well as national security men donning pins on their suit lapels indicating their affiliations with federal or state agencies. After a panel of community leaders detailed how local organizations worked to prevent young people from engaging in violent extremism, DHS host Nabil Soliman invited community members to an open discussion.

As people asked the panelists about CVE, I felt a palpable tension surface. The conversation about community efforts to counter violent extremism shifted to reports of an increasing number of white supremacist attacks on communities of color, their places of worship, and their bodies: How could communities combat these forms of violence? Were CVE policies also implemented in white communities and Christian institutions? As Soliman referred people who experienced white supremacist violence to the FBI and other law enforcement agents in the room, pressing uncertainties related to the violence against Muslims pulsated through the room. This exchange revealed that although community leaders served as, or worked closely with, national security actors, they, too, were exposed to intensified anti-Muslim violence in the hours, days, and months following President Trump's election.

As a project engaged in "studying up," I had considered the power relations involved in conducting research on national security actors prior to entering the field. During the DHS roundtable, however, I quickly recognized my failure to anticipate how people's elite status in, or associations with, the U.S. security state could not insulate them from anti-Muslim racism. Observing the DHS roundtable as a non-Muslim woman of color, I began asking: What does it mean to study people who both hold positions of power and are targets of state and vigilante violence? As a researcher, how did the Trump era—defined, in part, by ongoing threats to deport, incarcerate, and surveil Muslims—shape my responsibilities to research participants? At the time of my fieldwork, emerging research on CVE already had pitted "good" and "bad" Muslims against each other. In this context, how could I—as a researcher, writer, and teacher—militate against efforts to fracture Muslim communities while attending to community concerns with, and critiques of, CVE policies? What were the political and ethical implications of, and responsibilities in, "studying up" when people in power also occupied marginalized positions?

This chapter explores these methodological provocations, with attention to how the heterogeneity of power shapes the research encounter. To do so, I first outline the methodology that organized my fieldwork aimed at "studying up, down, and sideways," sometimes rearticulated as "studying through" or "studying power" (Nader 1997, 1972; Reinhold 1994). Second, I detail how I used eclectic methods to gather data that provided insight into the CVE policy world. Lastly, I explore how uneven and dynamic relations of power saturated every phase of this project, from designing the study to writing this book. In doing so, I seek to advance how social scientists theorize power in the methodological and epistemological projects of "studying up" and what these new understandings might mean for future research.

Making Sense of the CVE Policy World

When I first scrolled through the FBI's Don't Be a Puppet interactive website, my millennial sensibilities compelled me to ask, rather crossly, "Who made this?" The 1980s graphics seemed so remote from the 2016 gaming world with which I watched young people engage. I wondered how the website designers chose this interface and what they hoped to accomplish through young people's interactions with it. Through my initial encounter with the FBI portal, I began asking questions about Don't Be a Puppet's designers rather than its users: What did the website designers intend to communicate about violent extremism? What vocabularies did they, and the broader national security community, rely on to frame the problem of violent extremism? What did the website designers expect to achieve through young people's engagement with these national security vocabularies and frameworks?

Ever curious, I sought answers to these questions as I navigated the website. For example, I listened to FBI director James Comey introduce viewers to the Don't Be a Puppet theme. In this video, Comey warned that, through online terrorist recruitment, "young people become puppets used to spread a message of hate." Comey then urged young people to hone their critical thinking skills by engaging the website as a way "to be a part of the solution." "Don't be a puppet," Comey concluded, rather anticlimactically. As I watched this video, I noted how Comey framed young people as uniquely vulnerable to terrorist radicalization and suggested that Don't Be a Puppet could protect them from this vulnerability.

Next, I completed each of the learning modules, which defined violent extremism, listed "known violent extremist groups," discussed why people turn to violent extremism, explored how violent extremists recruit youth, and detailed "where to get help." By interacting with these learning modules, I came to understand the "twisted beliefs and values" and "warped principles" of violent extremists, the dangers of "groupthink," and the differences between "free speech" and "violent extremism." Despite its simplistic interface, the Don't Be a Puppet website provided extensive information on violent extremism from the perspective of the FBI.

As I completed Don't Be a Puppet's final assessment, I realized that although I was curious about how young people responded to the website, I wanted to know more about the perspectives of those who advanced the project, designed it, and advocated for its use in local communities. In addition, as interested as I was in what CVE policies said and what they sought to do, I also wanted to better understand how their makers came to think about national security: What is it? Who threatens it? Who secures the nation and how?

As these questions illustrate, my early encounter with Don't Be a Puppet provoked questions that focused on the website's creators rather than its users. I sought to uncover how Don't Be a Puppet and other initiatives came into being, particularly by investigating the perspectives and practices of those involved in the CVE policy world. Like Brenda Chalfin's (2010) ethnography of Ghana's Customs Service, this study sought to "probe the 'public face' of the state and how that face came to be constituted over time by shifts in policies, practices, and individual interests and understandings" (15). Such an approach recognizes that "before we can understand how the state is subverted or undermined, we need to consider how state power is manufactured, institutionalized, and recursively inscribed" (15). By researching the upper and lower echelons of the U.S. security state, I wanted to understand how CVE logics, norms, and discourses both shaped and were shaped by prevailing social contexts, institutional arrangements, and people's daily work.

Because the CVE framework has informed domestic war on terror debates, CVE policies have served as governing cultural texts, with CVE actors as the key authors of those cultural texts. I therefore sought to understand how federal policymakers, state law enforcement personnel, community leaders, street-level bureaucrats, and others in the CVE policy field defined for themselves what CVE was and how it worked, how they made sense of their roles in enacting CVE policies, and how they performed those roles. How did people negotiate competing theories of radicalization as they designed and implemented CVE policies? How did governing social, political, and economic contexts shape policy decisions and people's understandings of these policy decisions? How did differences in people's understandings of CVE and its broader national security context influence policy making and taking across CVE sites? As these questions indicate, I wanted to understand the prevailing "controlling processes," the "mechanisms by which ideas take hold and become institutional in relation to power" (Nader 1997, 711). That is, I sought to understand how the concept of countering violent extremism, and its attendant national security vocabularies and logics, came to be institutionalized and thus operationalized through people's everyday work. Politicians, street-level bureaucrats, community leaders, and local officials, after all, differentially understand, enact, and enforce policies, deciding for themselves what constitutes ethical and effective national security work.

To carry out this type of analysis, this research project heeded anthropologist Laura Nader's well-known call to "study up." Rather than follow disciplinary conventions of studying relatively powerless individuals, Nader (1972) urged researchers to analyze powerful institutional workers and their relationships to subordinated people. Social scientists have responded to this demand by studying Wall Street financiers (Ho 2009), J. P. Morgan bankers (Tett 2009), immigration bureaucrats (Mountz 2010), artificial intelligence scientists (Forsythe and Hess 2001), military strategists (Vine 2011; Lutz 2002), weapons manufacturers (Gusterson 1996; Nordstrom 2004), and police torturers (Huggins and Glebbeek 2003; Huggins 1998). Through an exploration of the everyday, these studies reveal the work of powerful people and their connections to larger systems, like racism and capitalism, that contour people's daily lives.

As a methodological imperative, "studying up" requires designing research projects that examine powerful institutions and their actors. As an epistemological demand, "studying up" necessitates historicizing and contextualizing power. This means undertaking additional work to "locate and analyze the connections between powerful institutions (particularly bureaucracies and corporations) and relatively powerless individuals" (Nader 1972, 13). That is, "studying up" is not "an either/or proposition" whereby researchers choose to study either powerful elites or powerless individuals (13). Instead, "studying up" requires "studying up, down, *and* sideways," which means that researchers investigate the networks of power that connect elite institutions, powerful actors, and everyday people (8).

Despite Nader's insistence on this nuanced framework, social scientists sometimes have reduced "studying up" to studying only the powerful. Given these tendencies, Sue Reinhold (1994) reformulated "studying up" as "studying through" in her dissertation research. "Studying through" means "tracing the ways in which power creates webs and relations between actors, institutions, and discourses across time and space" (Shore and Wright 1997, 14). "Studying through," as a conceptual frame, seeks to grasp the call to study up, down, and sideways.

Like Reinhold, Sarah Becker and Brittnie Aiello (2013) have worked to capture the complexity of "studying up" by reframing this methodological approach as "studying power." In this view, power is "not something one person has and another does not" but, rather, "contextually-bound and situationally variant" (64). This means that social scientists must trace how power operates as "a dynamic and negotiated process" that is "tied to pre-exiting status differences *and* context-specific factors" like race, class, gender, and sexuality (64). Given this understanding of power, social scientists who "study up" cannot research only those "who come[] from a high- or low-status position" because this "fails to adequately capture the complex nature of power in the field" (64). When Becker and Aiello studied institutions of crime control, for example, they needed to examine both "how individuals exercised power" and how this power "is implicated in the dominant cultural ideologies about gender, race, and crime control" (64). The researchers located individual power within the social histories, belief systems, and cultural ideologies that organized power relations and shaped how people acted within those power relations.

Whether conceptualized as "studying up," "studying through," or "studying power," this methodological approach to interpretive qualitative research emphasizes the socially mediated webs of power that connect elite actors, their institutions, and subordinated populations. Although research projects that "study up" investigate the everyday lives of powerful people, they do so to understand how power operates across time and space. As a methodological and epistemological approach, "studying up" was well-suited to capture the inner workings of U.S. national security power, policy, and practice. In doing so, this study locates key CVE actors in relation to the larger systems in which they conducted their daily work and the everyday people affected by that work. Accessing the organizing logics and labor of CVE actors offers a window into the cultural, political, and social machinations of the U.S. security state.

"Studying up" also aligned with the needs of local community organizations working to end the criminalization of youth of color. One community organization, for example, rejected a youth participatory action research project I proposed to examine and respond to how CVE affected local youth. Instead, this community organization sought more information on CVE that could contribute to their political education projects used to inform, empower, and mobilize youth to resist their criminalization. By providing insight into governing national security policies, "studying up" can support the work of community organizations contesting the constant criminalization, surveillance, and incarceration of their communities. This research study therefore concluded with a community convening through which I reported my findings to community organizations and conducted any additional research they needed, like filing Freedom of Information Act requests and tracking down additional policy documents.

Despite these aims, the ethical standards enforced by university institutional review boards limited my capacity to report my findings to community members. Mandated to protect the anonymity of research participants, I could not report which agencies said what about their local CVE practices. Under these dictates, I used interviews and participant observation as breadcrumbs, navigational tools to find public documents that revealed the CVE programs that participants discussed and used in their daily work. As public records, these documents could be shared with communities while adhering to the ethical standards that govern academic research. By leveraging my privileged status as a university researcher, which granted me access to national security experts, "studying up" supported grassroots organizing "from below."

An Eclectic Study of CVE Power, Policy, and Practice

From working as a floor runner for the Chicago Stock Exchange (Zaloom 2006), to hanging out with nuclear engineers in a singles club (Gusterson 1996), to following Customs Service workers across Ghana (Chalfin 2010), social scientists have relied on innovative methods to study complex layers of power. This is because powerful institutions like nuclear weapons laboratories often are inaccessible to the general public and thus not conducive to conventional ethnographic methods where researchers immerse themselves in a single setting for an extended period of time. Given these issues of access, some ethnographers undertake "polymorphous engagement," which means "interacting with informants across a number of dispersed sites" as well as "collecting data eclectically from a disparate array of sources in many different ways" (Gusterson 1997, 116). Rather than primarily rely on ethnography's tradition of participant observation, scholars who "study up" typically utilize an "eclectic mix" of research methods in multiple sites over time (Gusterson 1997). Drawing from broader approaches to interpretative qualitative research, these eclectic methods include participant observation, formal interviews and focus groups, document analysis of policy texts, and extensive attention to popular culture and online interactions. By blurring the genres of qualitative sociology and ethnographic anthropology, these eclectic methods can provide insight into the ideological and material work of the U.S. security state.

To "study power" within the CVE policy environment, this project undertook polymorphous engagement, employing eclectic methods in multiple sites of CVE policy making and taking over time. To understand the "full realm of processes and relations involved in the production of policy" related to countering violent extremism (Wedel et al. 2005, 34), this research project included participant observation, semi-structured interviews, informal conversations, and textual analyses of official documents and popular media.[1] Through these methods, my research assistant and I trafficked back and forth between policy hot spots to "uncover the constellation of actors, activities, and influences that shape policy decisions and their implementation, effects, and how they play out" (Wedel et al. 2005, 39). Taken together, these methods worked to obtain a "vertical slice" of how the

U.S. security state has operated in and through CVE policies and sites over time (Nader 1972, 8).

Entering the CVE Policy World

My first encounter with the FBI's Don't Be a Puppet website in 2016 sparked my curiosity about CVE and its makers. After completing the website's learning modules, my research assistant and I culled federal, state, local, and research databases for texts like policies, white papers, and reports related to countering violent extremism. Wanting to better understand what led to the creation and launch of the Don't Be a Puppet initiative, our initial review included more than a hundred documents. These documents included Cold War policies that provided a historical understanding of contemporary security regimes, research publications that first framed the problem of violent extremism in the early 2000s, and evolving policies that formalized the Obama administration's commitment to CVE in 2015. In addition, we read and analyzed policies and publications related to the United Kingdom's Preventing Violent Extremism initiative (now known as Prevent), which informed the making of CVE in the United States. We approached these policy documents as cultural texts as well as classificatory devices that sorted people into categories like "violent extremist." We also filed Freedom of Information Act (FOIA) requests, which compelled government agencies to disclose public records, such as CVE program evaluations, grant proposals, and operating budgets. These documents provided insight into the "official story" and dominant national security narratives circulated by agencies like the U.S. Department of Homeland Security (DHS) and Federal Bureau of Investigation (FBI).

In addition to these policy documents, we analyzed emerging reports issued by community organizations and popular media outlets like the Minneapolis newspaper *Star Tribune*. As anthropologists suggest, one way to monitor social life is to read local texts that regularly report on issues of national security. These documents provided insight into the debates over, and concerns about, the emerging CVE policy framework from writers across the globe with varying degrees of power and influence.

After conducting this initial document analysis in the early stages of this research project, we continued to collect, code, and analyze national security texts related to countering violent extremism. How people talk and write about the world in formal policies, research briefs, and online modules, after all, "reflect[s] wider ideological pressures and, ultimately, particular constellations of power relations" (Wooffitt 2005, 14). Within the national security policy environment, these documents offered a window into the contexts in which research participants operated and provided a historical understanding of contemporary CVE policies and practices.

Although this ongoing document analysis gave us insight into the official and popular texts and vocabularies that organized people's daily work and the logics of CVE policies, we also understood that researchers cannot "learn through records alone how an organization actually operates day-by-day" or "treat records—however 'official'—as firm evidence of what they report" (Atkinson and Coffey 1997, 47). Given these limitations, my research assistant and I supplemented our document analysis by observing industry conferences hosted by national security agencies and academic institutions, sitting in on web-based and in-person seminars related to CVE programming, visiting museum exhibits on national security issues, participating in conference calls organized by impacted community members, and attending community events like the DHS roundtable at the invitation of research participants. Through our observation of these events in different locations and attendant collection of distributed materials, we gained insight into how CVE actors framed the problem of violent extremism to various audiences and defined methods for combating the perceived rise of homegrown terrorism.

Industry conferences and trainings served as important sites for the circulation of CVE knowledges and practices. Observation of these spaces provided a window into "how (in)security professionals conceive of and inhabit knowledges of practice" through their participation in these events (Baird 2017, 2). Within these social settings, CVE actors performed for their peers or for targeted communities, allowing for the study of the "multiple meanings of discursive and non-discursive features of (semi)public events, including, symbols, relations, spaces, and objects, across the multiple talks and exhibits present at a certain event" (Baird 2017, 3). Erving Goffman's (1959)

Entrance to the 2016 College and University Peacebuilding Approaches to Violent Extremism and Youth Recruitment workshop hosted by Cleveland State University. Photograph by author.

formulation of front-stage/backstage "presentation of self in everyday life" instructs qualitative researchers to be attentive to how people strategically perform in different spaces to make particular impressions on the researcher, peers, supervisors, and community members. In this way, *multi-sited event ethnography* [was] an appropriate tool for understanding how knowledge of practice emerges, allowing the researcher to identify and record knowledge practices within and across particular events" (Baird 2017, 3). Although my research assistant and I could not conduct participation observation in one location for an extended period of time, this fieldwork provided insight into the vocabularies, knowledges, and norms of the CVE policy field and its actors through our strategic immersion into multiple sites.

Our inclusion in this range of CVE activities across the United States facilitated many informal conversations with CVE actors, who enjoyed varying degrees of privilege and influence, from political elites to powerful state actors to street-level bureaucrats.[2] These conversations helped us understand how people made sense of these activities in real time. Through these informal interactions, we began developing a network of CVE actors whom we came to formally interview.

In addition to meeting CVE actors at these public events, my research assistant and I observed college students who struggled to be taken seriously by adults. At my first industry conference, for example, we noticed that when two college students submitted formal "question cards" like other participants, the moderator discarded their questions. News reporters did not seek out youth participants and local news segments often privileged the voices of elite actors like DHS representatives rather than young adults directly affected by local CVE programming. In these instances, we wanted to know what these young adults wished to say and why, so we engaged with them through informal discussions and side conversations, sometimes in between sessions, over email, or during our next trip to the region.[3] When a Somali college student was denied an interview with a local reporter, for example, we hung around to learn more about what he intended to say to the reporter and why it was important to him.

As community organizing efforts against CVE intensified, we sought out these critical perspectives to clarify our thinking and to check our interpretations of CVE. Throughout this book, these voices and experiences provide additional insight into CVE, even though I never intended to formally include college students in this research project. Although not representative of all young adults targeted by CVE, these voices have sharpened my analysis of governing national security policies and the actors who create, implement, and manage them.

Through this eclectic mix of fieldwork and subsequent analysis, I realized that studying up requires rethinking the ethical conventions used to protect participants, particularly in reports about my findings. Although this book follows the ethnographic standard of referring to participants by their pseudonyms to maintain anonymity, I also have incorporated the real names of public figures whose actions or words are a matter of public record, with the exception of young adults.[4] This follows the naming convention used in Hugh Gusterson's ethnography of nuclear weapons scientists, where "some people appear under their real names while others appear only under pseudonyms. Others appear at one moment under their real name and later under a pseudonym. This is done, not to confuse the reader, but to maximize documentary verisimilitude and at the same time honor the privacy that properly lies at the heart of the ethnographic contract" (1996, xvii–xviii). In this book, I use real names when referring to information that is a matter of public record, like policy documents, newspaper interviews, or public forums. If the information I present came from an interview or private conversation, then I use a pseudonym. In addition, I have altered other information to further protect the identity of each participant. In some cases, this means using a pseudonym for a participant's workplace or changing a position title. These practices respond to the complex power relations that define "studying up," adhere to discipline-specific ethical mandates, and fulfill the confidentiality agreements rendered when formally interviewing participants.

Toward a Feminist Methodology

Shortly after responding to my research assistant's request for an in-person interview, potential participant Tanvir Rahman sent me an email. In this email, Rahman reiterated his interest in the study but first wanted to know more about me, my research, and my politics. As a part of his response, Rahman wrote:

> I told [your research assistant] during our telephone conversation today that I'd be interested in reading your work, and after visiting your webpage I found a number of articles that I would like to read. Unfortunately I don't have a budget for accessing these articles. Would you be willing and able to share these articles with me before I meet with [your research assistant] on Thursday so that I can read them? Would you be willing to speak with me about your work as well?[5]

As I compiled the published articles and book excerpts Rahman requested, I recognized that, unlike conventional ethnographic projects, this research study engaged people in positions of power, often with advanced education and training. Over the course of his professional career, Rahman had accumulated extensive experience and connections in the criminal-legal system. This follows Gusterson's (1996) reminder that when ethnographers "study up," we encounter research participants who are "powerful and literate" and who "read what we say" (117).

In our email exchange, Rahman confirmed his privileged status as a formally educated and well-connected CVE actor in a powerful, albeit underfunded, state agency. Research participant Adrian Baker similarly reported that he "read and strongly respected [my] work on militarization in the classroom." Exchanges like these illustrate how powerful participants can negotiate authority in the research encounter by limiting access, setting the conditions for meeting, directly showing that they "read what we say," and publicly questioning our findings on social media and other news outlets.

Despite these exercises of authority, power is not hierarchical, static, or something an individual person simply has or possesses. Power emanates from, and is defined by, broader social structures, historical processes, and cultural contexts. In addition, power often operates through workers, like intermediary bureaucrats, who, through their labor, come to embody, enact, and extend state power that is not of their own making. The power relations that "characterize any historically embedded society are never as transparently clear as the names we give to them imply" (Gordon 1997, 3). Power, after all, "can be invisible, it can be fantastic, it can be dull and routine. It can be obvious, it can reach you by the baton of the police, it can speak the language of your thoughts and desires" (3). Power is dynamic, constantly remade and reworked through governing institutions, dominant discourses, and people's daily work.

Because power operates diffusely, social scientists must "locate[] power relations and contextualize[] decision-making within workplace settings and life histories" (Mountz 2004, 328). When studying institutional power, researchers cannot assume that power inheres in elite actors; they must locate that power institutionally, historically, and socially. An analysis of power when "studying up" thus cannot be reduced to ethnographers studying elite actors within powerful institutions, as even powerful people report to authority figures, hold beliefs that can conflict with their jobs, are limited in the work they can do, and are shaped by prevailing social, political, and economic contexts. "Studying up" is more complicated than studying powerful people because power itself is dynamic and contextual. Qualitative researchers must be attentive to how elite actors carry out their work, and make sense of that work, within broader institutional contexts, social structures, and relations of power.

Social scientists have worked to account for these complex power relations through the application of feminist methodologies. Feminist methodologists acknowledge that our social location—our place in society—frames our research and shapes meaning-making processes (Harding 1993; Haraway 1988; Lather 1993; DeVault 1999; England 1994; N. Nguyen 2016). Lorraine Code (1995), for example, instructs that "differing social positions generate variable constructions of reality and afford different perspectives on the world" (52). This means that "knowers are always *somewhere*—at once limited and enabled by the specificities of their locations" (52–53). Like all people, my place in society informs what I know and how I have come to know it. In the research context, the social locations of the researcher, the researched, and the relations between the two shape the research process, including the interpretation and analysis of people's experiences, knowledges, and daily lives.

Understanding that all knowledge is situated and partial compelled me to ask: How did my status as a racial outsider—a non-Muslim woman of color interviewing U.S. Muslims like Rahman—shape my relationships with participants? How did my status as a university researcher and my intellectual politics inform the questions I asked, my interpretations of participant responses, and my analyses of how broader social contexts informed Rahman's everyday work? In a post-9/11 context, how did Rahman's status as an elite actor within a powerful institution influence his relationship with me and how he responded to my inquiries? How did our place in society organize our variable understandings of what constitutes national security, racial profiling, and violent extremism? These questions follow feminist methodologists who urge social scientists to account for the identities of researchers and research participants as well as the social contexts that frame the research process, structure axes of difference, and shape meaning-making. This meant that I needed to be reflexive about how my status as a racial outsider affected every stage of this study.

My status as a university researcher also influenced my rapport with participants who sometimes sought resources or connections through their inclusion in the study. Although I was read as a young (naïve) woman, my academic job indicated to research participants that I had the authority to report on CVE and represent their work. This invariably shaped my relationship with research participants, most evident in requests for my published manuscripts. By communicating their awareness of my research, participants like Rahman and Baker worked to manage the power relations that organized the research encounter.

Because I had no experience in law enforcement, some CVE actors treated me with suspicion, caution, and even disrespect. In interviews with law enforcement, for example, participants sometimes dismissed me when I raised community critiques of CVE, deeming them "unintelligent," "superficial," or "conspiracy theories." However, when I mentioned that a former FBI agent held similar concerns, some participants carefully thought about and responded to these concerns. Initially I interpreted these differential responses as racialized and gendered, whereby law enforcement personnel afforded a white man more credibility than Muslim critics. The former FBI agent, however, offered an alternative interpretation: "That's a law enforcement thing." From his perspective, "law enforcement don't respect the perspectives of anyone who hasn't walked in their shoes" (informal conversation, March 20, 2017). In this view, the former FBI agent's critiques had currency in the CVE policy world because of his prior experience with the FBI and his status as a white man. As a credible voice in the national security policy world, CVE actors needed to take seriously and manage the former FBI agent's role in pushing the CVE debate. Meanwhile, I struggled to gain respect during interviews with CVE actors, who sometimes took phone calls, visited with colleagues, or belittled me as I asked questions.

Although I was able to gain access to research sites by emailing potential participants and attending CVE events, some participants limited or abruptly terminated my access. Elliott Adams, for example, invited me to a DHS roundtable where he introduced me to other CVE actors and seemed eager to arrange a focus group with state law enforcement officials. After meeting me at the roundtable, however, he stopped responding to my emails and phone calls to schedule the focus group. Other participants refused to communicate with me after a local newspaper ran a story critiquing CVE, which included my own commentary on how the identification of potential terrorists relied on "racial and religious profiling practices" (as quoted in

Ruppenthal 2017). Despite regularly gaining access to research sites and participants, maintaining that access over time proved difficult, especially given my public commentary on CVE and association with local community organizations.

Like mine did, my research assistant's positionality shaped her fieldwork. As a white woman and graduate student, she primarily interviewed former white supremacists ("formers") and talked with college students about their perspectives on and experiences with CVE. As a racial insider, she was able to build rapport with "formers," who spoke freely about their past violences and struggles to leave white supremacist groups. In this study, being white did not automatically translate into trust in the research encounter, but the possibility of a shared understanding between anti-racist white people facilitated the interview process. Former white supremacist Amy Kerns, for example, stated that "*We* have a problem with white privilege in our society. I'm not one of those self-hating white people, but if you look around at how people of color are treated, and you hear things like, 'Oh, racism doesn't exist; we have a Black president now!'" As Kerns described how the current "hatred" made her "sick," my research assistant affirmed her, commenting, "I'm feeling what you're feeling." In this exchange, Kerns approached the interview as a conversation between two white people with a shared commitment to anti-racism, evident in her use of "we." My research assistant encouraged this sentiment by saying, "I'm feeling what you're feeling" (interview, January 5, 2017).

To build rapport with participants in positions of power, my research assistant highlighted her student status. To do so, she deferentially asked questions that presumed little prior knowledge or familiarity with industry jargon. Participants responded to my research assistant's questions as experts wanting to teach her about their work and the national security policies that drove that work. Because my research assistant positioned herself as a student who worked for a professor, participants rarely viewed her as a threat or as an academic with legitimate critiques of CVE.

As these examples indicate, like all researchers, our place in the world shaped how we interacted with, and interpreted the experiences of, CVE actors. "The production of ethnographic knowledge is shaped by the shifting, contextual, and relational contours of the researcher's social *identity* and her social situatedness or *positionality* (in terms of gender, race, class, sexuality, and other axes of social difference), with respect to her subjects" (Nagar and Geiger 2007, 267, emphasis in original). Feminist approaches to qualitative research recognize that our place in society frames our research and shapes meaning-making processes.

To account for how our social identities and positionality affect our research, feminist methodologists suggest that social scientists turn to "situating technologies" (Rose 1997, 308). Reflexivity is one such situating technology used to analyze and account for how power relations shape qualitative research. Reflexivity "is not a matter of looking harder or more closely, but of seeing what frames our seeing—spaces of constructed visibility and incitements to see which constitute power/knowledge" (Lather 1993, 675). Throughout this research study, I continually employed reflexive techniques like memoing and member-checking to recognize and account for what framed my seeing (Lincoln and Guba 1985). Through these practices, I interrogated my own assumptions, intellectual politics, and positionality, all of which organized my relationships with CVE actors, my interpretations of the data, and my writing of the study's findings.

Guided by these feminist contributions, critical approaches to "studying up" must attend to the relational power dynamics that infuse the research encounter. This reflexive process must include a "reconceptualization of how power operates in the research setting" and a "critical examination of researcher positionality and the micropolitics of the research encounter" (Conti and O'Neil 2007, 63). That is, feminist researchers "make central the complex workings of power in the research study" (Conti and O'Neil 2007, 65). Rather than ignore how power shapes fieldwork when "studying up," feminist methodologists call on ethnographers to examine how power relations affect research studies, how researchers may perpetuate power structures in the research setting, and how the relationality between the researcher and the researched influence the production of knowledge.

As a part of these feminist interventions, social scientists have explored some of the ethical and epistemological conundrums encountered when "studying up." Elise Edwards (2007), for example, struggled to evaluate the ethics of naming a CEO involved in a racketeering scandal at one of her research sites, the office of a Japanese soccer team. She examined how such reporting in academic publications and speaking engagements could harm others involved with the soccer team, from players to office staff with less power who could be punished or even fired. The "heterogeneity of power vectors" in Edwards's field site and the "multiplicity of positions" held by participants muddied the ethical and political demands of her research (574). Ultimately, Edwards determined that naming the CEO in her work "felt both historically and politically important," especially since "his name and documentation of his illegal activities were already part of the public record in countless newspaper articles and court documents" (580). Given the power differentials between people associated with the soccer team, the decision to preserve or abandon anonymity was not straightforward. Edwards maintained the authority to name, or not name, powerful people and to represent their actions in particular ways. Navigating these power relations and related ethical issues was a complex and messy process.

In addition to these negotiations of naming participants in positions of power, researchers who "study up" have explored different strategies to navigate these dynamic power relations. Some qualitative methodologists, for example, have examined how social scientists can leverage their status as researchers, experience with the military, or citizenship to manage research encounters with powerful military elites or national security agents (Gazit and Maoz-Shai 2010). Feminist researchers have investigated how women researchers of color negotiate racial difference when interviewing powerful white men (Anderson-Levy 2010). Additional studies have explored how women researchers manage sexual advances and violence when interviewing powerful people like police torturers and assassins (Huggins 1998; Huggins and Glebbeek 2003; Glebbeek 2003). Others have explored how research participants exercise their authority to govern the direction of an interview or question the credibility of the researcher (Conti and O'Neil 2007). In all these cases, "studying up" involved power relations that were more complicated and complex than simply less powerful researchers studying elite actors in powerful institutions. Given these complexities, researchers "studying up" must document, account for, and be reflexive about power relations during every stage of research, from designing the study, to gaining access, to writing.

Although "studying up" presents different power dynamics than more conventional qualitative studies, methodologists cannot ignore

or sidestep how power shapes fieldwork. Applying feminist methodologies and corresponding ethical guidelines to "studying up" conventions is one way to enhance how researchers acknowledge and
account for how power operates in projects on the elite.

"I Have Skin in the Game": Capturing Complex Personhood

Despite these contributions, few analyses fully address the heterogeneity of power within elite institutions where people occupy different positions of privilege, whether as managers, administrators, or
CEOs. Managers, administrators, and CEOs are also diverse in terms
of race, class, gender, sexuality, citizenship status, and dis/ability, axes
of social difference that generate particular power dynamics within
elite institutions as well as in the research encounter. Rahman, for example, held a powerful yet precarious position in a state institution
as his employment was contingent on continued state and federal
funding. He also was a Muslim man subjected to anti-Muslim racism.
Although socioeconomic status occasionally can mitigate the effects
of racism (Lacy 2007), Rahman's racial and religious identities complicated his status as an "elite" or "powerful" actor.

Given these complex power dynamics that define all workplaces,
Rahman's membership in and commitment to Muslim communities
organized his CVE work and his institutional standing. When my research assistant first met Rahman, for example, he declared, "I have
a criminal defense background. I've worked with youth. I've been, I
am a leader in the Muslim community. I have skin in the game." The
confluence of his experiences and identities as a legal scholar, youth
worker, and Muslim immigrant meant he had "skin in the game":
moral, ethical, and political responsibilities to engage CVE and respond to the needs of the communities to whom he was accountable,
from federal funders to Muslim youth. How Rahman thought about
and enacted his role as a CVE actor therefore could not be reduced to
his powerful position within an elite institution, as his multiple social
locations shaped his work and his understandings of that work (interview, November 10, 2016).

As an institutional worker, Rahman was not only a powerful CVE
actor. He also reported to supervisors and funders, was accountable
to community members who publicly critiqued or welcomed his ef-

forts, and experienced anti-Muslim racism in his everyday life. Power was contingent and dynamic in his workplace, in his community, and in the research encounter. As a qualitative researcher, I needed to be attentive to how these power relations structured national security work and shaped my research, particularly as I built rapport with research participants, negotiated authority during interviews, interpreted collected data, and reported my findings in media interviews and in my own writing. I also needed to engage in reflexive practices like sharing my findings with research participants during the interview process and participating in collaborative meaning-making sessions with other social scientists.

Rahman's affirmation that he had "skin in the game" not only caused me to rethink and reconceptualize power relations in the field. It also compelled me to ask additional research questions to better examine the "micro-processes" through which people "are influenced and persuaded to participate in their own domination or, alternatively, resist it, sometimes disrupting domination or putting the system in reverse" (Nader 1997, 712). Like policies themselves, CVE actors were producers of social categories that classified people as violent extremists, dangerous terrorists, or deviant criminals, typically through racialized forms of identification. Yet, the production of these social categories, in practice and in policy writing, sometimes generated disquiet and anxiety in their authors. As illustrated in Rahman's stated desire to "get CVE right," Muslim actors negotiated prevailing national security discourses, understandings of what constitutes "good citizenship" in the United States, their own experiences with anti-Muslim racism and racial profiling, and their career goals. These negotiations often created conflicting and contradictory logics and practices that research participants navigated in their everyday lives as CVE actors.

In our interactions with Rahman, I noticed strategies he used to smooth over these contradictions. Rahman, for example, nervously began the first few minutes of his interview by acknowledging that "in the wrong setting," the Don't Be a Puppet initiative "could be *really* problematic." Citing his own experiences as a Muslim immigrant in a predominately white community, Rahman criticized Don't Be a Puppet's narrow focus on Muslims as "the data clearly show that white supremacists, sovereign citizens, and violent militias are responsible for more violence and death than those who are inspired by al-Qaeda or now ISIS." Rahman also rejected CVE programs "focused exclusively on Muslim and Arab communities." Despite these critiques, Rahman helped "recruit mosques across the country" to participate in a CVE initiative "focused on the Muslim community nationally." Recognizing this contradiction, Rahman insisted that his own work "could be useful if it's done right," citing problems with the implementation, rather than the concept, of CVE. By distinguishing his work from other CVE programs, Rahman managed his own anxieties about the impetuses and implications of this emerging national security approach, particularly for Muslim communities (interview, November 10, 2016).

Our conversations with Rahman indicated that I needed to be attentive to how CVE actors nervously negotiated public objections to their work, which often generated contradictory logics to justify this national security approach. Rather than treat Rahman's fraught assessment of CVE as an internal struggle, I needed to locate these anxieties within broader contestations over how to define national security, identify a potential violent extremist, and ward off terrorist threats. As a qualitative researcher, I needed to look for how Rahman reacted when the ready-made narratives that organized his work ruptured. I needed to investigate how Rahman came to imagine his own CVE praxis as an effective and progressive national security strategy, despite community protests that argued otherwise. Yet, I could not undertake this analysis without being reflexive about the complex web of power relations that organized Rahman's work and his understandings of that work. This web was spun, in part, by national security funding streams that encouraged "talking points about jihad," histories of surveillance in communities of color, geopolitical struggles, prevailing cultural contexts that defined what counts as national security, and Rahman's own identities, beliefs, and personal experiences. I also needed to be reflexive about how my own status as a non-Muslim university researcher informed how Rahman discussed his work and how I made sense of his work.

As these negotiations illustrate, critical methodologists who "study up" must design research projects that capture the "complex personhood" of participants like Rahman. Complex personhood "is about conferring the respect on others that comes from presuming that life and people's lives are simultaneously straightforward and full of enormously subtle meaning" (Gordon 1997, 5). As a qualitative researcher, I needed to seek out how the "enormously subtle meaning" of participants' lives shaped their involvement in the CVE policy world. "Recognizing and portraying interviewees as complex and even sympathetic human beings disrupts easy or uncomplicated links between the social realm" of powerful institutions, their actors, and their impact on everyday people (Conti and O'Neil 2007, 79). Rather than reduce Rahman to a powerful elite who sought to advance CVE policies at any cost, I approached Rahman as a complicated figure—a Muslim, immigrant, legal scholar, husband and father, and careerist—who "possess[ed] a complex and oftentimes contradictory humanity and subjectivity" irreducible to his role as a CVE actor (Gordon 1997, 4; see also Tuck 2009). To apprehend this complex personhood, I worked to be attentive to the social, political, and personal contexts that organized Rahman's conceptualization of national security and his commitment to CVE. Through ongoing reflexive practices, my fieldwork pulled me closer toward the perspectives and lifeworlds of CVE actors like Rahman, whose complex personhood shaped their daily work.

Although I interviewed CVE actors in positions of power, I still needed to account for and be reflexive of my own authority throughout my fieldwork, especially as a non-Muslim woman of color. I maintained the authority to ask particular questions, interpret people's responses to my questions, and report those interpretations to the public. In a follow-up conversation with Rahman, for example, I tested out ideas about CVE, asked for clarification, and communicated my own critiques of CVE. This gave Rahman the opportunity to correct my misunderstandings or misinterpretations of his work. In fact, when a newspaper interviewed me about CVE, Rahman called me to critique my analysis and clarify his own position on CVE. Although Rahman could challenge or reject my ideas, I maintain the power to represent his work in my writing, including this book.

In crafting these representations, I also needed to consider how U.S. national security policies historically have pitted "good" and "bad" Muslims against each other. In this dominant framework, "bad" Muslims are "clearly responsible for terrorism" while "good" Muslims willingly comply with special registries, FBI investigations, and other forms of surveillance (Mamdani 2004, 15). The introduction of and contestations over CVE have intensified this divisive binary and fractured Muslim communities across the United States. As a qualitative researcher in a political context defined by renewed anti-Muslim racism, I needed to be reflexive about how my writing represents the heterogeneous experiences of Muslims involved in CVE. My representations, after all, can both reproduce and disrupt the good versus bad Muslim binary.

Like Carol Cohn's (2006, 1987) study of nuclear weapons intellectuals, I began this project because CVE troubled me and I wanted to better understand how people involved in this work came to understand CVE as a progressive alternative to conventional counterterrorism tactics. By "studying up," I sought to trace the webs of power through which national security ideas became institutionalized and enacted through the daily work of street-level bureaucrats and powerful actors. Yet, as my interactions with Rahman reveal, "studying up" involves more complex power relations than simply studying elite actors in powerful institutions. As a qualitative researcher I needed to craft reflexive practices that accounted for and responded to these dynamic power relations. I also needed to enhance my ethnographic toolkit to better apprehend and communicate the depth of institutional life and the constellation of effects it engenders in and through its elite workers with varying degrees of power, influence, and authority. Despite these efforts, I recognize the limitations of these reflexive practices and the need for qualitative methodologists to develop strategies that capture the heterogeneity of power when studying up.

Although reflexivity is an unfinished project, this book attempts to capture the complex personhoods of those involved in the CVE policy world, elevating their sometimes competing and contradictory understandings of justice, community engagement, and national security as central to this story. In doing so, I respond to the underdeveloped ethnographic demand to "retain the complex personhood of the informant," which "challenges dominant notions of how power operates when studying elites" (Conti and O'Neil 2007, 80). Too often social scientists "withhold from the very people they are most concerned with the right to complex personhood" (Gordon 1997, 4). Through my exploration of the CVE policy world, I work to render the complex personhoods of key actors as I explore the logics, norms, and structures of this new national security approach.

CHAPTER 2

LEFT OF BOOM
Remaking the Global War on Terror

"CVE is the squishy stuff," Tanvir Rahman abruptly explained as I settled into his office. For Rahman, if counterterrorism (CT) denoted the use of "human intelligence, surveillance, and kinetic means" to fight terrorism, then "CVE is *not* CT." Researcher Adrian Baker similarly described CVE as "different from counterterrorism." These common refrains defined CVE as an alternative to "law enforcement–centric" antiterrorism methods like FBI stings, preemptive prosecutions, surveillance, and "all kinds of things like that" (Baker, interview, January 27, 2017). Most practitioners distinguished CVE from counterterrorism, evident in Rahman's eager commentary.

National security experts similarly defined CVE in contradistinction to counterterrorism. Humera Khan (2015), for example, described CVE as "the use of *non-coercive* means to dissuade individuals or groups from mobilizing towards violence, and to mitigate recruitment, support, or engagement in ideologically-motivated or -justified terrorism by non-state actors in furtherance of political objectives" (para. 3, emphasis in original). Daniel Glickman characterized CVE as "the solution to the problem of violent extremism that looks to non-kinetic and non-coercive toolkits" because "you can't kill or arrest" every perceived threat (participant observation, March 29, 2017). Retired FBI senior advisor Matt Rogers more evocatively described CVE as the "fourth way," a viable alternative to "handcuffs, body bags, and the closed case file" (participant observation, October 7, 2016). These experts carefully defined CVE in opposition to more aggressive counterterrorism tactics.

To better understand CVE as "not CT," this chapter explores what constitutes counterterrorism and the contexts that led the United States to develop "squishy" national security methods. I map what Baker described as the "stylistic" and "substantive" shifts that ushered in a "new set of policies and strategies" now known as countering violent extremism. More specifically, this chapter locates CVE within the ongoing oscillations in the global war on terror, shifting between conventional warfighting, counterterrorism, and counterinsurgency. Through this genealogical excavation, I examine how the distinction between CVE and counterterrorism is "fuzzy at best" (Ayat 2017, para. 15).

Following the Squishy Stuff: From Conventional War to Counterinsurgency

In an August 2004 speech, President George W. Bush lamented that "we actually misnamed the war on terror" and proposed that the war "ought to be the struggle against ideological extremists who do not believe in free societies, who happen to use terror as a weapon to try to shake the conscience of the free world." Although the *Washington Post* reduced the proposed renaming to a "malapropism" and satirically suggested the abbreviation SAIEWDNBIFSWHTUTAAWTTTSTCOTFW, Bush's speech marked the beginning of a concerted but fitful effort to rebrand the global war on terror (Milbank 2004, para. 3). Secretary of Defense Donald Rumsfeld (2006), for example, traded the term "global war on terror" for "global struggle against violent extremism." National Security Advisor Steven Hadley similarly defined a "global struggle against extremism," which demanded more than military intervention to win (as quoted in Schmitt and Shanker 2005). Reframing the global war on terror as the global struggle against violent extremism—G-SAVE for short—initiated a strategic effort to recast the war and to widen its scope to include "all of the tools of statecraft, economic influence, and private enterprise" (Hadley, as quoted in M. Davis 2005). The attempted rebranding of the global war on terror indicated equivocation both in the U.S. military strategy and in the dominant narrative shaping the public's understanding of that military strategy. In this section, I examine these oscillations in the global war on terror, necessary precursors to the development of the CVE framework in the United States.

Counterterrorism: The Rise of the Intelligence Industry and Targeted Assassinations

After the September 11 attacks, President Bush invaded Afghanistan (2001) using special operations forces to assassinate terrorist leaders, aerial bombardments to destroy terrorist training camps, and the provision of financial and military aid to support the Afghan Northern Alliance. In his presidential address to the nation, Bush (2001d) reported that the U.S. military had begun "strikes against al-Qaeda terrorist training camps and military installations of the Taliban regime in Afghanistan." Bush argued that these "carefully targeted actions [were] designed to disrupt the use of Afghanistan as a terrorist base of operations, and to attack the military capability of the Taliban regime." Rather than engage in conventional warfare, Bush initiated a series of remote and special operations to kill terrorists and destroy their networks. To support these "kill or capture" efforts, Bush ordered the Central Intelligence Agency (CIA) (2012) to "collect real-time, actionable intelligence" that could guide targeted assassinations, drones strikes, and special operations raids. These intelligence-driven operations formulated the basis of the U.S. counterterrorism strategy in Afghanistan.

According to the counterterrorism paradigm, terrorism "is caused by specific individuals or groups that use violence to attack state interests" and "results from a lack of state capacity to maintain a monopoly on force" (Schirch 2015, 1). Given this understanding of terrorism, U.S. counterterrorism operations involve active measures to find and destroy terrorist organizations or cells, like drone strikes guided by signals- and human-intelligence. These "kinetic" and "enemy-centric" practices form the core of U.S. counterterrorism strategy, most evident in the 2001 invasion of Afghanistan.

The twenty-first century rise of U.S. counterterrorism marks a "discernible shift in combat into the shadow spaces of covert and robotic wars, and a focus on special operations, remote warfare, and intelligence-gathering" (Khalili 2015, 2). By deploying these counterterrorism operations, U.S. military strategists shifted war away from the battlefield and toward more nimble technologies, including drone strikes and special operations raids to "neutralize" terrorists. Despite legal bans on assassinations—"targeted killings" in counterterrorism parlance—the U.S. liberal political culture has justified and enabled these assassinations as progressive alternatives to more indiscriminate warfighting.

In a normalizing society, state racism intervenes to authorize killing "not only its enemies but its own citizens" in the name of national security (Foucault 2003, 254). Rather than only manage, regulate, and discipline populations, the U.S. security state exercises sovereign power—the right to kill—through these counterterrorism tactics, like President Obama's secret "kill list," a macabre catalog of suspected terrorists pursued by the U.S. military. Racism "justifies the death-function in the economy of biopower by appealing to the principle that the death of others makes one biologically stronger" (258). With "racism [as] the precondition that makes killing acceptable," the U.S. security state generates public support for its murderous functions by framing constant surveillance, drone strikes, and targeted assassinations as necessary methods to improve the health and security of U.S. society (256). The U.S. public accepts calibrated violence against populations that putatively pose a civilizational threat to the nation.

This approach is predicated on the principle of the lesser evil, "often presented as a dilemma between two or more bad choices in situations where available options are, or seem to be, limited. The choice made justifies the pursuit of harmful actions that would be otherwise deemed unacceptable in the hope of averting even greater suffering" (Weizman 2011, 6). As a cold political calculus organized around the economy of violence, the principle of the lesser evil suggests that moderated killing can arrest more lethal violence. In his 2015 State of the Union address, for example, President Obama declared that "we will continue to hunt down terrorists and dismantle their networks" and "reserve the right to act unilaterally, as we've done relentlessly since I took office, to take out terrorists who pose a direct threat to us and our allies." For Obama (2015c), the extrajudicial killing of a few preemptively prevented deadlier violence in the form of a terrorist attack, despite the growing number of civilian deaths his "surgical strikes" accrued.

To support these global efforts, the United States has enhanced its domestic counterterrorism operations, particularly through the passing of the Uniting and Strengthening America by Providing Appropriate Tools Required to Intercept and Obstruct Terrorism Act (USA Patriot Act). The 2001 Patriot Act "was the first of many changes to surveillance laws that made it easier for the government to spy on ordinary Americans" (American Civil Liberties Union, "Surveillience under the Patriot Act," para. 1). Through the Patriot Act, FBI agents could use self-issued subpoenas to obtain the phone, computer, credit, and banking histories of everyday people. In addition, NSA agents began conducting "warrantless surveillance" by monitoring phone calls, text messages, and internet activity without public or judicial oversight and in violation of Fourth Amendment protections against unreasonable searches and seizures. The Patriot Act expanded the U.S. security state's authority to surveil, monitor, and police Muslim communities in the United States.

Given the authorization of these expansive surveillance practices, the NYPD recruited "mosque crawlers" who acted as inside observers in mosques, reporting on sermons and employing a "create and capture" method to "create" conversations about terrorism and "capture" and report these responses to law enforcement (American Civil Liberties Union, "Factsheet," n.d.). The NYPD also tasked undercover police officers with "raking the coals" to find terrorist "hotspots" by monitoring conversations at sites frequented by Muslims, including restaurants and sports venues. The NYPD also surveilled Muslim students and student groups "far beyond the city limits" in the name of national security (Gilson, Park, and Vicens 2013). To do so, undercover informants trawled Muslim student websites, attended student group meetings, and participated in events, like a whitewater rafting trip, to record student names and the number of times each student prayed. Oftentimes, the FBI entrapped Muslims to force them to serve as informants in these covert operations under the threat of prosecution, incarceration, and/or deportation. Through these criminalizing technologies of control, the U.S. security state has treated Muslims as the enemy within—incipient homegrown terrorists (Aaronson 2013).

As these examples illustrate, the September 11 attacks authorized the massive expansion of domestic surveillance targeting Muslim communities, which articulates with global military operations. As Deepa Kumar (2012) observes, "While the foreign policy establishment oversees the war on terror enemy abroad, the law enforcement apparatus targets the enemy at home. The net result is a spectacle of terrorism that is constantly kept alive in the American imagination" (140). Domestic counterterrorism practices have contributed to broader global war on terror operations.

Within the United States, political leaders historically have utilized counterterrorism strategies like targeted assassinations, intelligence-gathering activities, and coercive policing to neutralize political dissidents and repress communities of color perceived to threaten state interests while supporting U.S. military operations abroad. In fact, the desire to deter, destroy, and disrupt subversive activities domestically facilitated the rapid growth of the FBI shortly after its inception in 1908. Across history, U.S. presidents and their attorneys general have "directed the FBI to investigate individuals and organizations engaged in what others might characterize as political advocacy," even if they did not violate federal law (Theoharis 2000, 2). These FBI activities eventually evolved into formal domestic counterterrorism programs used to dismantle "terrorist" groups perceived to threaten state interests like the Black Panthers and, more recently, Black Lives Matter organizers and Indigenous water protectors. Today, the FBI serves as the lead federal law enforcement agency in domestic counterterrorism operations, which have included the use of deadly force, as in the 2016 FBI killing of suspected extremist Usaamah Rahim. I track the FBI's genealogy to map the emergence of domestic counterterrorism within the United States, which informs contemporary security regimes.

With the 1914 onset of World War I, for example, President Woodrow Wilson feared that domestic protests could disrupt national efforts to mobilize an effective military response, increase military spending, and raise a conscript army. Wilson also worried that the U.S. public might commit espionage or sabotage military shipments, a growing concern after the discovery of explosive devices in ships bound for Allied countries. Given these concerns, the Wilson administration passed the 1917 Espionage Act, which, in part, prohibited oral and written statements "with the intent to interfere with the operation or success of the military or naval forces of the United

States or to promote the success of its enemies . . . or cause insubordination, disloyalty, mutiny, refusal of duty in the military or naval forces of the United States, or shall willfully obstruct the recruiting or enlistment service of the United States." Political organizers who protested the war or the newly instituted military draft faced prosecution.

During this time, the FBI convicted over two thousand individuals under the Espionage Act, "but none involved espionage or sabotage by German operatives or their American sympathizers" (Theoharis 2000, 7). Instead, the FBI targeted Socialist Party members, labor union organizers, and pro-German and pro-Irish activists. In 2013, the U.S. government charged whistleblower Edward Snowden with three felonies for leaking classified security documents to journalist Glenn Greenwald, including two counts under the Espionage Act. The U.S. government continues to use the Espionage Act to punish political dissidents in the name of national security.

The vocabularies of the 1917 Espionage Act drew from the 1798 Sedition Act, which prohibited public opposition to the U.S. government, punishing those who "write, print, utter, or publish . . . any false, scandalous, and malicious writing" intending to "stir up sedition." The Sedition Act guarded against insurrections by European immigrants following the French Revolution as well as Irish rebellions in the United States. The United States historically has criminalized political dissidents as threats to state interests and national security, particularly in times of imminent or ongoing war.

In 1919, Attorney General A. Mitchell Palmer established a special FBI "Radical Division"—renamed the General Intelligence Division (GID)—to "collect and collate all information about radical political activities" uncovered by the bureau and other law enforcement agencies (Theoharis 2000, 8). The newly formed GID quickly amassed over two hundred thousand dossiers on radical organizers, which the FBI used to raid the offices of the Union of Russian Workers in twelve U.S. cities and eventually deported 249 of the arrestees.

In 1920, FBI agents provocateurs—undercover agents who incite others to commit a crime to facilitate arrests—infiltrated communist organizations. These FBI activities led to the 1920 Palmer Raids, resulting in the arrest of some fourteen thousand communists in thirty-three cities across the United States. The FBI framed the raids as enforcing immigration laws rather than repressing the communist movement. Yet the raids sought to "publicize the seriousness of the radical threat" to gain support for the policing of political dissidence (Theoharis 2000, 9).

Through these raids, the FBI sought to dismantle the growing radical left in the name of national security. To discredit the communist movement following the raids, the FBI invited reporters "to view and photograph the unkempt and bearded radicals (confirming the stereotypical image of mad bombers)" (Theoharis 2000, 9). In addition, "press reports glowingly characterized the raids not as deportation proceedings but as the successful containment of a potentially revolutionary threat" (9). Despite these efforts to discredit the radical left, the U.S. public criticized the FBI's use of agents provocateurs to incite criminal activities and the "lack of legal authority to enforce immigration laws" (8). The Palmer Raids tarnished the FBI's reputation and diminished public approval for these tactics. Despite this fallout, the FBI continues to use agents provocateurs, undercover informants, and raids to manage and criminalize political organizers.

In 1924, J. Edgar Hoover was promoted to FBI director, an appointment that intentionally initiated administrative reforms to rein in surveillance, including illegal wiretapping. Despite these changes, Hoover continued the FBI's war on political dissidents by developing the 1956 Counterintelligence Program (COINTELPRO). Drawing from previous domestic counterterrorism operations, COINTELPRO tasked the FBI with conducting blanket surveillance by using undercover informants and agents provocateurs to "expose, disrupt, misdirect, and otherwise neutralize" the "terrorist" activities of groups like the Communist Party and, later, the Socialist Workers Party, the Black Panther Party, and the Ku Klux Klan (Hoover 1967). COINTELPRO therefore surveilled and sometimes assassinated community organizers like Black Panther leader Fred Hampton, ushering in an era of lethal force to manage political dissidents perceived to threaten the nation and its interests.

To achieve these goals, Hoover (1968) directed the FBI to "pinpoint potential troublemakers and neutralize them before they exercise their potential for violence" and to "prevent militant black nationalist groups and leaders from gaining RESPECTABILITY by discrediting them" (3). To do so, the FBI "replicated the tactics that had been employed during wartime operations against foreign intelligence agencies," including the use of informants, propaganda, and disinformation to delegitimize and destabilize targeted groups (Theoharis 2000, 127). As a repressive project that included lethal force, COINTELPRO sought to disrupt all political organizing that challenged the state's legitimacy and authority, from communists to the Black Panthers.

The 1976 Church Committee report on the FBI's COINTELPRO operations revealed that "nonviolent organizations and individuals were targeted because the Bureau believed they represented a 'potential' for violence." The FBI therefore "conducted a sophisticated vigilante operation aimed squarely at preventing the exercise of First Amendment rights of speech and association, on the theory that preventing the growth of dangerous groups and the propagation of dangerous ideas would protect national security and deter violence" (Select Committee to Study Governmental Operations with Respect to Intelligence Activities 1976). Today, the FBI and other agencies target Muslim communities through similar anticipatory tactics, on the same theory that political and religious organizing represent a "potential" for violence and therefore pose a possible if not imminent threat to U.S. national security.

This long legacy bears on contemporary FBI practices aimed at policing political and religious organizing through surveillance, entrapment, and lethal force, particularly in communities of color. The FBI (2018) continues to "neutralize terrorist cells and operatives here in the U.S., help dismantle extremist networks worldwide, and cut off financing and other forms of support provided to foreign terrorist organizations by terrorist sympathizers." U.S. intelligence agencies, for example, worked with private security firm TigerSwan to disrupt the 2016–2017 Indigenous NoDAPL protests of the Dakota Access Pipeline (DAPL), which transports (and leaks) crude oil across Indigenous lands. To do so, TigerSwan approached Indigenous organizers as "jihadists" engaged in an "ideologically-driven insurgency with a strong religious component." Despite the NoDAPL movement's use of peaceful resistance and civil disobedience, TigerSwan called for "aggressive intelligence preparation of the battlefield and active coordination between intelligence and security elements." Drawing from COINTELPRO tactics, TigerSwan also sought to delegitimize and disrupt the protests by exploiting "ongoing native versus non-native rifts, and tribal rifts between peaceful and violent elements" as well as filing an unsubstantiated racketeering lawsuit against environmentalist groups that have supported the NoDAPL movement (documents obtained by the *Intercept*).[1] By describing Indigenous water protectors as "jihadists," the U.S. security state authorized coercive, if not lethal, force to destroy the political movement.

Since the 1600s, the United States has surveilled, monitored, and punished political organizing by communities of color, including settler rebellions, Indigenous resistance, and slave revolts. These abusive systems of power continue to haunt domestic security regimes as well as global military operations focused more exclusively on targeted assassinations and remote warfare. One former FBI agent even explained that the U.S. security state has used "exactly the same terminology and methodology to suppress the labor movement and civil rights movement and now the Muslim community. It's political suppression" (participant observation, April 21, 2017). From this perspective, CVE has continued the U.S. legacy of "political suppression" by targeting politically active communities of color as terrorist threats, from Indigenous water protectors to Black Lives Matter organizers. Although racialization and colonization are neither analogous nor equivalent, these two distinct global systems of dominance, and the various technologies of control and degradation on which they depend, operate as conjoined state projects whose continuities bear on contemporary security regimes (Lowe 2015; Byrd 2011). As we will see, despite the common refrain that "CVE is *not* CT," this new antiterrorism framework has contributed to and articulated with ongoing efforts to neutralize perceived threats through coercive tactics on both domestic and global fronts.

Recalibrating the Global War on Terror: From Hard to Smart Power

Despite the primacy of counterterrorism, it is only one tactic that the U.S. security state deploys to maintain dominance. Unlike Afghanistan, the 2003 invasion of Iraq began as a conventional, albeit profoundly asymmetric, war. The United States deployed ground troops, which quickly conquered Iraq's major cities. Notwithstanding these early military victories, U.S. soldiers confronted Iraqi resistance fueled by growing civilian deaths and the prolonged military occupation. Given the increased attacks on U.S. troops and declining public support for the war, the Bush administration sought less lethal strategies that could engage civil society and mitigate resistance.

As radicalization theories gained prominence and the war raged on, the Bush administration ushered in new strategies for the "global struggle against violent extremism." Military strategists, for example, recognized that "you can't just confront terror on the battlefield, that if we really want people to stop people blowing themselves up— terrorist attacks—we have to continue the operational and tactical stuff . . . but we really need to prevent people from finding these ideologies and these narratives appealing in the first place" (Susan Bailey, participant observation, May 16, 2017). For the Bush administration, the "2005–2006 era" marked a concerted effort to recalibrate its war strategy to integrate more complex tools to prevent the "regeneration" of the radical ideologies perceived to fuel terrorism (Thomas Vincent, participant observation, May 16, 2017).

In 2006, President Bush announced his "Strategy for Victory in Iraq: Clear, Hold, and Build," a plan supported by a 2007 "troop surge." Instead of only killing and capturing its enemies, the U.S. military sought to clear a contested territory of insurgents; to hold, or defend, the city from insurgent influence; and to work with local leaders to rebuild local economic, political, and government infrastructures to "win hearts and minds" (Office of the Press Secretary 2006, para. 5). U.S. soldiers, for example, played soccer with Iraqi children, handed out coloring books, and developed relationships with Iraqi families. In addition, Bush deployed special operations forces, which covertly assassinated insurgents and detained enemy combatants, civilian suspects, and civilian populations inclined to support the insurgency (Khalili 2015, 2). Through its development of a "clear, hold, and build" strategy, the United States began redefining the global war on terror as an intimate struggle for legitimacy that prioritized political tactics over military aggression. As the U.S. public grew weary of the protracted military operations and soldiers' repeated deployments, the discursive shift toward the global struggle against violent extremism matched the (re)emergence of a new war strategy.

Although the 2007 troop surge initiated efforts to fight a smarter, more complex war, U.S. policymakers also planned to scale back military operations, ultimately authorizing a complete withdrawal of troops from Iraq in 2011 and increasing the use of technologies like drones to conduct assassinations without ground troops. The scaling up and scaling down of U.S. troops in Iraq reflects "on the fly" efforts to develop more effective global war on terror strategies, sometimes shifting or blending theories of change in the process (Kilcullen 2010, ix). As the U.S. war in Iraq indicates, these multiple approaches to the global war on terror have been messy, dynamic, and blurred. CVE is the result of the ongoing oscillations between global war on terror strategies and growing recognition that the United States could not "kill or arrest" every perceived threat, both domestically and globally. The United States needed to integrate more complex antiterrorism methods to support the "operational and tactic stuff."

An ideological shift from culturalist to reformist understandings of "Muslim extremism" facilitated this shift in war strategy.[2] Informed by Samuel P. Huntington's (1996) "clash of civilizations" thesis, culturalists frame Islam as inherently incompatible with the West, a cultural divide that provokes intractable conflict. Because "Muslim extremists are a threat to Western civilization," culturalists contend that "the state can legitimately use wide-ranging emergency powers to counter them," whether through drone strikes, special registries, or FBI stings (Kundnani 2014, 63). The cultural clash between Islam and the West demands an aggressive approach to national security both domestically and globally.

Reformist thinkers, however, reject the culturalist thesis, arguing that violent extremists rely on "distorted" or "perverse" interpretations of Islam. As reformist thinking has gained prominence within terrorism studies, U.S. military planners have sought a more complex war strategy aligned with these new understandings. A U.S.-Muslim Engagement Project report (2008), for example, explained that "policies and actions—not a clash of civilizations—are at the root of our divisions" (1). This report concluded that "it has become clear that military force may be necessary, but not sufficient, to defeat violent extremists in Iraq, Afghanistan, and Pakistan, or to prevent attacks elsewhere" (1). In this view, military strategists needed to elevate diplomatic efforts to resolve conflict, enhance local governance and civic participation, catalyze job growth, and improve mutual respect between Muslims and non-Muslims through the coordinated efforts of federal, state, local, and private institutions. In this view, the "kill or capture" military strategy had proven ineffective and even counterproductive, necessitating more complex methods of fighting global insurgencies, both at home and abroad.

Political scientist Joseph S. Nye Jr. (2009) similarly advised that "the United States and its allies cannot defeat Islamist terrorism if the number of people the extremists are recruiting is larger than the number of extremists killed or deterred" (160). Although "hard power" could "deal with" individual terrorists like Osama bin Laden through targeted assassinations, "soft power is needed to reduce the extremists' numbers and win the hearts and minds of the mainstream" (163). "Smart power" integrated both kinetic and non-kinetic measures to gain the support of "mainstream" Muslims and prevent insurgent regeneration similar to the clear, hold, and build method used in Iraq (163). Smart power narrowed its focus on gaining legitimacy, winning the approval of the "uncommitted middle," and supporting "mainstream" or "moderate" Muslims (U.S. Army/Marine Corps 2007). As the United States struggled to gain legitimacy in Iraq and Afghanistan, its war strategists pursued alternative approaches that relied on both military force and rebuilding civil society to quell insurgent regeneration.

Shifting the Center of Gravity: The Counterinsurgency Turn

This more complex approach to warfighting is known as counterinsurgency, a distinct state struggle to regain legitimacy and quash dissent through "military, paramilitary, economic, psychological, and civil actions" (U.S. Army/Marine Corps 2007, 1–2). In the counterinsurgency paradigm, problems in the state-society relationship drive "non-state armed groups"—insurgents—to "use violence to attack state interests" (Schirch 2016, 150). "Insurgency" therefore refers to "an organized, protracted politico-military struggle designed to weaken the control and legitimacy of an established government, occupying power, or other political authority while increasing insurgent control" (U.S. Army/Marine Corps 2007, 2). The counterinsurgency theory of change involves destroying, isolating, and undermining insurgents and their narratives as well as winning the hearts and minds of the general population. Recognizing the limits of lethal force, this approach integrates humanitarian, development, and diplomatic efforts with military, intelligence, and police operations. This means that counterinsurgency combines enemy-centric methods to destroy insurgents with population-centric efforts to listen to, understand, and win the support of local communities.[3]

Remaking earlier U.S. counterinsurgency strategies of the mid-1900s,[4] these efforts seek to "secure the civilian, rather than destroy the enemy" (Sewall 2007, xxv). In contrast to an enemy-centric war strategy that relies only on lethal and coercive force, a population-centric approach engages in "perception-shifting" to "influence attitudes and alliances with the population at large" (Bhungalia 2015, 2312). According to counterinsurgency doctrine, "the civilian population is the center of gravity—the deciding factor in the struggle. Therefore, civilians must be separated from insurgents to insulate them from insurgent pressure," ultimately "isolating, weakening, and defeating the insurgents" (Sewall 2007, xxv). Instead of destroying the enemy on the battlefield, this type of warfighting works to persuade civilians to denounce the insurgency. These efforts "defeat the regenerating capacity" of insurgent networks, making this approach more effective than the "kill or capture" strategy (Vincent, participant observation, May 16, 2017).

Although the counterinsurgency turn in the global war on terror ushered in softer antiterrorism tools, it did not abandon remote warfare or other counterterrorism tactics, evident in the rise of drone strikes, targeted assassinations, dragnet surveillance, and FBI stings under both the Obama and Trump administrations. For an established, interim, or occupying government to regain legitimacy and authority, it must "eliminate[] those extremists whose beliefs prevent them from ever reconciling with the government," isolate the general population from insurgent pressures, gain the support of the "uncommitted middle," "provide the security and rule of law that allow establishment of social services and growth of economic activity," and facilitate "people taking charge of their own affairs and consenting to the government's rule" (U.S. Army/Marine Corps 2007, 2). U.S. counterinsurgency operations therefore deploy both kinetic and non-kinetic methods to suppress insurgent movements.

The pivot toward counterinsurgency signified a broader "cultural turn" in the global war on terror. War strategists blamed U.S. soldiers' misunderstandings of Iraq's cultural terrain for their early military failures. The U.S. military therefore sought greater "cultural awareness" to improve its global war on terror operations (Scales 2004, 2). U.S. Major General Robert Scales (2004), for example, explained that "intimate knowledge of the enemy's motivation, intent, will, tactical method, and cultural environment has proven to be far more important for success than the deployment of smart bombs, unmanned aircraft, and expansive bandwidth" (2). The U.S. military has committed significant resources to anthropologically studying the cultural and social aspects of its targets of war with the help of academics. The U.S. Army's Human Terrain System (2007–2014), for instance, deployed social scientists alongside combat troops "to support operationally relevant decision-making, to develop a knowledge base, and to enable socio-cultural understanding across the operational environment" (U.S. Army 2013). By building relationships with local communities, social scientists curated intimate cultural knowledge not as a "substitute for killing" but, rather, as a "prerequisite for its refinement" (Gregory 2008, 8).

Consonant with this cultural turn, counterinsurgency operations depend on "conflict ethnography," whereby the "professional counterinsurgent" engages in a "close reading" of the "physical, human, informational, and ideological setting[s] in which the conflict takes place" (Kilcullen 2007, para. 11). The cultivation of "cultural capability" depends on "extensive partnership with, and reliance on, local populations and security forces" as "only locals have the access to the population and deep understanding of a particular insurgency that is necessary to combat it" (Kilcullen 2010, 224). Community engagement serves as a key feature of the cultural turn in the global war on terror, as it fosters relationships with the local community, facilitates intelligence gathering, and fortifies the legitimacy of the U.S. military, all critical in the struggle to win hearts and minds. As we will see, CVE similarly has relied on community engagement to advance its mission through both kinetic and non-kinetic antiterrorism methods. In fact, the shift to the "global struggle against violent extremism" shaped both global and domestic war on terror operations through the introduction of hard and soft technologies of control to prevent the regenerating capacity of extremist ideology.

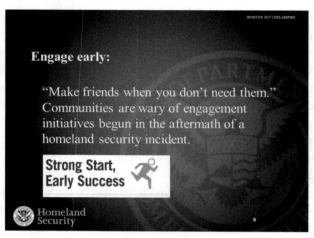

Screenshot of the PowerPoint presentation used at a law enforcement–
sponsored CVE workshop featuring a representative from the
Department of Homeland Security's Office for Civil Rights and Civil
Liberties.

"Picking Who Is a Terrorist and Who Is an Ally": Securitizing Humanitarian Aid

To facilitate this community engagement, the United States has
worked domestically and globally to build partnerships with local
populations and enhance national security through the strategic
provision of humanitarian aid and other social services. In principle,
humanitarian aid reduces suffering and responds to crises through
the administration of life-sustaining services like medical assistance,
food and water, and shelter to those most in need. In this framing,
humanitarian aid mitigates the effects of war, violence, or prolonged
conflict.

The strategic delivery of basic provisions to win hearts and minds,
however, securitizes humanitarian aid. Historically and presently, humanitarian aid can justify, advance, or fuel war, as the United States
decides who receives aid, for what purposes, and under what conditions. As a key tactic in perception-shifting, the securitization of humanitarian aid contributes to grander counterinsurgency strategy.

Although humanitarian aid organizations like the International
Committee of the Red Cross (ICRC) uphold principles of impartial-

ity and neutrality, John Cosgrave (2004) reports that "aid decisions are increasingly being weighted in terms of security and foreign policy rather than on humanitarian goals" (1). The "changing patterns of who gets aid can only be explained in terms of broader foreign policy" (Cosgrave 2004, 2). In 2003, for example, the United States directed $20 billion in humanitarian aid to the reconstruction of and regime change within Iraq, despite ongoing humanitarian crises in sub-Saharan Africa. Aid diversions from Africa to Iraq highlight just one example of this shift.

The securitization of humanitarian aid involves "picking who is a terrorist and who is an ally," a political determination that dictates the distribution of aid, eschewing the humanitarian commitment to neutrality. As foreign policy, humanitarian aid, and war cohere, agencies evaluate the "importance and usefulness" of potential recipients in the global war on terror, a key metric in determining who does and does not receive aid (participant observation, April 21, 2017). Geopolitical selectivity undermines humanitarianism's core principles of impartiality and neutrality (however flawed) and refashions aid as a critical global war on terror tool.

Contravening "traditional" humanitarians who view aid as apolitical and neutral, "new" humanitarians connect their aid efforts to development, democratization, and the general improvement of the human condition (Burde 2007; Nan 2010). These emerging efforts include the provision of educational services, thereby refuting the notion that education is "an indulgence that can be postponed till the development phase of reconstruction" (Cahill 2010, 1). Although new humanitarians view education in emergencies as a means to protect children, rebuild communities, and address the psychosocial needs of children, educational aid can be instrumentalized in the service of foreign policy or used to fuel conflict (Sobe 2007; Novelli 2010b). Since militaries and insurgents often attack and close schools as a part of their war strategy, the provision of educational services is a political act that can garner support, shift perceptions, and win hearts and minds.

In addition, the United States has mobilized education to Americanize aid recipients through the inculcation of U.S. beliefs, cultures, and ways of life. Donor states, for example, can impose certain conditions for the delivery of educational aid, including the importation of U.S. textbooks, languages, teachers, and pedagogies. In the current context, educational aid can be used to "induce policy change" by "using education as a means of socializing target populations towards accepting Western and capitalist hegemony" in ways that support the political agendas of donor states (Novelli 2010b, 453). Given the inherently political nature of education, educational aid can be "reduced to a political commodity" or "used by politicians to manufacture the consent of loyal supporters or to deprive societies of progress" (Her Highness Sheikha Mozah Bint Nasser Al Missned 2010, 7). The delivery of educational aid can be, and is, strategically deployed in the development, security, and economic interests of donor states.

Taking this tack, President Obama (2010) appealed to the U.N. Development Summit for continued investment in global development, particularly related to poverty, health, and education. Obama proffered that "in our global economy, progress in even the poorest countries can advance the prosperity and security of people beyond their borders, including my fellow Americans." Obama also argued that "when millions of fathers cannot provide for their families, it feeds the despair that can fuel instability and violent extremism," thereby inextricably linking national security and global development. Through such a gendered call, Obama refuted the "old myth" that "development is mere charity that does not serve our interests." Economist Jishnu Das (2010) more poignantly asked, "Why bother with humanitarian aid if you have no chance of winning the hearts and minds of recipients?" (para. 2). For both Obama and Das, humanitarian aid, including education, is a critical counterinsurgency tool domestically and globally.

To justify this development approach to national security, Obama appealed to the U.S. public through humanitarian and democratic ideals. Obama (2010), for instance, argued that U.S. investment in global development was "rooted in America's enduring commitment to the dignity and potential of every human being." This liberal rhetoric, however, "has long been deployed in the interest of imperial aims" (Kumar 2012, 123). Today, U.S. empire depends on liberal commitments to human rights, democracy, and national security rather than the "civilizing mission" of the eighteenth and nineteenth centuries. These liberal precepts justify war as well as the humanitarian, development, and diplomatic interventions that support U.S. military operations.

The securitization of humanitarian aid contributes to grander counterinsurgency strategy, evident in the continued "comingling of militaristic and humanitarian forces, coercion and governance, destructive and productive technologies, and war and law" (Bhungalia 2015, 2312). As a theory of war guided by liberal precepts, counterinsurgency emphasizes managing civilian populations and winning hearts and minds through economic development, service provision, humanitarian aid, and calculated violence. As a recalibrated military strategy, counterinsurgency doctrine responds to the perceived failures of the global war on terror and advances a perceptively less lethal approach to warfighting.

Playing Nice: Toward Full-Spectrum Dominance through Community-Oriented Policing

Through the domestic application of counterinsurgency principles, the U.S. security state deploys a "careful balance of hard and soft controls," including a reliance on community outreach and the securitization of social services to support domestic and global antiterrorism operations (Insolacion 2013, 188). To prevent the regenerating capacity of insurgent networks within the United States, law enforcement agencies have renewed their community policing efforts. In the community-oriented policing paradigm, community members serve as coproducers of public safety. In this view, coproducing public safety amounts to "democracy in action" by empowering local communities to collaboratively solve local problems with law enforcement agencies (Community Policing Consortium 1994, 4).

In the United States, this "democratic" approach to policing dates back to the mid-twentieth century, although national commitments to community policing have fluctuated with shifting political, cultural, and social contexts from the civil rights movement to the war on drugs. The early rise of community policing models in the United States represented a pivot away from "incident-oriented" policing and toward "problem-oriented" policing. Leading police strategists James Q. Wilson and George L. Kelling (1989), for example, explained that "the conventional police strategy is 'incident-oriented'—a citizen calls to report an incident, such as a burglary, and the police respond by recording information relevant to the crime and then trying to solve it" (para. 4). Incident-oriented policing, however, fails to address the underlying community conditions that cause these crimes. Given these limitations, Wilson and Kelling called for a more complex "problem-oriented" approach to policing that directly addressed the root causes of crime.

Community policing also emerged as a response to national critiques that coercive policing violently suppressed the 1960s Black freedom struggle. As mass protests and political assassinations grew during this time, national commissions identified the police as the source of social tension. The "police force's inability to handle urban unrest in an effective and appropriate manner brought demands by civic leaders and politicians for a reexamination of police practices" (Community Policing Consortium 1994, 7). Like the military occupation of Iraq, both the U.S. government and its public indicted the police as the cause of political instability. Confronting increasing social unrest, emerging community policing models sought to repair the police's image, reputation, and capacity to solve crimes, particularly in communities of color contesting police brutality, racial profiling, and constant surveillance.

After the 1992 Los Angeles uprisings, for example, President George H. W. Bush initiated Operation Weed and Seed to "weed" out criminals and to "seed" community revitalization projects. This community-oriented policing initiative "bridge[d] weeding and seeding strategies: officers obtain[ed] cooperation and information from area residents while they assist[ed] residents in obtaining information about community revitalization and resources" (Department of Justice 2014b). By enhancing the police's intelligence-gathering capabilities, community cooperation facilitated the "weeding" out of criminals. In this model, population-centric tactics like community revitalization projects can strengthen the police's capacity to arrest, detain, and incarcerate.

Despite the progressive framing of Operation Weed and Seed, some warned that "this is a program that use[d] a disproportionate share of its resources on the weed side of the formula in communities of color, and use[d] a disproportionate share of its resources on the seed side in communities that [were] predominately white"

(Kanigher 1996). Operation Weed and Seed also forced communities to comply with local policing to gain access to sorely needed "community revitalization and resources." Even though the Bush administration pitched Operation Weed and Seed as a program responsive to local needs, organizers argued that this community policing initiative merely intensified misdemeanor arrests and police brutality against people of color while securitizing the provision of community resources. Resistance to Operation Weed and Seed revealed contestations over who counted as "the community" and what constituted "policing," particularly as some residents experienced increased police brutality in the name of social order.

Given the perceived rise of homegrown terrorism and intensifying concerns about the abrogation of civil liberties in the pursuit of national security, the U.S. security state has sought to apply community policing models like Operation Weed and Seed. In fact, community policing "is understood today, and increasingly promoted as, an effective approach to preventing terrorist activity" as "it builds on community-police relationships and collaborative ownership of security issues" (United States Institute of Peace 2014, 5). Cultivating community partnerships and developing community trust "may lead to increased reporting of suspicious activity as well as sharing of information, target hardening, and improved coordination" by "leveraging the strength of communities and their members" (International Association of Chiefs of Police 2014, 2). In this view, community members "are an important force multiplier," especially as local law enforcement agencies "have become increasingly important in providing for the national security of the United States" (1–2).

In 2007, for example, the Los Angeles Police Department's counterterrorism bureau "proposed using U.S. census data and other demographic information to pinpoint various Muslim communities and then reach out to them through social service agencies" (Winton, Watanable, and Krikorian 2007, para. 2). Through this initiative, the LAPD sought to map Muslim communities under the auspices of providing social services while documenting what the department perceived to be "hotbeds of extremism" (Winton, Watanable, and Krikorian 2007, para. 1). In doing so, Deputy Police Chief Michael Downing reported, "It is also our hope to identify communities, within the larger Muslim community, which may be susceptible to violent ideologically based extremism and then use a full spectrum approach guided by an intelligence-led strategy" (as quoted in Winton, Watanable, and Krikorian 2007). By aligning its community outreach with broader national security goals, the LAPD pursued a "full spectrum," "intelligence-led" counterterrorism approach, particularly in Muslim communities perceived to be uniquely vulnerable to terrorist radicalization. This process securitized social service providers, whose work contributed to and enhanced the U.S. security state and its counterterrorism agenda. As we will see, this community policing approach has anchored the Los Angeles CVE model, which treats Muslim communities as uniquely vulnerable to becoming "hotbeds of extremism" and social service providers as critical foot soldiers in the domestic war on terror.

Community engagement continues to support coercive policing operations dedicated to territorial control and national security. In 2016, for example, U.S. Immigration and Customs Enforcement (ICE) established a new Office for Community Engagement staffed with ICE community relations field officers. According to one field officer, this new office "has expanded and strengthened ICE within all of civil society." In addition, the local field officers "increase local and national understandings and support of ICE's mission," which bolsters trust and collaboration with communities. Through strategic community outreach efforts, these officers cultivate relationships that generate more referrals that report "national security threats" to ICE "before an attack materializes" (participant observation, November 10, 2016). By enhancing ICE's reputation within targeted communities, these community engagement activities have strengthened ICE's border enforcement capacities.

To facilitate these community engagement tactics, ICE relies on "third-party policing," a strategy whereby law enforcement agencies or local legislation require government employees like teachers to report undocumented immigrants. A 2004 Arizona statute, for example, mandated that social workers report "any violation of federal immigration law by any applicant for [public] benefits" like college scholarships and imposed criminal misdemeanor charges on social workers who failed to comply with this reporting mandate (Ariz. Rev. Stat. § 46–140.01). These tips facilitated immigration raids, making undocumented families "afraid to pick their kids up from school, shop, and otherwise go about their daily lives" (Insolacion 2013, 197). Law enforcement officials therefore have exploited social service providers to intensify border enforcement.

Because immigration raids have a "chilling" effect on the local community, ICE "plays nice" and establishes "good relations" through community collaborations that "manufacture support for ICE" and therefore strengthen its border enforcement capabilities (Insolacion 2013, 196). U.S. Customs and Border Patrol agents, for example, have created activities like "Shop with a Cop" where law enforcement personnel take children to local stores to buy clothing or shoes (Miller 2014, 71). The Border Patrol Explorer program provides young adults aged 14–20 with "the opportunity to work with dedicated law enforcement professionals throughout their formative years," which drums up support for Border Patrol and encourages children of color to consider law enforcement careers (Department of Homeland Security 2014). Rather than rely solely on immigration raids that intensify local resistance, federal law enforcement agencies have developed strategic relationships with local communities who coproduce territorial and national security through their own reporting of potentially undocumented individuals assumed to threaten the United States. By managing resistance, ICE's community engagement efforts have complemented more coercive enforcement methods, like incarceration, torture, and even murder by Border Patrol agents. In this way, community policing integrates counterinsurgency doctrine, utilizing both kinetic and non-kinetic methods to defeat perceived insurgencies and win hearts and minds.

These community policing methods slowly crept into the early stages of CVE planning. In 2010, for example, DHS formed a CVE Curriculum Working Group led by LAPD's counterterrorism expert, Michael Downing. This working group sought to adapt community-oriented policing models to "address the dynamics of Violent Extremism and the associated convergent threats, particularly those that emanate from Diaspora communities" (Department of Homeland Security CVE Curriculum Working Group 2011, 5). Following the recommendations of the working group, the 2011 White House Strategic Implementation Plan detailed the importance of integrating CVE efforts into existing community-oriented policing models and building law enforcement expertise in CVE methods.

This work has informed the development of the LAPD's "countering violent extremism tailored community policing" model (CVETCP). CVE researchers argue that "adopting a community policing model is a necessary approach to better protect and serve communities at risk for violent radicalization," including "Muslim immigrants and refugees from countries where the police were feared and citizens learned to turn away" (Weine, Younis, and Polutnik 2017, 1). Like more traditional community policing models, CVETCP has "leverage[d] existing community partnerships to counter violent extremism and violent crime," ultimately enhancing police legitimacy, capacity, and power, especially in diasporic communities (White House 2016, 16). Furthermore, CVETCP assumes that "Diaspora communities" are uniquely vulnerable to violent extremism and reaffirms the police as problem-solvers rather than violent forces to be feared.

Despite the rapid emergence of CVETCP, some security experts have argued that these "government-led and government-sourced" initiatives have threatened the integrity of CVE. These critiques have created calls for CVE programs to maintain a strict "division of labor" where law enforcement "deal with crime" and communities "deal with non-crime." According to Baker, "the evidence is suggesting that it would be civil society-sourced and -led efforts . . . that are the most promising approach to essentially ameliorating" the complex factors "associated with entry into non-state ideologically-motivated violence." Baker argued that transferring CVE duties to civil society organizations "seems to be a much more promising direction" than police-led initiatives (interview, January 27, 2017).[5]

Given these concerns with "government-led and government-sourced" programs, some cities have developed CVE initiatives with ostensibly minimal collaboration with law enforcement agencies. In Chicago, for example, the Illinois Criminal Justice Information Authority presented its Targeted Violence Prevention Program (TVPP) as distinct from police-led initiatives. Rather than rely on law enforcement, TVPP practitioners sought to "educate a broad cross-section of communities in Illinois on how to off-ramp individuals who exhibit warning signs of radicalization to violence as well as those who exhibit behaviors signifying they may be in the early stages of planning an act of ideologically inspired targeted violence" (Illinois Criminal Justice Information Authority 2016, 3). In this "community-led" model facilitated by a state law enforcement agency and funded by the Department of Homeland Security, TVPP practitioners trained social service providers like mental health professionals to identify and work with individuals vulnerable to or in the process of radicalizing. These efforts, however, also incorporated local police officers "eager to participate" and garnered support from the Chicago Police Department, Elgin police chief, FBI, DHS, and Illinois Terrorism Task Force (obtained documents). Advertisements for a training for mental health professionals, for example, listed FBI special agents and a DHS representative as speakers. Despite public-facing documents that framed TVPP as a community-driven initiative, practitioners necessarily relied on law enforcement agents who helped design and implement the program.

"Community-led" CVE programs have called on social service providers to coproduce national security in cooperation with local, state, and federal law enforcement agencies. Practitioners have contended that this approach offers an alternative to more coercive counterterrorism practices. Critics, however, have argued that this new generation of CVE programs enhances police power by deputizing social service providers as law enforcement agents who identify, report, and off-ramp individuals on the perceived pathway to violent extremism. In addition, the introduction of these programs has not led to the suspension of conventional counterterrorism practices, like FBI sting operations. Despite ongoing claims that "CVE is not CT," CVE has served as one component of a multipronged antiterrorism approach that deploys a careful balance of hard and soft technologies of control to achieve territorial security and full spectrum dominance.

The Wake-Up Call: Facing the Threat of Homegrown Terrorism
When President Obama formally launched CVE in 2015, he explained that this national security approach "encompasses the preventative aspects of counterterrorism as well as interventions to undermine the attraction of extremist movements and ideologies that seek to promote violence" through community engagement. More specifically, Obama reported that the "underlying premise" of CVE is that "communities provide the solution to violent extremism" and that "CVE efforts are best pursued at the local level, tailored to local

dynamics, where local officials continue to build relationships with their communities through established community policing and community outreach mechanisms" (Office of the Press Secretary 2015). As this explanation indicates, the U.S. security state has developed new domestic antiterrorism methods by integrating (and sometimes conflating) the principles of community-oriented policing, counterterrorism, and counterinsurgency. By deploying both kinetic and non-kinetic tactics, this integrated strategy has sought to disrupt, deter, and/or destroy insurgents "left of boom": before they build and activate bombs within the United States or travel abroad to fight for designated foreign terrorist organizations.

This multipronged national security approach has drawn from President Bush's earlier efforts to mobilize Muslim youth in the United States as "active messengers" who could counter extremist propaganda and "identify people who were in danger of being radicalized" (Bailey, participant observation, May 16, 2017). Bush's "global struggle against violent extremism" strategy, however, "didn't resonate so they just stuck with the 'global war on terror,'" both "stylistically" and "substantively" within the United States (Baker, interview, January 27, 2017). CVE therefore "went dormant" until the Obama administration redesigned and repackaged this national security approach (Bailey, participant observation, May 16, 2017).

Even after Obama announced his 2011 Empowering Local Partners to Prevent Violent Extremism in the United States plan, emerging domestic CVE programs still were "not well-funded" and lacked "political support." As an underfunded initiative with little political support, CVE "remained more of an activity that was on the bookshelf rather than something that really galvanized the U.S. government" (Bailey, participant observation, May 16, 2017). The 2013 Boston Marathon bombings, however, reignited governmental and public interest in domestic CVE programs as a key global war on terror strategy:

> After the Boston bombings, all of a sudden people within the government *really woke up* to the fact that there is a domestic threat, despite a lot of the work the Obama administration had done addressing some of the big-picture foreign policy grievances that helped motivate terrorist narratives like having

troops on the ground in the Middle East or having what people perceived as sort of a negative or a confrontational relationship with various countries in the Middle East. We still had people who were attracted to these ideologies, domestically. So that was a wake-up call. (Bailey, participant observation, May 16, 2017)

For government officials, the Boston bombings signaled a rising "domestic threat" that could destabilize the United States economically, politically, and territorially. Shortly after, ISIS "really began its march, territorially" and started "splashing" sophisticated videos across U.S. news screens during the summer of 2014 (Bailey, participant observation, May 16, 2017). Despite the fluctuating commitment to CVE and other non-kinetic antiterrorism methods, the Boston bombings and growing ISIS presence generated a sense of urgency in the U.S. public, which demanded an immediate response to the perceived crisis of homegrown terrorism. CVE came to serve as that response, evident in the 2014 launch of pilot programs in Boston, Minneapolis, and Los Angeles. As in Iraq, the U.S. security state recognized the limitations of its "kill or capture" approach and therefore pursued a more complex domestic war on terror strategy that could support its military pursuit of ISIS.

Following the Boston Marathon bombings, U.S. news outlets pointed to a growing homegrown terrorist threat, heightening fears of an attack in local communities, venues, or schools. In a fear-filling report, Fox News warned that "Boston is just the beginning," provocatively suggesting that the U.S. public should expect additional attacks (Erickson 2013). Local CVE actors harnessed palpable fears of a homegrown terrorist attack to advance their agenda.

In Illinois, news of an FBI sting operation that led to the arrest of teenager Adel Daoud rapidly circulated and "stunned" Muslim communities (Shah 2014a). Referencing the Daoud arrest, Targeted Violence Prevention Program director Junaid Afeef (2014) urged "Muslims in America" to help "halt extremism" in a local op-ed piece. In fact, Afeef reported that he was "more concerned about the future of Muslims in America" than ever before. In his compelling message, Afeef (2014) implored "the Muslim leadership of our mosques" to "wake up" to the "reality that our young people are vulnerable to extremist ideologies" and to "take control of this nightmare" (para. 2).

Like others, Afeef reaffirmed that violent extremism was a dangerous problem that Muslim communities needed to solve collectively.

At a 2016 U.S. Department of Homeland Security Quarterly Roundtable, community leader Masoud Kaleel similarly reported that in his community, "ten young Muslims were arrested over the past two years" for terrorism-related crimes. Kaleel poignantly described how "the families of these people were devastated." He also explained that since these arrests, local Muslim organizations "have been involved in developing programs to build the resilience" to terrorist radicalization. Despite concerns that an "overreaction" to homegrown terrorism could lead to racist arrests like Ahmed the clockmaker, Kaleel affirmed CVE as an important intervention given the number of "devastating" terrorism-related prosecutions across the United States (participant observation, November 10, 2016). In this view, CVE could protect Muslim children from terrorist influences.

Like Kaleel, Tanvir Rahman expressed deep concerns about the preemptive arrest of Mohammed Hamzah Khan, a teenager who allegedly tried to fly overseas to join ISIS. For Rahman, if the FBI understood that "a kid is going down this path . . . there's got to be a better way" to address the issue than simply arresting him. Khan's arrest and sentencing generated an urgent desire to develop nonpunitive solutions to the intimately local problem of violent extremism.

Muslim leader Bassem Ali also described how the radicalization of his former student, Samir Khan, affected him and drew him into CVE work. Ali described Khan as "this kid who was this cyber jihadi who was working out of his parents' basement and eventually he left and went to Yemen and then he resurfaced publishing, or allegedly publishing, *Inspire*, which was this English-language magazine about al-Qaeda." Ali kept in irregular contact with Khan until he was killed in a 2011 U.S. targeted drone strike alongside fellow U.S. citizen Anwar al-Awlaki. As his teacher, Ali "watched [Khan] transform from this nerdy kid into this guy who is full of rage and such over the years. So, it's a lot that is very close to my heart" (interview, March 16, 2017). For many Muslim leaders like Ali, Kaleel, and Rahman, these "devastating" arrests close to their hearts compelled them to "do something about this." As community leaders, they felt a sense of duty to protect Muslim children from terrorist influences. Researching, developing, and implementing CVE programs became one way these leaders worked to create healthy communities resilient to terrorist radicalization.

Law enforcement official David Greene similarly framed home-grown terrorism as a deeply personal issue. In a public forum, Greene delivered a provocative speech that communicated the imminent and terrifying danger of violent extremism taking hold of youth in nearby coffee shops, community centers, and schools. As a part of his call to action, Greene offered an anecdote that illustrated the intimate urgency of this perceived problem, saying:

> About a mile from here, on an average afternoon kind of like this, a group of young Somali teens were at a restaurant. And while they were at the restaurant, they were on a Skype telephone call with a terrorism recruiter from Somalia, from, excuse me, from Syria. And the conversation was tape recorded, so we know what was said and we know what happened. And as they were sitting in the restaurant—just like my kids would do when they were teens, talking amongst themselves, talking to the server about what they wanted to eat and drink—they were also Skyping with someone who was trying to destroy their lives. He was a terrorist recruiter from ISIL. And during that call, he's explaining to them how they can get to Syria—through Mexico, through Canada, and other means. And they're listening, they're engaging, because that's what *they* had decided they wanted to do.
>
> And I tell you that because as we spend the day speaking about countering violent extremism, or as they call it in Minnesota, building community resilience, this is what we're trying to stop. Luckily, none of those young men made it to Syria. But a number of their friends did. And those friends are dead, before they reached, for the most part, their 21st birthday. And so, for me, when we talk about countering extremism, building resilience, stopping terror recruiting, it's not a theory. It's not a concept. It's personal, and it's real, and it's something we all need to care a great deal about. (participant observation, August 18, 2016)

Through repeated narratives of how parents in the Twin Cities "lost young sons to terrorist recruiters" in nearby restaurants and coffee shops, Greene evoked a palpable sense of urgency, grief, and fear. After citing the names of recently arrested youth, Greene declared that "it's my goal to work with our community, to work with our civil society, our Somali community, our law enforcement to make sure that when we're done . . . no one else will have to know the pain of losing a son or daughter to terrorism before they turn twenty or twenty-one" (participant observation, August 18, 2016). By narrating the threat of losing a loved one to terrorist recruiters, Greene framed CVE as a progressive effort to protect the community and defend the nation.

As an outsider to local politics, I found Greene's storytelling evocative. As I traveled the country, I heard other CVE actors rely on similar storytelling to elicit the approval and consent of community members seeking to protect their children from terrorist influences. Through these provocative stories, political actors like Greene "do not seek merely to purchase or compel others' assent to specific policies"; they also "aim to shape the linguistic axes that define the scope and substance of political debate" and "fix the terms in which debate is conducted, policy legitimated, and events interpreted" (Krebs 2015, 9). Greene thus strategically employed storytelling to gain support for his controversial CVE policies and programs, shape how communities interpreted the problem of homegrown terrorism, and limit the terms of the CVE debate.

The centrality of these national security narratives, however, did not mean that local communities agreed to CVE policies or circumscribed their interpretations to the terms advanced by politicians like Greene. College student Hodan Hassan, for example, argued that Greene "caused so much destruction" through both his recitation of these maligned narratives and the CVE practices they came to justify (participant observation, April 21, 2017). Like Hassan, college student Bashir Cilmi criticized a Somali elder who "pushed the notion that hoards and swarms of Somalis are becoming radicalized and if you don't send them on camping trips, they're going to radicalize." Cilmi concluded that, through these oppressive narratives, "you lose or are stripped of your identity and voice for ourselves" (participant observation, April 21, 2017). U.S. media, for example, began portraying Minneapolis as "a city gone mad" and "the Islamic State of

Minnesota." Somali organizers like Hassan and Cilmi rejected these narratives as dehumanizing and destructive accounts.

Despite these critiques, these dominant narratives resonated with CVE actors who mobilized to "halt extremism" in the United States. From their perspective, CVE offered a way to protect their children from terrorist radicalization without relying on FBI stings, as in the case of Adel Daoud. Framed as a liberal alternative to conventional counterterrorism, CVE gained currency in communities as a therapeutic approach to solving the problem of violent extremism.

As these examples illustrate, the Boston bombings and preemptive prosecutions of Muslim youth like Adel Daoud ushered in a new commitment to and rearticulation of CVE within the United States. Through a process Foucault (2003) calls "eventalization," incidents like the Boston bombings take on historical significance as "events" by transforming structures of meaning. These events usher in the diagnosis of new problems to be managed through new forms of knowledge. The Boston bombings and FBI stings disrupted prior modes of understanding, diagnosed a new problem of domestic radicalization, and installed new epistemologies to make sense of and respond to homegrown terrorism. These new modes of understanding have informed emerging national security approaches like countering violent extremism. Politicians have capitalized on these devastating events to advance CVE as a viable strategy to fight homegrown terrorism without criminalizing Muslim communities. Through these fear-filling and grief-stricken national security narratives, political leaders have shaped how the U.S. public thinks about the problem of homegrown terrorism and solutions to this perceived problem.

Left of Boom: Toward a Hybrid Antiterrorism Theory of Change

As these observations indicate, news of local arrests encouraged political leaders, law enforcement officials, and community members to develop a "left of boom" strategy that prevents violent acts before they are planned and executed within the United States. Learning from its early global war on terror failures, security experts recognized that they could not "kill or arrest" every perceived threat, domestically or globally. The U.S. security state therefore has turned to a more complex antiterrorism approach through the variable integration of counter-terrorism, counterinsurgency, and community policing paradigms.

Across the United States, CVE actors have contributed to this new approach by developing a portfolio of ostensibly "soft" antiterrorism programs that differentially support, and incorporate, more kinetic measures like community policing. As with the U.K.'s CONTEST program, this multipronged approach has sought to eliminate the threat of homegrown terrorism, prevent terrorist regeneration, and protect children from terrorist influences while pursuing military operations like drone strikes and targeted assassinations. As the "squishy stuff," CVE programs have bolstered support for the very institutions that historically have criminalized communities of color by appearing to attenuate coercive policing, racial profiling, and political exclusion.

To develop CVE in the face of unrelenting community resistance, security experts have produced new scholarship that examines the terrorist radicalization process and the "macro-, meso-, and micro-level" factors that facilitate that process (Baker, interview, January 27, 2017). Although social scientists, community organizers, and national security experts disagree on the validity of this radicalization research, this scholarship has shaped how CVE practitioners organized and made sense of their work. To do so, they rigorously read and interpreted radicalization models, rejecting, accepting, and negotiating prevailing national security frameworks for themselves. Given the continued saliency of, and contestations over, radicalization theories in CVE policies, I now turn to the main tenets of this research.

CHAPTER 3

"THE R WORD"
Radicalization Theories and Their Discontents

Scholar Yassir Morsi (2017) warns that under CVE

> every aspect of the Muslim life is brought under the microscope of this scientific, "evidence-based" approach. The gaze utterly shatters and makes fragments of its subject matter. It quarters us and the life of the pre-radicalized into categories for intellectual pontifications. Personal traumas, economic deprivation, social alienation and discrimination, and even our consciousness of conflicts with Muslims become topics for scholarly thought police. (17)

The study of the radicalization process dissects Muslims by treating every aspect of personhood as an object of analysis that can inform the U.S. antiterrorism agenda. Some scholars defend this dehumanizing research agenda as the necessary means to identify tomorrow's terrorists today. In this view, studying the cultural, psychological, and theological conditions that facilitate the radicalization process can guide the identification of individuals at risk of turning into terrorists. Yet, by focusing on individuals and communities, rather than broader political contexts, radicalization research conveniently "forgets colonialism" (Morsi 2017, 17) and "precludes any wider discussion of foreign policy" (Kundnani 2014, 14). The narrow focus on individuals dehumanizes Muslims, ignores the political aims of violent actors, and dismisses the role of Western state violence in the production of "what governments call extremism," which "is to a large degree a product of their own wars" (Kundnani 2014, 25). Given these critiques, the concept of radicalization has become so controversial that some CVE practitioners referred to it as the "r word." This contentious concept has remained hotly debated in and intensely relevant to the CVE policy environment.

In this chapter, I explore the evolution of radicalization research. I also document how this research has influenced the CVE policy world through the development of indicators, factors, and early warning signs used to detect individuals perceived to be vulnerable to or in the process of radicalizing. Through this analysis, I argue that radicalization research pathologizes Muslims by "marking the origins, causes, developments, consequences, and manifestations of deviation from some imagined norm," turning common human experiences into objects of study and surveillance (Erevelles 2014, 84). Radicalization research therefore functions as a technology of biopower, which seeks to "qualify, measure, appraise, and hierarchize" populations (Foucault 1976, 144). Knowledge generates statistical measures to identify the "normal" and the "deviant." Through this process of normalization, "power is both 'totalizing,' because it controls all aspects of life by creating pressure to conform to norms, and 'individualizing,' because those who fall outside the norm are marked as deviant and targeted with disciplinary strategies designed to neutralize their deviance" (Pylypa 1998, 23–24). Radicalization research has produced new knowledge used to identify and correct deviant subjects perceived to threaten national security.

Defining Radicalization: New Theories for a New Breed of Terrorism

In 2016, U.S. security agencies defined radicalization as "the process through which an individual changes from a nonviolent belief system to a belief system that includes the willingness to actively advocate, facilitate, or use unlawful violence as a method to effect societal or political change" (Department of Homeland Security and Federal Bureau of Investigation 2016, 1). Struggling to understand "homegrown terrorists," these U.S. security agencies have shifted their scale of analysis from the broader social contexts that generate political violence to the psychology, culture, and theology of individual actors.

The study of individual pathologies has generated new conceptual frameworks to understand and respond to an evolving terrorist threat.

Historian Walter Laqueur (2006) first examined the perceived "changing face of terrorism," identifying a "new breed of terrorism" distinct from older forms of terrorism enacted by "social revolutionaries driven to desperate actions by intolerable conditions, oppression, and tyranny" (48). This new breed of terrorism is "different in character, aiming not at clearly defined political demands but at the destruction of society and the elimination of large sections of the population" (Laqueur 1999, 81). Applying his new terrorism thesis to contemporary events, Laqueur (2004) argued that "Al-Qaeda and September 11 occurred not because of a territorial dispute or the feeling of national oppression but because of religious commandment—jihad and the establishment of shari'ah" (para. 8). In this view, new terrorists have abandoned the political orientation of previous revolutionaries in favor of "religious fanaticism" and "excessive indiscriminate violence" (Spencer 2006, 13).

Laqueur (2004), however, also wanted to better understand why only a few "militants" turned to violence if many "believe[d] with equal intensity in the justice of their cause" (para. 15). Although he admitted that "imponderable factors might be involved" in the turn to violence, Laqueur determined that "neither economic nor political analysis will be of much help in gaining an understanding" of this new breed of terrorism (para. 15). Instead, Laqueur hypothesized that a "cultural-psychological predisposition" could explain why only a few "militants" turn to violence (para. 16).

To test his cultural-psychological predisposition hypothesis, Laqueur (2004) analyzed Europe, which he considered to be the "most vulnerable battlefield" in the global war on terror. Through his case study, Laqueur (2004) concluded that Muslim newcomers refused "cultural and social integration" so they could "preserve their religious and ethnic identity and their way of life" while in Europe (para. 23). Unlike their parents who sought to "live in peace and quiet," second generation immigrants were "superficially acculturated (speaking fluently the language of the host country)" yet also driven by acute feelings of "resentment and hostility" (para. 25). In this context

it is not necessarily the power of the fundamentalist message . . . which inspires many of the young radical activists or
sympathizers. It is the feeling of deep resentment because,
unlike immigrants from other parts of the world, they could not
successfully compete in the educational field, nor quite often
make it at the work place. Feelings of being excluded, sexual
repression . . . , and other factors led to free-floating aggression
and crime directed against the authorities and their neighbors.
(Laqueur 2004, para. 26)

The presence of and interplay between these cultural and psychological factors contribute to the radicalization of frustrated, sexually
repressed, and aggressive youth. The culture, theology, and psychology of individual actors outweigh any political factors driving violent
extremism. By anchoring his theory of radicalization in a "cultural-
psychological disposition," Laqueur generated interest in identifying
cultural and psychological indicators of a vulnerability to, or propensity for, violent extremism.

Through an intensive case study of Al-Muhajiroun in the United
Kingdom, for example, CVE architect Quintan Wiktorowicz (2005)
detailed a three-step psychology-based radicalization process. First,
a "cognitive opening . . . shakes certitude in previously accepted beliefs," catalyzing an individual's "initial interest" in extremist groups
(5). For individuals "willing to expose themselves to new ways of
thinking and worldviews," a "cognitive opening" can "facilitate possible receptivity" to radical ideas and actions (5). There "is no single
catalyst for initial interest" as "any number of things can prompt a
cognitive opening," from discrimination to political repression (5).

This cognitive opening "sparks a process of religious seeking in
which [individuals] search for answers to pressing concerns through
religious meaning," oftentimes with friends (Wiktorowicz 2005, 5).
"Not every individual who experiences a cognitive opening," however, "will engage in religious seeking and not every individual who
becomes a religious seeker" explores "radical Islamic groups" (5).
During this time, extremist groups may mobilize their social networks to contact and expose individuals to their mission and gain
credibility. Lastly, extremist groups socialize individuals to "incul-
cate" their ideology and convince individuals to "engage in risky ac-

tivism" (6). Through this three-step psychological process, individuals mobilize toward violent extremism.

As Wiktorowicz's study indicates, continued struggles to understand why a small percentage of the population turns to violent extremism ushered in a new generation of radicalization scholarship that has sought to study the possible "cultural-psychological predisposition" to violent extremism. In fact, Laqueur's (2004, 2006, 1999) initial publications generated an explosion of studies seeking to better understand the radicalization process, particularly by examining the role of culture, theology, and psychology. These theories would provide the scientific evidence needed to support surveillance practices to detect actionable indicators of violent extremism based on these cultural, psychological, and/or theological dispositions.

Jihadization: The Perceived Role of Theology in the Radicalization Process

In 2007, the NYPD published one of the most influential reports on "radicalization in the West," which created new ways of knowing and policing the "homegrown threat." More specifically, the study examined the "threat from Islamic-based terrorism to New York City" and developed a "conceptual framework for understanding the process of radicalization in the West" (Silber and Bhatt 2007, 5). Through this study, the NYPD identified four phases of the radicalization process, each with "its distinct set of indicators and signatures": pre-radicalization, self-identification, indoctrination, and jihadization (7).

To map this radicalization process, the NYPD conducted case studies of five prominent terrorist plots and groups: the 2004 Madrid attack, the 2005 London bombings, Amsterdam's Hofstad Group, the 2006 "Toronto 18" thwarted terrorist plan, and the 2005 Operation Pendennis raids that prevented attacks in Australia. After handpicking these five cases, the NYPD "dispatched detectives and analysts to meet with law enforcement, intelligence officials, and academics at each of these locations to enhance [its] understanding of the specifics of these events as well as the phenomenon of homegrown radicalization" (Silber and Bhatt 2007, 15). Using this information, the NYPD identified "common pathways and characteristics among these otherwise different groups and plots" to guide its policing (15).

To test these findings, the NYPD applied its framework to the observable radicalization process in five operational cells in the United States: Lackawanna, New York; Northern Virginia; Portland, Oregon; New York City, New York; and the Hamburg, Germany, cell that organized the September 11 attacks. Through these cases, the NYPD confirmed its hypothesized four-phase radicalization process with identifiable "indicators and signatures." Although social scientists have noted that the NYPD's study "relies on [an] inadequate sample set," its findings of a four-phase radicalization process have informed CVE programming and community policing across the United States (Patel 2011, 14).

The role of theology anchors the NYPD's framework, which defines each phase of the radicalization process by a changing relationship with Salafism (a strand of Sunni Islam). In fact, the NYPD claimed that "radicalization in the West is, first and foremost, driven by: jihadi-Salafi ideology" (Silber and Bhatt 2007, 16). In addition, the NYPD report reduced the perceived radicalization "phenomenon" to an individual, not political, struggle "for an identity and a cause" (82).

According to the NYPD, the pre-radicalization phase refers to an individual's "life situation before they were exposed to and adopted jihadi-Salafi Islam as their own ideology" (Silber and Bhatt 2007, 6). During this time, economic, social, political, or personal crises like job loss could trigger a "cognitive opening," which "shakes one's certitude in previously held beliefs and opens an individual to be receptive to new world views" (6). This cognitive opening facilitates the self-identification phase, in which individuals "begin to explore Salafi Islam" and "gravitate away from their old identity and begin to associate themselves with like-minded individuals and adopt this ideology as their own" (6). Crises catalyze this "religious-seeking" behavior, indicated by "giving up cigarettes, drinking, gambling, and urban hip-hop gangster clothes," "affiliating with like-minded individuals," and regularly attending a Salafi mosque (31). These perceived indicators tie increased (Islamic) religiosity to progression in the radicalization process.

In the indoctrination phase, "an individual progressively intensifies his beliefs, wholly adopts jihadi-Salafi ideology and concludes, without question, that the conditions and circumstances exist where action is required to support and further the cause. That action is militant jihad" (Silber and Bhatt 2007, 36). In this phase, individuals accept a "religious-political worldview that justifies, legitimizes, encourages, or supports violence against anything *kufr,* or un-Islamic" (36). For the NYPD, the withdrawal from a mosque or development of new identities based on Salafi ideology may indicate that an individual is progressing through the indoctrination phase.

Lastly, in the jihadization phase, group members "accept their individual duty to participate in jihad and self-designate themselves as holy warriors or mujahedeen" (Silber and Bhatt 2007, 19). The group begins operational planning and preparation for a terrorist attack, which can occur gradually or rapidly. Traveling abroad, participating in "Outward Bound-like activities" like camping or whitewater rafting, or "researching on the internet" could indicate that a person has committed to and is planning a terrorist attack (7).

Through its development of this linear four-stage radicalization process culminating in "ATTACK," the NYPD report indicts the theology and psychology of violent extremists, irrespective of broader political, social, and economic contexts (Silber and Bhatt 2007, 9). To guide its counterterrorism operations, the NYPD looks for the perceived "typical signatures" of the radicalization process, such as "giving up cigarettes," "growing a beard," "wearing traditional Islamic clothing," and "becoming involved in social activism" (31). In fact, the NYPD argues that the "consistency in the behaviors and trajectory" of each terrorist plot "provides a tool for predictability" (82). These perceived indicators of radicalization therefore have informed the NYPD's predictive policing practices.

Although the NYPD's study has informed its predictive policing practices that target "radical Islam," radicalization is not a linear process with identifiable "signatures" that can be detected by law enforcement. Legal scholar Faiza Patel (2011) instructs that "despite the impetus to find a terrorist profile or hallmarks of radicalization to hone in on incipient terrorists, empirical research has emphatically and repeatedly concluded that there is no such profile and no such easily identifiable hallmarks" (8). Even the FBI (2015a) concedes that "there is neither one path or personality type, which is prone to adopting extremist views or exhibiting tendencies, nor is there a singular path or personality that leaves an individual vulnerable to others who may seek to impress these views or tendencies upon them" (2). Despite the growing number of CVE programs that rely on this understanding of the radicalization process and use these "typical signatures" to identify individuals vulnerable to violent extremism, CVE actors admit that there is no single terrorist profile and no scientifically proven warning signs of radicalization to violence (Jenkins 2007; Horgan 2008; Patel and Koushik 2017).[1]

In addition to these concerns, the NYPD study utilized a flawed methodology. The absence of a control group—a cohort of similar but nonviolent individuals—means that the NYPD cannot conclude which factors facilitate radicalization and which "typical signatures" indicate progression in this process. Accepted social science methodology, after all, "requires a comparison between behaviors and beliefs common to terrorists and a control group" (Patel and Koushik 2017, 14). This means that "contrary to social science norms, the NYPD report fails to consider whether the religious conduct and expressive activity that it characterizes as early signatures of radicalization occur with any more frequency among terrorists than among all American Muslims" (Patel 2011, 16). In fact, the NYPD later conceded that "during the early stages of radicalization, the behaviors associated with a greater degree of religiosity . . . cannot be used as a signature of someone becoming a terrorist" and "so law enforcement would be doing itself a disservice and wasting significant resources on tracking individuals who simply exhibit behaviors that at this stage are perfectly benign and in the vast majority of cases not associated with terrorism" (Silber and Bhatt 2009, 12). Despite these documented limitations, radicalization researchers still fail to "employ basic scientific principles, such as the use of a control group, to test the specificity and validity of terrorism-related measures" (Sageman 2015).

Terrorism scholars themselves have raised this methodological issue on several occasions. Marc Sageman (2015), for example, testified:

> Any attempt to assess the validity of indicators or factors that might lead an individual to commit political violence would require a study including both (a) individuals who actually carried out acts of political violence, and (b) individuals (the control group) who are similar to the first set in all respects ex-

cept that they did not engage in violence. Use of a control group is critically important because it is only by a comparison with this control group, in which the indicator of actual violence is absent, that one can make the argument that other indicators specific to the subject group are valid. In short, a control group helps to lower the probability of generating a false positive, that is, falsely identifying someone as a future terrorist when he is not. (9)

As a terrorism scholar, Sageman objected to the faulty methodologies used to determine the indicators of violent extremism, calling these predictive judgments mere "guesses" and "hunches" (9). These flawed studies therefore cannot be used to accurately identify individuals vulnerable to or in the process of radicalizing.

Even as these radicalization theories matured, they continued to commit the same methodological errors as the NYPD's early report. In 2016, for example, Sageman again concluded that "Western states' indicators of 'radicalization' . . . are really indicators of the generally nonviolent Islamist protest community in the West, and not its violent members" (167–68). Sageman (2016) repeated his warning that these indicators could not accurately identify radicalizing individuals and, instead, alienated Muslim communities and criminalized political protest.

CVE researcher Adrian Baker described similar methodological concerns with radicalization research, noting that "one of the biggest criticisms of certain radicalization models has been from a social science perspective" because of "the fact that there's a lack of a control group and there's reliance on the dependent variable." For Baker, this was an "*entirely valid* methodological critique" that "has largely gone unaddressed in radicalization research." Baker also confirmed that "long story short, basically, we don't necessarily have evidence yet that can speak to causality. For instance, a lot of people at an individual level have said, 'Oh, extremist ideology causes people to engage in violent extremism.'" Without a control group, however, social scientists cannot claim a causal relationship between extremist ideology and violent extremism (interview, January 27, 2017, emphasis in original). In fact, "most people who hold radical ideas do not engage in terrorism, and many terrorists—even those who lay claim to a 'cause'—are not deeply ideological and may not 'radicalize' in any traditional sense" (Borum 2011, 8).

Given these scientific shortcomings, Baker reported that "we can say that there's certain factors that are *associated* with [violent extremism], that they may be necessary or near necessary conditions, but we can't say, for instance, that they directly cause these kinds of things. At most we can say that they're associated to some degree, whether weakly, moderately, or strongly." For Baker, this meant that "as social scientists, we don't want to engage in those kinds of very strong *causal* claims, in large part because, again, as CVE critics and radicalization critics have rightly pointed out, there are no . . . comparison and control groups from which we can begin to adequately isolate some of those variables and tease out causality" (interview, January 27, 2017, emphasis in original). Baker conceded that radicalization research could not reliably identify the indicators, risk factors, or early warning signs of violent extremism.

In recognizing these methodological shortcomings, Baker still asserted that "in the domestic context," CVE "*is* an attempt to try and address what I would call macro-, meso-, *and* micro-level factors that are *associated*—again, not causing, but *associated*—with entry into nonstate ideologically-motivated violence, aka violent extremism." Like the NYPD, Baker acknowledged the methodological shortcomings of radicalization research while affirming that these studies had identified factors "associated to some degree with," but not causally linked to, violent extremism. Practitioners therefore could develop CVE programs organized around these factors "associated with" violent extremism while recognizing "we don't necessarily have evidence yet that can speak to causality" (interview, January 27, 2017, emphasis in original).

Despite Marc Sageman's warning, radicalization researchers still conduct studies and develop antiterrorism programs using the same flawed methodology (see, for example, Gartenstein-Ross and Grossman 2009). In 2018, the FBI used this same faulty methodology to outline a series of "concrete, observable pre-attack behaviors of many active shooters," "warning signs" communities could use to identify individuals "moving towards violence" (Silver, Simons, and Craun 2018, 6). To determine these "pre-attack behaviors," the FBI undertook a "descriptive study," meaning it "cannot postulate on the probability as to whether some of the behaviors and characteristics seen here would also have been seen in other populations," such as those who do not commit mass shootings (26). Despite these scientific limitations, the FBI determined that these "concerning behaviors" include "amount or quality of sleep," "changes in weight or eating habits," "sudden and/or recent use of changes in use of alcohol," and "indications of depression, anxiety, paranoia, or other mental health concerns"—all common behaviors and experiences in the United States (29). Although radicalization researchers have recognized the methodological shortcomings of such descriptive studies, some scholars have continued to undertake this research and use their findings to inform national security policy.

Unfortunately, these flawed findings have guided CVE programming across the United States. This is evident in the growing number of initiatives that have called on social service providers, community members, and law enforcement to learn about and use these early warning signs to identify individuals vulnerable to terrorist radicalization. The Illinois Criminal Justice Information Authority (2016), for example, planned to train community members to "be more alert to warning signs," to "be more proactive when these warning signs are observed," and to "engage effectively with individuals who exhibit warning signs of radicalization to violence and/or to targeted violence" (4). As we will see, CVE actors both acknowledged the limits of radicalization research and used the concept of radicalization to organize their work.

A Social Autopsy: Toward a Middle-Level Analysis of the Radicalization Process

Responding to these well-documented critiques, some terrorism scholars have acknowledged that "attempts to profile terrorists have failed resoundingly" and have called for more complex analyses that examine the pathways to violent extremism rather than the profiles of violent extremists (Horgan 2008). Like Laqueur's early formulation of the "cultural-psychological predisposition" to radicalization, these scholars have sought to account for factors beyond theology that contribute to the radicalization process. In this approach, CVE researchers must conduct a "social autopsy" to understand the radicalization process and potential points of intervention (Guillermo Cespedes, as quoted in Slutzker 2016). New radicalization studies have undertaken this work by conducting, cataloging, and analyzing the "social autopsies" of known violent extremists to taxonomize the terrorist mind.

Critical of past radicalization research like the NYPD study, Marc Sageman (2008) rejects micro-level, or psychological, analyses that assume that "there is something different about terrorists that make them do what they do" (16). Sageman also discredits macro-level, or sociological, analyses that only examine the "root causes" of terrorism while missing the "collective dimension of terrorist behavior" like "how people get together and what motivates them to carry out the work of the abstract terrorist organization" (22). Instead, Sageman calls for a "middle-range analysis" that examines "how the terrorists act on the ground: how they evolve into terrorists; how they interact with others (terrorists and non-terrorists); how they join terrorist groups; how they become motivated to commit their atrocities; how they are influenced by ideas; and how they follow orders from far-away leaders" (16, 23). Through this "middle-range analysis," Sageman has pursued a more complex rendering of terrorism that can inform national security policy and practice.

To develop this "middle-range analysis," Sageman (2008) built a database to generate and test his hypotheses about the radicalization process. The database includes information about "people and their relationships with other terrorists, non-terrorists, ideas, and the social, political, economic, cultural, and technological context" (25). This database also can "trace the evolution of these relationships to see how they form, intensify, and fade so as to describe them over time" (25). Although think tanks have developed "incident-based databases," Sageman argued that they "do not help us answer questions about terrorism and its processes, such as radicalization, mobilization, recruitment, and motivation" (27). Rather than catalog terrorist incidents, Sageman's database mapped the complex processes perceived to facilitate the turn to violence.

To map the radicalization process, this study focused on "the people who carried out September 11, and all those like them who pose a threat to the United States" (Sageman 2008, 27). After curating and analyzing a database of five hundred case studies, Sageman concluded that there are "four prongs" to the radicalization process: a sense of moral outrage, the interpretation of this moral outrage, the resonance of that moral outrage with the individual's own lived experience, and the mobilization by terrorist networks to convert moral outrage to violence. This four-step process, however, does not always progress linearly or uniformly: "One cannot simply draw a line, put markers on it, and gauge where people are along this path to see whether they are close to committing atrocities" (72). With a narrow focus on Muslims, Sageman encouraged readers to think about the interplay between these multiscalar prongs rather than interpret them as distinct or discrete factors that drive the radicalization process (as with the NYPD report).

In this view, a sense of moral outrage initiates the radicalization process. Personal or political tragedies "brought about by human hands and seen as a major moral violation such as killing, injury, rape, or arrest" can generate this moral outrage in Muslim communities (Sageman 2008, 72). Moral outrage, however, is insufficient to radicalize individuals or mobilize them to violence. To rise to the formation of an "Islamist terrorist," this moral outage must also "fit into a moral universe," "resonate with one's own experience," and "be amplified within a group." Through an "enabling interpretation," a person can "make sense of the violation and put it into a context that affects him personally and leads to his personal involvement" (75). To justify violence, individuals must undertake an interpretive process that bridges global tragedies with local grievances. This "interpretive bridge" can make young Muslims "feel personally involved" and thus "more likely to join this fight" (83). To propel terrorist radicalization, global tragedies must be interpreted in relation to Muslims' own everyday lives and sense of morality. This interpretive process therefore is political, despite the vocabularies that make radicalization appear religious in character.

These interpretive processes, however, do not amount to brainwashing as Muslims take on an active role in making sense of their environment and their lives. Radicalizing individuals are agentic rather than passive recipients of the beliefs and interpretations of group leaders. In addition, "global Islamist terrorist ideology is not unified," particularly given the differing assessments of which types of violence are permissible and effective (Sageman 2008, 82). These interpretations, however, help individuals make sense of their moral outrage and direct it toward action.

Finally, to help them "cross the line from venting their anger to becoming terrorists," radicalizing individuals need "other people who share their outrage, beliefs, and experiences, but who are further along the path to violence or who are willing to explore it with them" (Sageman 2008, 84). According to this "bunch of guys" thesis, social networks—including those formed through "radical student associations" and "radical mosques"—are central to the radicalization process (85). In this view, "political violence is the natural result of evolutionary cognitive mechanisms that make us identify and favor our group at the expense of strangers" (Sageman 2016, 174). Social bonds therefore precede any ideological commitment to terrorism. This conclusion justifies the policing and surveillance of sites that cultivate these social bonds, like schools, student associations, and mosques.

Through this "middle-level analysis" and "bunch of guys" thesis, Sageman treats terrorism as "the product of a socialization process of friendship and kinship, progressive intensification of beliefs leading to acceptance of the Salafi ideology, and a link to know-how and support" (Kundnani 2014, 130). Yet, "claiming social bonds to be the root cause of terrorism is inadequate" as CVE practitioners still have no way of knowing how radical beliefs transform into violent methods, unless they rely on the assumption that radical beliefs are inherently violent (Kundnani 2014, 129). Despite his desire to develop a more nuanced understanding of the radicalization process, "at the heart of [Sageman's] model remains an unexamined assumption that violence has its origins in dangerous theological ideas," an assumption that has plagued radicalization research since its inception (130). Despite this limitation, Sageman advocates for a "managerial approach to Muslim grievances," using soft power methods like community policing to identify tomorrow's terrorists through today's associates of terrorists "without asking too many questions about where that radicalism comes from" (Kundnani 2014, 129). In this view, Sageman's analyses do not bring us closer to understanding homegrown terrorism while reaffirming the primacy of the concept of radicalization as a theological, cultural, and/or psychological process facilitated by social bonds.

Like other radicalization researchers, Sageman admits that there is no single profile of a terrorist and no discernable warning signs of radicalization. The radicalization process remains mysterious, as individuals follow different pathways toward violence and are mobilized by a range of factors that cannot be distilled into a single comprehensive model. As CVE practitioner Humera Khan concludes, "This is not about rational explanations. This is about dealing with humans where they are" (as quoted in Slutzker 2016).

Locating Violent Extremism in the Global War on Terror

Although radicalization case studies typically dismiss broader economic, political, and social conditions in their examination of the theological, cultural, and/or psychological factors driving the turn to violence, some continue to call for less individualizing analyses. The United States Agency for International Development (USAID), for example, studied the global "drivers of violent Islamist extremism," working from the premise that "terrorists and other violent extremists do not exhibit common psychological attributes," nor do they "share a psychopathology" (Denoeux and Carter 2009, 51). Rather than engage in an "elusive search for a 'terrorist personality,'" USAID explored other contexts that drive violent extremism, distilling its findings into three main categories: (1) enabling environments like weak states with ineffective security services and state support for violent extremist groups; (2) pull factors that cultivate the appeal of violent extremism like terrorist groups with a "compelling narrative and attractive objectives" and the "lucrative economic opportunities" in exchange for participation; and (3) push factors that drive individuals to violent extremism like social exclusion, "real or perceived" discrimination, the denial of political rights and civil liberties, foreign occupation, and the "perception that the West is attacking Islam and Muslims" (Denoeux and Carter 2009, 2–4).

After providing a summary of these factors, USAID concluded that "there is ample evidence to suggest that foreign military occupation—and, more generally, large-scale external political and military intrusion—represents a significant driver of VE" (Denoeux and Carter 2009, 19). For USAID, military occupation facilitates and intensifies the push and pull factors of violent extremism. This report, however, still normalizes the concept of radicalization, treats political violence as epiphenomenal to U.S. foreign policy, and reaffirms the

"bunch of guys" thesis. Today, USAID's concepts still organize some
CVE work in the United States, noted in the continued use of "push
and pull factors" to describe the drivers of violent extremism.

The U.K.'s Joint Intelligence Committee (2003) similarly warned
the British prime minister that "the threat from al-Qaeda will increase at the onset of any military action against Iraq. . . . The worldwide threat from other Islamist terrorist groups and individuals
will increase significantly" with such military aggression (1). The
report further cautioned that "the broader threat from Islamist terrorists will also increase in the event of war, reflecting intensified
anti-U.S./anti-Western sentiment in the Muslim world, including
among Muslim communities in the West" (2). Like USAID, the U.K.
Joint Intelligence Committee feared that increased military operations would intensify retaliatory acts by violent extremists in Britain,
signaling a more complex understanding of radicalization than a mere
psychological process lubricated by social bonds.

Contrary to these concerns raised by the U.K. intelligence community and the USAID report, radicalization studies primarily investigate the cultural, psychological, and theological drivers of violent
extremism. The reliance on such an individualizing understanding
of the radicalization process means that political violence is never
placed within the context of the global war on terror and radicalism
is never treated as a serious political orientation. For example, after
the brutal machete killing of a British soldier in Woolwich, South
London, "it remained taboo to suggest any connection between the
killing of a British soldier on the streets of London and the killings by
British soldiers in the villages of Helmand [Afghanistan]" (Kundnani
2014, 19). Media restricted their coverage to the "official narrative
of radicalization by a dangerous ideology," while ignoring how "the
perpetrators offered a clear statement of what they were doing" (19).
Like Tsarnaev's testimony etched into a Boston boat, one Woolwich
attacker proclaimed that "the only reason we have killed this man
today is because Muslims are dying daily by British soldiers. And this
British soldier is one. It is an eye for an eye and a tooth for a tooth.
By Allah, we swear by the almighty Allah, we will never stop fighting you until you leave us alone. . . . So, leave our lands and we can all
live in peace. That's all I have to say" (as quoted in Jamieson 2013).
These comments locate the brutal attack in a broader political con-

text by drawing attention to the United Kingdom's ongoing violence in Afghanistan.

Given these findings, USAID concluded that violent extremism "typically results from the confluence of several factors and dynamics" such that "mono-causal explanations," like theology or psychology, "should be viewed with particular skepticism." Lastly, USAID reported that "from a programmatic perspective, there is no 'magic bullet' for the many challenges posed by VE" (Denoeux and Carter 2009, 84). By studying the role of military occupation in the rise of violent extremism, these scholars suggested that radicalization is a far more complex political process than conventional radicalization studies suggest. Rather than exonerate violent extremists, this approach explores the conditions that make violence seem like a justified tactic to achieve specific political goals.

For some CVE practitioners, however, these studies also engage the same methodological flaws as similar studies of the cultural, psychological, and theological drivers of violent extremism. Baker, for example, explained that, "when it comes to the issue of foreign policy and economic conditions—especially when it comes to causality—there's insufficient evidence to suggest that foreign policy, at least by itself, causes people to enter into ideologically-motivated violence" (interview, January 27, 2017). Although the USAID study never claimed that foreign policy itself drives violent extremism, it also did not use a control group to test its theories. Like other radicalization studies, USAID could not draw a causal link between U.S. military occupation and violent extremism. Instead, USAID approached violent extremism as a response to military aggression that fueled "anti-U.S./anti-Western sentiment in the Muslim world."

Even though CVE actors expressed interest in the "micro-, macro-, and meso-level factors *associated with* violent extremism," they used this methodological shortcoming to dismiss the role of "foreign policy and economic conditions" while focusing on cultural, psychological, and theological factors identified through similar methods. CVE programs therefore have focused primarily on identifying struggling individuals perceived to be "at risk" of radicalization, with little attention to the broader contexts that organize political violence or the political goals violent actors may pursue. Unlike other radicalization research, USAID examined the interaction between multiscalar factors from individual experiences to foreign policy. USAID, however, still viewed radicalization as an individual process facilitated by broader political and social contexts.

Like the U.K. Intelligence Committee's finding, this approach encourages an analysis of U.S. foreign policy to understand the political orientation and objectives of violent actors. A narrow focus on how individuals radicalize misses the factors that "are politically inconvenient for governments, such as the impact of state violence, both domestic and foreign" (Patel and Singh 2016, para. 14). CVE practitioner Bassem Ali also questioned the politically expedient focus on theology, asking:

> If there's theology, if theology is a major part of this, if theology is somewhere in there, if it is a major part of this, then why is all this stuff beginning now? Why didn't this begin 50 years ago, 60 years ago? As a society, we're still not ready to have an honest conversation about why 9/11 happened. We need to talk about our foreign policy. . . . I don't know when we'll be ready to talk about 9/11, meaning what I'm saying is, I don't know when we'll be ready to really talk about our foreign policy. (interview, March 16, 2017)

Given the perceived role of foreign policy in the rise of domestic terrorist attacks, Ali incorporated a political analysis in his religious teachings to Muslim youth. This view, however, does not dismiss the interplay of other factors that propel individuals toward violent extremism. Instead, it locates violent extremism in a broader set of social, political, and economic contexts, thereby indicting U.S. foreign policy in the turn to political violence. These more complex analyses, however, still pathologize violent actors, particularly by reaffirming the concept of radicalization and arguing that broader political contexts like war produce deviant behavior, such as violence.

In addition to these shortcomings, studies like USAID's introduce new analytical problems. Anthropologist Darryl Li (2015) cautions that although "a critical understanding of imperial practices and the U.S. role in particular is absolutely indispensable," analytically "reducing jihadi groups to mere epiphenomena of U.S. actions is a dead end for analysis" (para. 12). These approaches unfortunately "give rise to a kind of Frankenstein theory of jihad, which insists that the US can manufacture such groups but then somehow always loses control over them without ever really explaining how" (para. 15). In addition, "the political logic of the complicity charge can be all too easily appropriated by warmongers, such as the late columnist Christopher Hitchens, who maintained that U.S. support for Saddam Hussein in the 1980s made Washington all the more obligated to overthrow him in 2003" (para. 15). In a world organized by nation-states, framing violent extremism simply as the blowback of imperial policies refuses to take radicalism seriously as a political project undertaken by non-state actors. In this view, terrorism scholars do not need better studies to map the radicalization process; they must challenge "jihad talk as demonology" by reconceptualizing radicalism as a political orientation (para. 17).

Toward a Public Health Model: Recalibrating Violence Prevention Programs

Recognizing the limitations of radicalization theories, some CVE practitioners and policymakers turned to other violence prevention programs as additional models for their work. The U.S. Department of Homeland Security (2015), for example, identified a need to "learn from intervention approaches in other situations, such as gang prevention," to solve the problem of violent extremism (13). Although committed to teaching social service providers to identify the early warning signs of radicalization, CVE practitioner Tanvir Rahman also referred to suicide- and gang-prevention programs to guide his work. In fact, the utility of gang prevention models compelled Rahman to "focus on the V not the E," meaning he sought to deter violence rather than criminalize extremism (interview, November 10, 2016). For Rahman, focusing on violence, rather than ideology, avoided the shortcomings of radicalization research, making other violence prevention models more applicable to his own CVE work. Rahman and other CVE practitioners, however, typically did not abandon conventional radicalization research as a guiding frame for their work.

Despite the increasing popularity of gang-prevention programs in the CVE policy environment, some warn that "the track record of gang reduction programs is mixed" and that "gang violence and terrorism are radically different in scope" (Patel and Koushik 2017, 18). Violence prevention expert Guillermo Cespedes, for example, observed, "It appears to me that while the diagnosis seems to be somewhat different, we seem to be applying the same solution that did not work [with gangs] to violent extremism" (as quoted in Slutzker 2016). CVE practitioner Seth Rogers also admitted that "there's criticism about following the gang intervention model because the vast majority of people say it hasn't worked. . . . If we're thinking about just replicating a wheel that hasn't worked before, how are we building on lessons learned?" (interview, November 9, 2016). Sociologist David Pyrooz similarly concluded that "on an individual level, policies and programs designed to prevent and intervene in gang membership might not translate very well to domestic extremism" (as quoted in National Consortium for the Study of Terrorism and Responses to Terrorism 2017a).[2] Given these two critical issues, some CVE practitioners refused to incorporate gang-prevention models into their work.

Seeking additional guidance on violence prevention, some CVE practitioners turned to the "violence-as-infectious-disease" model, which treats violence like a contagious disease that spreads, as "one event leads to another, leads to another, leads to another" (Slutkin 2016). This infectious spread occurs in "all kinds of manifestations of violence, whether we're talking about riots or we're looking at gangs or tribes or militias that fight each other with repeated retaliations" (Slutkin 2016). Like infectious diseases, proximity and exposure to violence influence an individual's susceptibility to committing an act of violence, meaning violence must be contained and quarantined to prevent its spread.

Despite the effectiveness of this approach in controlling infectious diseases, it provides little guidance in understanding political violence. As Arun Kundnani (2014) explains, "even if we accept the implication that terrorism spreads like a virus from a person already infected to his associates, all we have done is explain the process of infection; we have said nothing of why the virus exists in the first place" (129). More perniciously, "the use of the discourse of contamination and disease is used to reaffirm colonial ideas about the inferiority and bodily degeneracy of colonized people," namely diasporic communities (Murdocca 2002, 20). Under these enduring colonial logics, the "diseased is represented as both a moral danger and as a bodily danger to otherwise law-abiding, legitimate citizens" (20). As a threat to the social order, the diseased must be quarantined, corrected, or eliminated through "therapeutic" measures.

Given the perceived parallels between infectious disease and violence, epidemiologist Gary Slutkin (2016) "began to apply some of the same methods and applications of public health to reducing the spread of violence, which means detecting and interrupting events and changing behaviors. . . . This system or method that we've used for other contagious processes works very well for reducing violence." Given the limited occurrence of violent extremism, Slutkin has advocated for methods that "find potential cases or very urgently likely cases, for example, a case of [tuberculosis] to prevent it from spreading to others and the family or to friends. And it's important to find a potential person who is about to do violence or is considering doing violence because those acts cause more as well as the friends and the contacts pick up the ideas in proximity as well." In this view, a violence-as-infectious-disease model can prevent the spread of violent extremism by first identifying "a potential person who is about to do violence"—the diseased—and then providing interventions to stop the spread of violence.

Other practitioners and scholars have developed a "public health model" of CVE to reduce susceptibility to, and contain the spread of, violence using the same methods to prevent epidemics. These methods include primary prevention, secondary prevention, and tertiary prevention. Primary prevention "aims to prevent injury and disease before it occurs by preventing exposure to the causes and promoters of injury and disease," like healthful eating to prevent diabetes (Weine and Eisenman 2016, para. 3). Applied to the problem of violent extremism, primary prevention counters radicalization through "community-level strategies that mitigate modifiable risk (e.g., availability of extremist media) and leverage protective factors (e.g., parenting support and education) that are empirically or theoretically associated with violent extremism" (para. 4). Secondary preventions treat a disease before it "manifests and progresses" (para. 3). In the CVE context, secondary preventions are "directed at individuals who have been identified as having some characteristics that render them at elevated-risk for violent extremism" like "exposure to extremist ideologies" (para. 4). Secondary prevention strategies include counseling and mentoring. Lastly, tertiary prevention efforts like psychotherapy and intensive case management target radicalizing individuals before they engage in acts of violence. To deliver these resources, this approach tasks social service providers with amplifying the protective factors that support healthy individuals and reducing the risk factors associated with violent extremism. Through these measures, this public health model attempts to "move to a more proactive and positive paradigm to address violent extremism through non-coercive means in the pre-criminal space" (para. 1).

Despite the growing popularity of these public health approaches to CVE, critics questioned their utility in understanding and responding to violence. Gang prevention specialist Teddy Howard, for example, cautioned that this public health model failed to consider the social, political, and economic conditions under which "guys get caught up" in violence, making the infectious disease analogy "bullshit" (interview, November 2, 2016). Critics also warned that the public health model still organizes the delivery of social services on the assumption that certain factors, like "mental health/psychosocial troubles," contribute to the radicalization process, even while recognizing "there has yet to be a statistical evaluation of these factors" (Weine, Eisenman, Kinsler et al. 2017, 212). By acting on these perceived risk factors, mental health professionals come to view their clients through an antiterrorism lens and enhance the relationship between law enforcement and the provision of social services. Despite these critiques, the CVE policy world has advanced this public health model as a viable method for preventing and quarantining the problem of violent extremism.

Drawing from this public health framework, in 2016 the Los Angeles Police Department (LAPD), Department of Mental Health, Sheriff's Department, and FBI launched a CVE program called Recognizing Extremist Network Early Warnings (RENEW) (later renamed Providing Alternatives to Hinder Extremism [PATHE]). RENEW was designed to "find a potential person who is about to do violence" and intervene immediately. To support this objective, RENEW created pathways for communities to report individuals "about to do violence" and for law enforcement to respond in multiple ways, thereby containing the threat of violence and its infectious spread.

When LAPD officers or community members encountered an individual exhibiting certain "early warnings of potential violent behavior," they reported this person to the Joint Terrorism Task Force/ LAPD Major Crimes Division liaison. This liaison then notified the LAPD's RENEW program coordinator, who contacted the Joint Regional Intelligence Center (JRIC). The JRIC conducted a "full workup on the subject," after which the subject was directed to different services, like counseling and outpatient therapy. By opening a criminal investigation under "reasonable suspicion . . . that a crime was about to take place," this process putatively prevented the spread of violent extremism (National Academies of Sciences, Engineering, and Medicine 2017, 31–40). This meant that law enforcement intervened in noncriminal cases in the name of national security.

Although social scientists have determined that there are no reliable indicators of violent extremism, RENEW deputized community members as the police by encouraging them to report individuals using "early warnings of violent behavior" like "exhibiting signs of mental illness" (National Academies of Sciences, Engineering, and Medicine 2017, 32). LAPD counterterrorism expert Michael Downing insisted that this program prohibited the profiling of people, only "criminal behaviors," despite intervening in noncriminal cases specifically in "diasporas and other communities" (32, 29). Furthermore, this reporting process engaged several law enforcement agencies, including the LAPD Major Crimes Division, Joint Terrorism Task Force, and Joint Regional Intelligence Center, three units primarily engaged in counterterrorism investigations and prosecutions. Given this police involvement, the incorporation of mental health professionals to prevent the spread of violent extremism does not address community concerns related to anti-Muslim surveillance or the criminalization of individuals with psychiatric disability labels in the name of national security.

Although a "public health" model sounds like a less punitive and more therapeutic approach to countering violent extremism, this model necessarily has relied on punitive institutions like the criminal-legal system, even opening criminal investigations of referred individuals before they commit a crime. This preventative approach has further tethered the provision of social services to law enforcement and encouraged providers to view their clients through an antiterrorism lens. Rather than serve as an alternative to coercive counterterrorism methods, RENEW increased police contact and facilitated information sharing across law enforcement agencies, using and therefore securitizing mental health professionals and other social service providers who participated in RENEW. Lastly, RENEW still relied on disproven early warning signs of violent extremism to detect and refer individuals "about to do violence" for services.

Although CVE actors have borrowed from gang prevention programs and infectious disease control, these new approaches do not eschew the problems with earlier iterations of CVE as they continue to securitize social services, facilitate police involvement, and use early warning signs with no evidentiary basis. These CVE programs have reinforced state power by adding onto, rather than transforming, dominant institutions of control that historically have criminalized communities of color.

Terrorist Watchdogs: Policing Pre-Criminal Behaviors

Guided by their interpretations of radicalization research as well as other violence prevention models, some CVE actors have developed programs that increase community participation in the prevention of violent extremism. To do so, CVE actors have mobilized social service providers, parents, and friends to detect individuals perceived to be vulnerable to or in the process of radicalizing. This "third way" has offered a "path between doing nothing and calling the police" by "empowering community members to help these individuals before they engage in criminal acts (the pre-criminal space)" (obtained documents). One CVE practitioner argued that, although "there are no known profiles of people who will become radicalized to violence," he could train community members to "identify individuals who may be on a path towards becoming radicalized to violence or on a path towards engaging in acts of ideologically inspired targeted violence" (obtained documents). By taking on this role, community members could coproduce national security while reducing the role of preemptive prosecutions and other carceral solutions in the prevention of violent extremism. Despite their noted flaws, radicalization research, gang prevention programs, and public health models have supported CVE initiatives by providing guidance on the early warning signs communities could use to identify individuals "on the path toward becoming radicalized" and the types of multidisciplinary programs to "help these individuals." This approach has deputized social service providers and community members as the police who watch out for, report, and work with individuals vulnerable to violent extremism.

In Minnesota, the Hennepin County Sheriff's Office applied for a 2016 DHS CVE grant, proposing, in part, two workshops with the Voices of East African Women community organization. These proposed workshops would be "specially designed for area women and their children" to "understand the nature and danger of the threats, the processes and signs of radicalization, and aid in discussion of available resources for protecting their children and others in the community" (Hennepin County Sheriff's Office 2016, 6). These workshops intended to mobilize Muslim mothers as critical national security agents who protected their children from predatory terrorist recruiters by understanding the "processes and signs of radicalization."

The Hennepin County Sheriff's Office (2016) also sought to replicate the London Metropolitan Police Department's Red Stop Program, an online system for individuals to "easily and anonymously report extremist internet content to law enforcement" (11). This approach would "allow residents and community partners to share the responsibility of policing the internet" and "create a clear opportunity for law enforcement to engage the community in partnership," particularly within Somali communities (11). Moreover, the Sheriff's Office proposed a "new staffing model for law enforcement" by hiring "community liaisons" who would "develop relationships with growing immigrant diaspora communities that face challenging cultural and language barriers" and "vouch for our Agency credibility" (Hennepin County Sheriff's Office 2016, 8). In this proposal, the Sheriff's Office called on "women and their children," community liaisons, and social service providers to watch out for the perceived signs of radicalization, strengthen community-police relationships, and enhance police credibility, all in the name of "addressing the threat of radicalization." Bashir Cilmi even reported that, after years of CVE programming in Minneapolis, a psychologist consulted with him to determine if a struggling Somali child "was radicalized." Psychologists came to view and evaluate their Somali clients through a radicalization lens, even if they had never "worked with this population before" (informal conversation, December 2, 2017). The racialized concept of radicalization creeped into the minds and practices of mental health professionals such that they came to view Somali youth as incipient terrorists.

Like the Sheriff's Office, New Jersey's Global Peace Foundation submitted a 2016 DHS CVE grant application similarly proposing "train-the-trainer" programs for law enforcement agents and community leaders. These trainings intended to "promote knowledge and awareness of Violent Extremism (VE) and Countering Violent Extremism (CVE)" and were "designed to help communities to assess at-risk persons, inform communities about when it is appropriate to notify law enforcement about individuals at risk, make the environment resistant to violent extremism, and to encourage the development of community-led prevention and intervention" (Global Peace Foundation 2016, 4). The City of Houston (2016) also proposed "Empowered Parents workshops" to educate parents about the "risk factors" of violent extremism (11). In Colorado, the Denver Police Department (2016) announced plans for a "community-led" CVE model to "help facilitate community-police trust and relationships as together we seek to recognize and prevent radicalization of at-risk populations in the Denver Metro area." To do so, the Denver Police Department (2016) partnered with Goodwill Industries to provide additional mentoring to youth identified as "at risk" of radicalization organized around the "concept of community-oriented policing" (4–5).

In Michigan, the Dearborn Police Department (2016) pursued DHS CVE funding to "help raise awareness on recognizing disturbing behaviors which warrant non-criminal intervention by well-trained law enforcement personnel and mental health professionals" (2). Citing Dearborn's large Arab Muslim population, the police department emphasized the need for "partnering with citizens and the community as the first line of defense in both homeland and hometown security" (4). From the department's perspective, "the marriage of community policing and countering violent extremism has proven effective in meeting the needs of the City of Dearborn" (4). This marriage contributed to the creation of the department's "Intervention Model" whereby "family, friends, or acquaintances" who are "worried about a person's behavior" can "tip[] off the police" (6). The police department suggested that terrorism awareness and prevention trainings could equip community members with the tools to identify and thwart potential threats by knowing the behaviors or activities that may lead to criminal activity.

Dearborn's approach aligns with broader CVE practices that police the "pre-criminal" space presumed to be a precursor to criminal violent extremism. In this "preventative" or "public health" approach, family, friends, and acquaintances use their CVE trainings to spot and report suspicious behaviors "*before* the line of criminal activity is crossed" (Department of Homeland Security 2015, emphasis added). Redefining noncriminal behaviors like extremist thought as "pre-criminal" facilitates the criminalization of racialized communities, whereby certain behaviors are identified, reported, and treated as proven precursors to criminal violence.

These "pre-criminal" community policing approaches have gained increasing acceptance in the CVE community even while recognizing that scientific studies routinely demonstrate that there are no known indicators, warning signs, or risk factors of violent extremism. Despite these scientific limitations, the social construction of a "pre-criminal space" has enhanced policing powers by reframing noncriminal behavior as pre-criminal and then training community members to report such noncriminal behaviors to law enforcement and support individuals identified as vulnerable to violent extremism.

Each of these community policing–oriented CVE programs has relied on community partners to give local police legitimacy, credibility, and access to targeted communities. The City of Houston's planned CVE program, for example, included "government partners, academia (Rice University and University of Houston), and non-profit partners (the Islamic Society of Greater Houston (ISGH), Interfaith Ministries of Greater Houston (IMGH), and the United Way)." In Boston, the Police Foundation (2016) identified the North American Family Institute, the Somali Community and Cultural Association, and the Boston Police Department as critical partners in implementing its Youth and Police Initiative Plus program aimed at fostering "community resilience to violent extremist recruitment and radicalization among Somali families in the Boston metropolitan area" (1). In addition to these religious, academic, and community institutions, CVE community-police partnerships increasingly include mental health providers like the Illinois Department of Human Services Division of Mental Health, Oakland's Mind Body Awareness Project, and the New Jersey Division of Mental Health and Addiction Services, to name just a few. In these collaborations, the FBI encouraged mental health professionals to "tell us if you think there's a large threat to something" (participant observation, October 27, 2017). Although CVE practitioners referenced suicide prevention strategies to justify the policing of this "pre-criminal space" by mental health professionals, behavioral scientists contributing to CVE discussions admitted that "in the realm of suicide prevention work, there are no interventions in place to screen people for (or prevent) *thoughts* of killing oneself, because of the difficulty in distinguishing between those who are thinking about killing themselves and those who go on to kill themselves" (Rajeev Ramchand, as referenced in National Academies of Sciences, Engineering, and Medicine 2017). Given their concerns with the validity, ethics, and impact of this approach, some mental health professionals and community partners, such as the Ta'leef Collective, have withdrawn from CVE programs, despite their initial support.

Within the CVE policy world, policing institutions have enhanced their power by training social service providers and community members to identify, report, and work with individuals vulnerable to violent extremism using disproven indicators, risk factors, and warning signs. This process aligns with academic calls for preventative interventions that "serve youth and adults who are believed to be at risk of committing a violent act but are still in the pre-criminal space" (Weine, Eisenman, Kinsler et al. 2017, 3). Researchers suggest that "a consensus of policymakers and practitioners have called for developing community-based capacities that proactively address those vulnerable to violent extremism in the pre-criminal space through mental health and psychosocial programming, rather than waiting for them to cross the line, or involving them in sting operations that take them in a direction where they never have dreamed of going" (Weine, Eisenman, Kinsler et al. 2017, 8). By encouraging communities to police certain noncriminal behaviors and thoughts as precursors to criminal violence ("pre-criminal"), CVE practitioners have criminalized common immigrant experiences, constitutionally protected acts, psychiatric disabilities, radical thought, and "Muslim and refugee communities" perceived to be uniquely vulnerable to violent extremism.

Although the U.S. security state's collaboration with community institutions suggests a softer, friendlier approach to fighting homegrown terrorism, Kristian Williams (2004) warns that "the dangers of allowing the state to co-opt community institutions, especially those of oppressed minorities, should be clear enough" (501). In Nazi Germany, for example, "whenever the extermination process was put into effect, the Germans utilized the *existing leadership and organizations* of the Jewish community to assist them. . . . In the face of German determination to murder all Jews, most Jews instinctively relied on their own communal organizations to defend their interests whenever possible" (Rubenstein 1978, 72, emphasis in original). Yet, "these very organizations were transformed into subsidiaries of the German police and state bureaucracies" such that the Jewish organizations "undertook such tasks as selecting those who were to be deported, notifying the families and, finally, of sending the Jewish police to round up the victims" (Rubenstein 1978, 74). The incorporation of community institutions and social service providers into state projects thus can increase, not mitigate, state violence. This means that "by organizing on a sufficient scale, the police can greatly enhance their own power—not only *over* these agencies, but *through* them—while acquiring relatively few additional burdens for themselves" (Williams 2004, 339). Rather than frame CVE as an alternative to law enforcement activities, communities must approach CVE as a security strategy that has enhanced policing powers by deputizing community partners as coproducers of public safety and legitimizing local police agencies.

On Killing: The Radicalization of the State

Although radicalization research has informed CVE work, it has not been used to prevent or mitigate state-sanctioned violence. U.S. police trainings, for example, emphasize the necessity of killing, an unquestioned tactic framed as public safety rather than state terrorism. Radicalization research therefore reinforces the state's monopoly on legitimate violence by pathologizing, criminalizing, and demonizing violence committed by nonstate actors.

In his popular police training "On Combat," Lieutenant Colonel David Grossman informed police trainees that to "serve and protect," they must "deter and then stop the threat." Grossman argued that "the most effective way to stop someone is to fire a bullet into his central nervous system. It is up to God and the paramedics as to whether the man dies. Your job is to stop the deadly threat and the most effective way to do that is to make that threat die" (participant observation, June 28, 2017). In 2016, U.S. police killed 1,093 people in the name of public safety (*Guardian* 2018).

Rather than advance a "bunch of guys" thesis or theorize a three-step psychological process to understand what drives law enforcement to violence, the United States positions police violence—including firing a bullet into a person's central nervous system—as a necessary strategy to "serve and protect." The U.S. public largely does not question how its soldiers or law enforcement officials come to enact violence even when, as I detail below, this violence has included the indiscriminate slaughtering of civilians for sport. Despite increased opposition to police killings of people of color, the U.S. public views this violence as a necessary instrument to ensure national security and social order.

Given the state's monopoly on legitimate violence, violence perpe-

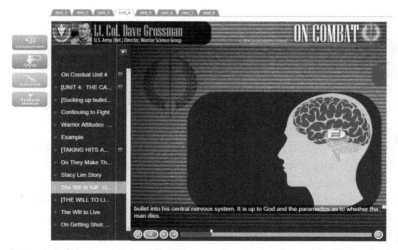

Screenshot of Lieutenant Colonel David Grossman's police training module, "On Combat."

trated by state actors does not qualify as "evil" acts. In a 2007 video leaked by Chelsea Manning, for instance, U.S. soldiers in two Apache helicopters began killing unarmed Iraqi civilians, commenting, "Hahaha. I hit 'em" and "Oh yeah, look at those dead bastards." Rather than question the culture, theology, or psychology of these soldiers, U.S. media suggested Manning's gender identity contributed to her "traitorous decision" to leak classified documents. Manning (2013), however, argued that she was "depressed with the situation we were mired in [in Iraq]" and by U.S. military operations "obsessed with capturing people." Leaking the documents could "make the world a better place" by sparking a public debate about the vicious violence deployed by the U.S. military (Manning 2013). Despite Manning's efforts, the U.S. public often defends war, drone strikes, and targeted assassinations as critical national security tools rather than contesting them as acts of state terror. Radicalization models limit the concept of violent extremists to "nonstate actors," effectively eliminating state actors from the radicalization rubric and "violent extremist" label.

Despite the mass violence U.S. soldiers inflict on local populations, we do not reduce soldiers to irrational evildoers or indict soldiers' culture, psychology, or theology in their capacity to kill. Li (2015) assesses that, although radicalization research reduces political violence to individual pathologies, scholars "would never write a cogent analysis of the invasion of Iraq by focusing on why soldiers volunteer to join the U.S. military" (para. 25). Ultimately, "the absence of politics leaves accounts" of radicalization "rather empty" (para. 25).

To Think Otherwise: Unsettling Radicalization Research

Today, radicalization research advanced by psychologists, social scientists, and terrorism experts organize domestic security policies. What these radicalization models seek to, but cannot, demonstrate is "how an otherwise normal individual becomes a murderous terrorist" (Puar and Rai 2002, 123). Despite these scientific limitations, this research indicts individual psychologies, cultural deficiencies, or theological perversions in the radicalization process. "Terrorism, in this discourse, is a symptom of a deviant psyche, the psyche gone awry, or the failed psyche; the terrorist enters this discourse as an absolute violation" (Puar and Rai 2002, 124). CVE programs informed by this radicalization research encourage community members and law enforcement agents to identify these "deviants" and provide therapeutic, or corrective, services.

Following these normative assumptions, Los Angeles's RENEW program could place individuals perceived to be at risk of or in the process of radicalizing on an involuntary psychiatric hold. In Minneapolis, CVE practitioners described psychological factors like "disaffection" and "internal identity crises" as indicators of radicalization and hired youth intervention workers to "spot" these "root causes of terrorism" in schools. In Chicago, the Illinois Criminal Justice Information Authority trained mental health professionals to "identify when a person close to them appears to be in crisis and at risk for committing a violent act." These narratives, and the carceral practices they authorize, implicate these perceived deviations from hegemonic norms in the mobilization to violence, particularly when expressed by Muslim youth. In fact, "over 70 percent of federally-supported CVE programs are premised on the unsupported conclusion that diversity and the experience of discrimination in America are suggestive of a national security threat" (Patel, Lindsay, and DenUyl 2018b, para. 3). These programs therefore treat difference as a source of danger.

According to philosopher Michel Foucault (1999), abnormality is a relational concept that defines the norm through differentiation. This means that the "normal" is defined by constructing the abnormal—the mad, the sick, the criminal, the deviant, the terrorist. For Foucault (1999), "racism against the abnormal" is distinct from but interlinked with ethnic racism, evident in the rise of German psychiatry simultaneous to the rise of Nazism (317). This "internal racism" has authorized "the screening of every individual within a given society" to detect "all those within a group who may be the carriers of a danger to it," ultimately defending society against its "abnormal individuals" (Foucault 1999, 317). Grafted onto ethnic racism, these categories of abnormality demonize, pathologize, and criminalize individuals of color as "monsters" if they appear to deviate from hegemonic social, cultural, and psychological norms. This process historically has facilitated the development of practices to defend society from these monsters, including incarceration and psychiatric intervention that disproportionately target communities of color.

Today, these monsters "haunt the prose of contemporary counterterrorism," particularly in the monitoring of entire communities to detect potential threats (Puar and Rai 2002, 124). More specifically, "the knowledge and form of power that is mobilized to analyze, taxonomize, psychologize, and defeat terrorism has a genealogical connection to the West's abnormals, and specifically those premodern monsters that Western civilization had seemed to bury and lay to rest long ago" (Puar and Rai 2002, 124). In the 1850s, for example, psychiatrists "believed that African American slaves who ran away from their white masters did so because of a mental illness called *drapetomania*" (Metzl 2009, ix). During the 1960s Black freedom struggle, psychiatry similarly "positioned itself as an authority that made sense of the crisis posed by angry, protesting Black men" by labeling these men as "crazed Black schizophrenic killers" (108, xv). "Anxieties about racial protest catalyzed associations between schizophrenia, criminality, and violence," ultimately equating Black political protest with insanity (xix). These narratives have resurfaced in the contemporary treatment of Black organizers as "Black Identity Extremists" who must be monitored, surveilled, and controlled in the name of public safety. Today, "psychiatric definitions of insanity continue to police racial hierarchies, tensions, and unspoken codes in addition to separating normal from abnormal behavior" (ix). By indicting a deviant or failed psyche, these pathologizing discourses strategically have erased what slave insurrections, the Black Panthers, and the Movement for Black Lives sought to accomplish, politically, through their struggles, while shoring up support for policing institutions to manage these perceived threats.

Through her exploration of how "colonial constraints and imperial dispositions have a tenacious presence" in the geopolitical and spatial distribution of inequities, anthropologist Ann Stoler (2016) argues that today's "colonial configurations are different, as are the actors, but the tactics of instantiating difference and forging an 'internal enemy' are colonial reverberations with a difference—and with more than a distant semblance to earlier racial logics, engendered fears, and counterinsurgent tactics from which they gained their support" (4, 28). Organized around "internal enemies," these reworked colonial concepts contribute to contemporary security regimes that service U.S. empire. Rather than treat the anti-Muslim logics that inform radicalization models as a byproduct of the global war on terror, we must locate these dynamic racial formations within a longer genealogy of defining, taxonomizing, and criminalizing terrorist-monsters, particularly in nondominant communities. The ready-made narratives we reach for to make sense of "homegrown terrorism" did not simply emerge after the instantiation of "terrorism studies" or after the September 11 attacks. The concepts we call on to understand violent extremism are rooted in colonial histories that bear on the present through the rearticulation of the dangerous terrorist-monster lurking in our communities who must be detected and corrected.

Pulsating through an iteratively receding and resurfacing "colonial presence," CVE policies depend on a "seamless continuation of colonial practices that pervade the present," like the reworked counterinsurgency tactics to neutralize the perceived civilizational threat posed by "merciless Indian savages" who resisted colonial rule (Stoler 2016, 25; Estes 2017). Because colonial entailments "wrap around contemporary problems," these "colonial counterinsurgency policies rest undiluted in current security measures" (Stoler 2016, 4). These continuities reveal the complex temporalities of colonial relations in the development of CVE that draws on, supports, and remakes domestic counterinsurgency, counterterrorism, and community policing doctrines to advance U.S. empire "over here" and "over there." If radicalization theories reactivate and remake colonial taxonomies, how might we decolonize terrorism studies and think otherwise?

Because these colonial impingements are not overdetermining, the next chapter examines how CVE practitioners interpreted and negotiated prevailing radicalization research, remaking for themselves what constituted progressive and ethical national security work.

CHAPTER 4

PATRIOT ACTS
Managing Public Objections to CVE

On a hot summer day, my father eagerly assembled my brother, mother, and me for a family photograph. My father staged the photograph, placing us in front of our two-car garage. Above us waved a crisp U.S. flag that my father dutifully displayed each national holiday. Looking at the photograph some twenty-five years later, the prominence of the flag, and its centrality in our lives, cannot be missed.

As a curious child, I often followed my father as he put up, and took down, our flag. I watched him carefully affix the flag to our suburban home and listened as he discussed the importance of this patriotic symbol to our own filial identity. Although as a child I ascribed no exceptional value to this ritual, I cataloged my father's sometimes conflicting narration of the flag's role in our suburban lives. Family photographs, for example, worked to capture a realized American dream, complete with a house with a white picket fence, two cars, and two children. At the same time, my father sometimes grumbled that the flag served as reassurance to our neighbors who questioned our Americanness, an antagonistic sentiment harnessed to nativist understandings of citizenship and belonging. Our family photograph thus signified a proud yet anxious American family seeking to continually reassert its social value materially and symbolically. In the long shadow of the Vietnam War, my multiracial immigrant family sought to visibly prove our loyalty to the United States in a "culture of proof" often tethered to a "neoliberal ethos that demanded a commitment to the core American value of capitalism" (Silva 2016, 58). Flanked by symbols of suburban consumption, the U.S. flag compensated for our racial difference by communicating our patriotism and indicating our willingness to assimilate to dominant U.S. culture. U.S. symbols, rituals, and performances reasserted our social value while reminding us that our belonging was contingent on continually proving deserving citizenship.

My own childhood experiences growing up in the United States reflect the fraught and often contradictory experiences of immigrant families who negotiate dynamic geopolitical, social, and cultural contexts. In the wake of the Iranian revolution and the September 11 attacks, U.S. Muslims have deployed similar tactics to navigate shifting racial formations that mark their bodies as perpetual foreigners, incipient terrorists, or impossible subjects. This charged context compels "Muslim-looking" people to perform patriotic acts that minimize their racial difference and demonstrate their love for the United States.

These patriotic performances work to ward off the terrorist label and the violence such a label authorizes. Some Muslim women, for example, have donned hijabs embossed with the U.S. flag, a practice iconicized through a 2017 anti-Trump protest poster.

The Americanized hijab militates against the racialized trope of the terrorist that facilitates the exclusion, demonization, and criminalization of anyone who "looks Muslim." To navigate the political terrain partially wrought by the global war on terror, some racialized populations enact public performances of U.S. loyalty while others engage in a politics of refusal.

Given its increasing national security concerns, the U.S. government has called on Muslims not only to denounce homegrown terrorism but also to actively thwart it. For U.S. Muslims at this historical juncture, performing patriot acts now involves serving as key operatives in the fight against domestic terrorism. CAIR-Los Angeles director Hussam Ayloush even declared in the aftermath of the September 11 attacks that "Muslims in America are the first line of defense against terrorism conducted falsely in the name of Islam" (as quoted in Silva 2016, 67–68). Four years later, Ayloush would retract this charge, warning that the intensifying arrangements between mosques and law enforcement eroded trust by deepening the surveillance, monitoring, and prosecution of Muslim communities across the United States (Aaronson 2013, 112). Racist assumptions about

Portrait of Munira Ahmed, by Shepard Fairey for the We the People project coordinated by the Amplifier Foundation. Artwork by Shepard Fairey for Amplifier.org.

who is dangerous drive the demand for all Muslims to denounce—and now prevent—terrorism as a part of their patriotic duties.

As Ayloush's own shift in understanding indicates, Muslim communities differentially interpret, negotiate, and respond to these demands, especially as families consider the possibilities, limitations, and risks of various approaches. In the current security context, the U.S. public marks Muslims who work with law enforcement in the fight against terrorism as "good Muslims." Collaborating with the police as terrorist watchdogs, however, advances the criminalization of Muslims and therefore can destroy community relationships, erode trust, and harm friends and family. Conversely, resisting the role of terrorist watchdog risks the "bad Muslim" label, which exposes communities to heightened surveillance, monitoring, and threats of arrest.

Given this "impossible dilemma" manufactured by the U.S. security state, some targeted communities that objected to FBI stings have welcomed CVE as an alternative to more coercive forms of policing imposed on Muslim communities after September 11 (Cacho 2012). Some Muslim leaders have viewed CVE as a compromise between protecting civil liberties and pursuing national security. Others, however, have rejected any collaborations with the U.S. security state, especially projects that assume Muslims are more susceptible to violent extremism or that uniquely hold their communities responsible for preventing terrorism. Like my own family, Muslim communities have found different ways to navigate these complex contexts and made strategic decisions about how to keep their loved ones safe from state and vigilante violence.

Since its inception, the U.S. government has struggled to manage the real and perceived tensions between national security and civil liberties. When the 2002 Homeland Security Act established the Department of Homeland Security, for example, it required the Homeland Security Secretary to appoint an Officer for Civil Liberties and Civil Rights. This officer must "review and assess information concerning abuses of civil rights, civil liberties, and profiling on the basis of race, ethnicity, or religion" and then report all findings to Congress (Pub. L. No. 107-296). In a 2004 report regarding the Homeland Security Civil Rights and Civil Liberties Protection Act, Congress reaffirmed its commitment to "provide[] checks and balances to protect civil rights and civil liberties" (S. Rep. 108-350 [2004], 2). The report, however, also warned that DHS had become the "country's biggest law enforcement agency," employed "more Federal officers with arrest and firearm authority than the Department of Justice," and installed many programs and policies, all of which "have the potential, if not scrutinized, to affect individual liberties" (2). The report cautioned that "in this post-9/11 world, the Department must be especially sensitive to maintaining civil liberties as it works to strengthen security and detect and deter terrorist attacks" (3). The September 11 attacks intensified debates about ensuring national security without eroding civil liberties, evident in the legislative provisions that expanded and regulated the reach of the U.S. security state.

Although the September 11 attacks and their aftermath amplified attention on the continued abrogation of civil liberties in the name of national security, these concerns predate the establishment of the Department of Homeland Security. The 1988 Civil Liberties Act, for example, granted reparations to U.S.-based Japanese people incarcerated in camps run by the Department of Justice following the 1941 Japanese bombing of Hawaii's Pearl Harbor (Pub. L. No. 100-383). In the 1940s, President Franklin D. Roosevelt justified the forced relocation and incarceration of more than one hundred thousand U.S.-Japanese people as an effective national security strategy. Four decades later, the prosecution of eight pro-Palestinian organizers revealed a similar DOJ "contingency plan" to round up and detain thousands of legal "alien activists" from Algeria, Iran, Jordan, Lebanon, Libya, Morocco, Syria, and Tunisia.

As with these forms of planned and actual mass incarceration, prevailing yet dynamic racial formations continue to shape antiterrorism policies and their corresponding national security vocabularies, norms, and logics. Throughout history, the United States has installed policies, laws, and programs that suspend the civil liberties of some, whether by criminalizing dissent, immigration, or people on the basis of race, religion, gender, and other axes of difference. The United States uses ongoing national security concerns to justify these marginalizing efforts.

Informed by these histories, human rights, civil liberties, and community-based organizations have challenged CVE, particularly by calling attention to how this national security framework "stigmatize[s] American Muslims and cast[s] unwarranted suspicion on innocuous activity" (American Civil Liberties Union 2014). CVE expert Susan Bailey, for example, affirmed that "there's a lot of controversy about CVE domestically. There are concerns about civil liberties. There's concerns about stigmatization of entire communities." Political scientist Seth Michaels similarly worried that "we don't want a plane blown out of the sky, but we need to find a balance between protections of civil liberties as well as security. I don't think we found it here in the United States." Given these concerns, Lieutenant Colonel Ryan Simpson asked, "How we can strike the right equilibrium between civil liberties and security?" As these examples illustrate, the elusive struggle to "strike the right equilibrium" between civil liberties and national security has palpated CVE conversations (participant observation, May 16, 2017).

This tension also surfaced in local national security programming, including educational initiatives. A 2017 Chicago History Museum teacher workshop titled Spies, Traitors, Saboteurs: Fear and Freedom in America even asked these central questions: "How do we identify the 'enemy'? How do we keep our country safe without compromising civil liberties?" For this teacher workshop, the museum highlighted the tensions between national security and civil liberties, particularly in the identification of the "enemy."

Given these ongoing debates, CVE actors often confronted critics who questioned their work and its impact on the civil liberties and civil rights of targeted communities. Competing definitions and practices pulled CVE actors in different, and sometimes contradictory, directions as they struggled to address public opposition to their work. As CVE researcher Ron Stuart reported, "Not surprisingly, DHS and FBI are huge bureaucracies and the people who work in them don't see things all the same way. So, depending on who you talk to, you get very different outlooks and perspectives on how much we should be emphasizing things like intervention versus just being law enforcement only." In fact, Stuart explained that an FBI agent recently rejected CVE, insisting that "we don't want to do [CVE] interventions. Our job is to arrest people. We're going to arrest. We're not going to do anything other than that." Yet, that same FBI agent later said, "We can't arrest our way out" of the problem of violent extremism. From Stuart's experience, "even the same person isn't necessarily consistent with what they're saying" (interview, February 17, 2017). Rather than flatten the complex personhood of CVE actors, this chapter explores how these workers acted on their own intellectual conceptualizations of national security and civil liberties, thereby understanding and performing their roles differently. By positioning national security workers as complex and sometimes contradictory people, this chapter queries how CVE actors differentially defined for themselves what constituted ethical national security work and responded to public opposition to their work.

CVE Meets Its Critics: From Unintelligent Analyses to Conspiracy Theories

In a 2015 *Patheos* article, Junaid Afeef and Alejandro Beutel (2015) argued that "CVE critics are right" and that "CVE is still necessary" (para. 1). In this piece, Afeef and Beutel (2015) recognized that, although the Obama administration branded CVE as "an alternative paradigm to the excesses of the War on Terror," many civil liberties groups "have raised important criticisms and concerns about CVE that must be addressed to the satisfaction of the public" (para. 1). Given these concerns, Afeef and Beutel (2015) concluded that "it is necessary for American Muslim communities to take up the challenge of developing programs that incorporate these lessons in order to prevent Muslims from succumbing to ISIS's powerful online recruitment efforts. The legitimate grievances of Americans—including Muslims—cannot be a reason to not do the right thing" (para. 2). Rather than reject CVE, Afeef and Beutel offered remedies to fix CVE's programmatic flaws while offloading redesign responsibilities onto Muslim communities. In reading this article, I realized I needed to explore how CVE actors managed community concerns, like racial and religious profiling, in ways that reaffirmed, rather than threatened, the primacy of CVE on the national security stage.

I quickly learned that by managing national security narratives and corresponding community concerns, CVE actors set the terms of the national security debate, which, in turn, shaped the legitimation and formation of policy outcomes. Although some social scientists address the power of national security narratives in the legitimation of public policy, I contend that managing public objections is integral to sustaining controversial national security policies like CVE. Social scientists must pay careful attention to the discursive maneuvers national security workers deploy to control the terms of the national security debate, organize public understandings of national security, and pressure Muslim communities to uphold, rather than contest, the U.S. security state as "good citizens." It is to these maneuvers I now turn.

"Little CVE": Learning from Past Mistakes

In 2017, I observed a public CVE workshop for mental health professionals, which included a DHS representative, FBI special agents, and local practitioners. A small group of protestors disrupted the beginning of this workshop, holding signs and shouting chants that contested CVE's reliance on racial and religious profiling. Through my observation of this workshop, I learned, firsthand, how some CVE actors responded to public objections to their work.

After the protestors left, DHS representative Nabil Soliman introduced himself to workshop participants as "not a typical DHS person" given his prior experience as a "civil rights attorney who prosecuted crime [committed] by DHS." Like Afeef and Beutel, Soliman acknowledged past abuses by DHS. Yet, he also insisted that DHS was now a "different agency" dedicated to "advancing civil rights and civil liberties," which "will help us reach our goal of securing our communities and campuses." Legitimized by his status as a former civil rights attorney, Soliman sought to bolster support for security agencies whose past crimes fueled distrust in communities of color by framing DHS as a "different agency" that had learned from past mistakes. Practitioners like Tanvir Rahman similarly argued that they had learned from the "behaviors and practices that have been objectionable" and struggled to prove their work differed from these past efforts that "securitized relationships between law enforcement and these minority communities" (interview, November 10, 2016). Throughout my fieldwork, the concept of "learning from past mistakes" sought to manage public objections to local CVE programming (Emily Evans, participant observation, October 7, 2016).

Meanwhile, on Twitter, co-facilitator Alex Russo described the protestors as "well-intentioned, though misinformed," even asserting that they were all "on the same team." Through this narrative, Russo suggested that he shared similar objections to past CVE programs and therefore offered an alternative approach that did not rely on law enforcement. In fact, Russo described his work as "little cve"— denoted by all lowercase letters—to distance himself from federal CVE programs that often collaborated with the police, despite applying for a DHS grant. Like Rahman, Russo managed public objections to his work by distinguishing it from the "objectionable practices" of other CVE programs. The presence of FBI agents, however, called into question Russo's narrative that his approach differed from other police-led programs.

Co-facilitator Tanvir Rahman also asserted that "we're all on the same team" and that the protestors—"kids"—were simply "wasting our time." Protestors, however, identified serious concerns with local CVE programming, shouting, "What markers are there that lead to violent jihadism? What markers are there? There are none! There's no real science behind this except . . . racism. That's why we're here." After the protestors left, Rahman explained to participants that his work "educated communities to identify behaviors outside of the norm that we should be concerned about," which "is not about racial profiling and stereotyping." Like Russo, Rahman argued that protestors wrongly conflated his work with past CVE practices, despite his insistence that mental health professionals could learn the "warning signs of radicalization to violence." An FBI special agent then confirmed that, through their observations, mental health professionals could report individuals indicating "movement toward violent ideology." Local CVE programming therefore employed the same techniques as other initiatives by seeking to identify, report, and off-ramp individuals vulnerable to violent extremism in collaboration with law enforcement, even though Rahman framed his work as different from these past practices. Despite using similar practices and organizing logics, Rahman objected to the conflation of his work with other harmful CVE programs.

By reducing the protestors to misinformed kids and rejecting their critiques through simple denials, these practitioners managed how participants interpreted public objections to their work. These brief statements effectively minimized the impact of the protest on workshop participants, evident in their continued engagement in the training. In fact, only one participant walked out of the workshop to provide jail support for the two protestors arrested on a trespassing charge after another co-facilitator called the police (participant observation, October 27, 2017).

As these examples demonstrate, practitioners like Rahman and Russo managed community dissent by identifying ways security agencies had "learned from past mistakes," distancing their work from other "objectionable practices," and discrediting protestors as "kids" who misunderstood the new generation of CVE programming. This approach positioned CVE as a progressive response to past abuses by the U.S. security state, a narrative that resonated with the personal experiences of public officials like Nabil Soliman. Through these strategic maneuvers, practitioners sought to reaffirm the concept of homegrown terrorism and increase public support for and cooperation with government agencies that historically have criminalized Muslim communities, including the Department of Homeland Security.

Like other community organizers, the 2017 protestors refused CVE collaborations because they shored up the U.S. security state. Some practitioners, however, encouraged the "voluntary and ongoing cooperation" between the government and civil rights organizations to "build resources for communities that can be truly useful in preventing violence whilst safeguarding civil liberties" (Afeef 2018, paras. 11–12). In their efforts to distinguish current CVE practices from past abuses, some practitioners missed the broader critiques related to enhancing the very institutions and organizing logics that have harmed, and continue to harm, Muslim communities. The introduction of CVE, after all, has not stopped the use of FBI stings and other coercive methods to prevent violent extremism. Rather than advocate for national security reforms, community organizers sought to develop new forms of public safety independent of the U.S. security state, a strategy often misunderstood by CVE actors as they managed public objections to their work.

From Prediction to Prevention: Negotiating CVE's Scientific Limitations

CVE actors like Adrian Baker also managed the credibility of their work in the face of social science research that routinely demonstrated that there are no scientifically proven indicators, risk factors, or warning signs of violent extremism. Given these scientific limitations, CVE actors argued that, although these indicators could not predict who will become a terrorist, they could help identify individuals "vulnerable to" or "at risk of" violent extremism. The use of these indicators became one "alternative fact" practitioners and researchers sought to manage.[1]

Baker, for example, used his interview to dispel the "false narratives" about CVE's predictive functions. To do so, Baker explained throughout his interview that critics wrongly concluded that CVE sought to predict, rather than prevent, violent extremism. For Baker, "CVE itself is not attempting to do violence prediction. That has also been a narrative based on alternative facts. It is about prevention rather than prediction." Given these circulating "alternative facts" and "false narratives" about violence prediction, Baker refrained from using the "r-word"—radicalization—which he reported "was almost like dropping the f-bomb in some communities" (interview, January 27, 2017). Because the r-word "sets off alarm bells" and signals predictive policing, Baker preferred the term "entry into violence."

In his discussion of "entry into violence," Baker conceded that radicalization research could not draw a causal link between the early warning signs of radicalization and violent extremism. Practitioners therefore could not use these warning signs to predict who might commit an act of terrorism. Baker, however, also argued that these warning signs were "associated with entry into violence," meaning they could help identify individuals *vulnerable to* violent extremism. This strategy allowed CVE actors to use these warning signs in their everyday work while affirming the research studies that disproved them. Critics, however, argued that using these factors to identify individuals "at risk" of violent extremism posed the same problems (and scientific limitations) as employing these factors to predict who will commit an act of terrorism (participant observation, April 21, 2017).

Leading CVE partners like the now defunct World Organization for Resource Development and Education (WORDE) created manuals, practices, and programs that followed these contradictory logics. WORDE (2016), for example, published a CVE instructor's manual that detailed how "radicalization to violent extremism is multifaceted, interconnected, and often entails overlapping potential factors" (42). WORDE (2016) also argued:

> This framework was developed using terms such as "risk factor" or "indicators of vulnerability" in the colloquial sense. It is important to note that, scientifically, "risk factors" may assume that risk is quantifiable, or that there is a proven causal link between two factors (for example, smoking is a common risk factor of lung cancer). However, because there are no studies to date that have demonstrated a causal link between any one risk factor, or combination of factors, and an individual becoming a terrorist, *our use of the term "risk factor" is not predictive of who will become radicalized.* Instead, it represents a structured guide to explore variables that have a *potential* to contribute to one's radicalization. (44, emphasis in original)

Although WORDE admitted (2016) that no research studies had demonstrated a causal link between its listed risk factors and violent extremism, it suggested that these risk factors could serve as a "structured guide" in identifying individuals vulnerable to violent extremism (44).

WORDE employee Nazanin Zaghari also reported that despite "millions of dollars of research" that demonstrated that "there is no single factor that can predict who will become a terrorist," empirical research on "convicted terrorists" suggested that "some common indicators . . . exist in many of those cases, which *may* make an individual more vulnerable to recruitment and radicalization" (participant observation, August 18, 2016). Even though Zaghari recognized that scientific studies had disproven the utility of these "common indicators," she proffered that their mere presence in some "convicted terrorists" imbued these indicators with the power to identify individuals "at risk of" or "vulnerable to" violent extremism. Following these contradictory logics, WORDE's CVE programming taught community members how to identify individuals vulnerable to terrorist radicalization and recruitment using the very warning signs WORDE conceded had no scientific basis.

Adhering to this model, community members referred more than twenty-five individuals for interventions, citing "homesickness," "acculturation-related stress," "feelings of alienation," and "economic stressors" as signs these individuals "*may be* at risk of violent extremism." A partner agency, for example, worried about a "young Afghan male" who had "withdrawn from family and friends and had failed to attend school for several months." With the assistance of WORDE (2014), the agency determined the young man was "severely homesick and needed help adjusting to his life in the U.S." and therefore possibly at risk of violent extremism (4). By associating common immigrant experiences with violent extremism, WORDE encouraged adults to view Muslim, Arab, and other immigrant children through a radicalization lens, without considering the impact of marking individuals at risk of violent extremism.

Critics have identified these contradictory logics as scientifically suspect, ethically questionable, and practically flawed. Legal scholars, for example, contend that "WORDE in fact seems to use these factors to do just what the group says they cannot"—identify individuals as vulnerable to violent extremism based on "potential risk factors" (Patel and Koushik 2017, 26). Given the public opposition to CVE, "policymakers are being forced to admit that the science does not support their policy, but instead of changing the policy, they're keeping it, and then inevitably having to contradict themselves when explaining the policy's scientific credentials" (Kundnani, as quoted in Mirza 2016). In this view, the indicators of violent extremism could neither predict who will become a terrorist nor identify individuals vulnerable to violent extremism.

The Illinois Criminal Justice Information Authority (ICJIA) (2016) similarly worked this tension as it created and instituted bystander-gatekeeping trainings to "educate community members on how to identify warning signs of radicalization to violence and warning signs that someone may be in the early stages of planning an act of targeted violence" (18). In its 2016 DHS CVE grant proposal, for instance, ICJIA framed its bystander-gatekeeper training as a preventative, not predictive, approach to violent extremism while still relying on "warning signs of radicalization." ICJIA advanced this training despite recognizing that "there are no known profiles of people who will become radicalized to violence or who will engage in acts of ideologically inspired targeted violence" (obtained documents). In this view, the absence of a single profile of a violent extremist did not preclude the possibility of using early warning signs to detect individuals "radicalizing or mobilizing toward violence." Like WORDE, ICJIA (2016) conceded that these "potential risk factors *correlated with* violent extremism" and "risk factors *associated with* radicalization toward violent extremism" had no predictive power while using them preemptively to identify individuals who may be vulnerable to violent extremism (9, emphasis added). CVE actors used qualifying vocabularies like "*potential* risk factors *correlated with* violent extremism" and "*may be* early indications to *possible* violence" as a way to recognize and then sidestep scientific studies that demonstrate that there are no known indicators that can be used to identify individuals vulnerable to violence.

CVE actors also relied on public health metaphors to manage the contradictory logics that organized their work. Researchers Alejandro Beutel, Asma Shah, and Mimi Yu (2016), for example, proposed that "violence prediction and violence prevention can be understood using an analogy: Doctors cannot precisely say when a person is going to have a heart attack (prediction); however they can confidently identify when someone is at serious risk for one and what steps can be taken to lower that risk (prevention)" (para. 28). Predictive efforts "focus on determining the accuracy of whether or not an individual will commit a future act of violence" (para. 29). Preventive measures, however, "focus on 1) developing a rapid and context-specific analysis of a potential threat posed by an individual and 2) connecting the person of concern to protective resources that will mitigate their specific issues driving them toward violence" (para. 29). By distinguishing prediction from prevention, the researchers asserted that CVE "does NOT seek to 'predict' who will be a violent extremist and who will not" (para. 26). The doctor analogy, however, obfuscated how CVE actors have identified "persons of concern" or individuals at risk of violent extremism. This analogy also erased the scientific studies demonstrating that there are no early warning signs of violent extremism and no indicators that reliably can detect individuals "at serious risk" of violent extremism.

In practice, these nuanced arguments flattened into self-contradictory statements that criminalized individuals using disproven indicators of violent extremism. The NYPD, for example, acknowledged that it is "difficult to predict who will radicalize" while routinely questioning, investigating, and arresting individuals exhibiting "typical signatures" of radicalization, like growing a beard, wearing traditional Islamic clothing, or experiencing social disenfranchisement (Silber and Bhatt 2007, 20). These warning signs also have "criminalize[d] the normal human experiences of Muslims and open[ed] the door to people acting on prejudices and stereotypes in tagging individuals as potential terrorists" (Patel, Lindsay, and DenUyl 2018a, 1). Aysha Khoury, for example, warned that "showing signs of withdrawing or isolation" sometimes triggered a CVE intervention, even though withdrawn youth usually are "just struggling to grow up," a common U.S. experience with no connection to violent extremism (interview, January 25, 2017). For these critics, the distinction between causality and correlation and the debate about prediction and prevention were meaningless. The NYPD and other organizations have responded to disproven warning signs that may, or may not, indicate an individual is vulnerable to radicalizing *as though the individual is, or may become, dangerous.*

To support their work, organizations like ICJIA turned to studies that curated risk factors "associated with" violent extremism. The DHS-funded National Consortium for the Study of Terrorism and Responses to Terrorism (START) (2017b), for example, developed a terrorist database called Profiles of Individual Radicalization in the United States (PIRUS). This database contains "individual-level information on the backgrounds, attributes, and radicalization processes of nearly 1,500 violent and non-violent extremists who adhere to far right, far left, Islamist, or single-issue ideologies in the United States covering 1948–2013." Even though PIRUS can identify the "backgrounds, attributes, and radicalization processes" common among violent extremists and compare them to nonviolent extremists, researchers still have no way of knowing if any of these behaviors and characteristics correspond to terrorist radicalization. The database also employs questionable categories, such as classifying the Black Panther Party as a terrorist organization. CVE critics reject this troubling strategy, reporting that "government programs try to get around the lack of predictive markers via checklists of 'push' and 'pull' factors that identify individuals at risk of violent extremism" (Patel and Singh 2016, para. 6).

Given these limitations, radicalization theorist Marc Sageman (2014) concedes that "after all this funding and this flurry of publications, with each new terrorist incident we realize that we are no closer to answering our original question about what leads people to turn to political violence" (569). Despite understanding that "credible empirical studies amply demonstrate that there are no predictive markers of who is likely to become a terrorist," CVE strategists have "promoted programs that rely on such markers" to identify individuals "at risk" of violent extremism (rather than predict who will go on to commit terrorism) (Patel and Singh 2016, para. 17). This self-contradictory practice defined many CVE programs.

As these examples illustrate, researchers and practitioners negotiated the scientific limitations of CVE by defining their work as a preventative, not predictive, approach to violent extremism. In addition, CVE actors admitted that the warning signs "associated with radicalization" could not predict who will become a terrorist while arguing that these warning signs could help identify individuals at risk of violent extremism. Through these discursive maneuvers, CVE actors worked to maintain the credibility of this approach and the security agencies leading it, which they viewed as effectively balancing national security and civil rights.

"Our Criminal Justice System Works": Denying Racial and Religious Profiling

Given the continued charge that CVE relied on racial and religious profiling to identify individuals "at risk of" or "vulnerable to" violent extremism, organizations and practitioners often made direct statements to acknowledge their commitment to protecting the civil liberties of targeted communities. The Los Angeles Interagency Coordination Group, for example, placed civil liberties at the heart of its published materials. Its 2015 publication enunciated that "the preservation of civil rights and civil liberties is a key pillar of the Los Angeles CVE Framework" and that "the Framework is designed to mitigate the risk presented by violent extremist groups while preserving individual liberty, fairness, and equality under the law" (Los Angeles Interagency Coordination Group in collaboration with community stakeholders 2015). To assuage community concerns, the Los Angeles CVE Framework openly expressed a commitment to balancing civil liberties and national security in all lines of effort.

Despite this stated commitment, Muslim organizations in California publicly opposed local CVE programming. A coalition of Muslim Student Associations (2015) at twenty-seven college campuses across California, for example, wrote that as "advocates for social equity and protection of civil liberties for all Americans, we firmly stand in opposition to the Countering Violent Extremism programs." Although CVE organizations sought to minimize public objections to their work through their verbal commitments to civil rights and civil liberties, communities still contested CVE because it "solely targets and stigmatizes the Muslim community" (Muslim Student Association-West 2015). In fact, consistent pushback from community organizations led Los Angeles mayor Eric Garcetti to turn down the city's $425,000 DHS CVE grant in 2018.

Other CVE actors similarly affirmed the importance of ensuring the protection of civil liberties through blunt arguments that stymied debate. For example, when local critics accused Minneapolis officials of targeting Somali youth through CVE programming, David Greene publicly asserted that "I'll pledge to you as your senior law enforcement official, at the federal level and at the state, we are abiding by all the civil liberties and human rights that all of us, including me, cherish and hold dear. So, our criminal justice system works. It's got all the right checks and balances, and I pledge to you, we are not profiling. We never will." Given the ongoing resistance to local CVE programming, Greene emphasized that "the criminal justice system works" and reaffirmed his commitment to protecting the civil liberties of "all of us" (participant observation, August 18, 2016).

In addition to these verbal assurances, Greene met with people across Minnesota who had been "victims of Islamophobia" to demonstrate his commitment to "standing up to Islamophobia," which he "cared about deeply to [his] core." Greene personalized this commitment, describing how,

> as a Jew, what it sounds like to me when I hear people denouncing Muslims, it sounds like what my forefathers and foremothers lived with many years ago. When my great-great-grandfather was required to change his name because it sounded too Jewish, he couldn't live in the community in Austria they lived in. . . . Coming from that background and living with that history, I will stand up to anybody in Minnesota who tries to reinvent that against our Muslim community. (participant observation, August 18, 2016)

Greene's primary audience of national security workers met his personal narrative with resounding affirmation, evident in a sudden round of applause. For this audience, this narrative assuaged any fears of racial discrimination, harassment, or profiling CVE might engender through local programming (participant observation, August 18, 2016).

Community organizers, however, questioned Greene's commitment to their civil liberties, particularly given local CVE programming's "laser focus" on Somali youth. Public declarations, after all, are often "non-performative" in that "they do not do what they say" (S. Ahmed 2004b, para. 1). A stated commitment "does not necessarily commit the institution to doing anything" and, simultaneously, can be used to "block the recognition of racism within institutions"

(S. Ahmed 2012, 116–17). Institutional workers can refer to these strategic public statements to deny their impingement on the civil liberties of targeted communities, regardless of their actual practices. These public statements therefore can serve as evidence of an organization's commitment to civil liberties without necessarily enacting that commitment.

Some community members, for example, questioned Greene's commitment to "not profiling," citing the recent arrests and prosecutions of Somali youth on terrorism-related charges (participant observation, August 18, 2016). CVE practitioner Yasir Ahmed even urged Greene to "stop going after the Somali community" and "stop targeting them." Ahmed fumed, "You're a prosecutor! You're not there to help people" (informal conversation, April 12, 2017). Refusing to enroll local youth in CVE-oriented sports programs endorsed by Greene, another CVE practitioner insisted that "we're not going to send our children to law enforcement" (informal conversation, April 13, 2017). As these examples demonstrate, some practitioners objected to Greene's role in CVE, particularly because he was a federal prosecutor "who will prosecute you." From their perspective, local CVE programs intensified, not mitigated, the criminalization of Somali youth by "seeing the Muslim community as having a Muslim problem" in need of interventions conducted in collaboration with law enforcement (participant observation, April 21, 2017). From the perspectives of these CVE practitioners, Greene's passionate speeches about how the "criminal justice system works" sinisterly masked his role in targeting and arresting Somali youth.

Somali organizers also dismissed Greene's stated commitment to their civil liberties and civil rights, pointing to the continued use of racial profiling to identify children perceived to be at risk of violent extremism. College student Axado Isnino reported that local CVE programs were "predicated on the idea that Muslims have a higher propensity for violence than the general population," a premise that "dehumanized" Somali youth. Given their experiences, youth organizers rejected CVE as a racist project that targeted them because they were "Black and Muslim and poor and refugees" (participant observation, April 21, 2017). CVE practitioner Aysha Khoury affirmed these comments, saying that, in Minneapolis, "It doesn't matter where you look. There's so much resentment to even the idea of doing CVE programming. And civil rights groups have been protesting that this is actually just a glorified way of targeting Muslims anyway. And if you ask to confirm that? I'd say, 'Actually, yes, we are. That is what we do'" (interview, January 25, 2017). Statements like Greene's therefore "can be described as non-performatives: they do not bring into effect that which they name," even while appearing to attenuate racial and religious profiling (S. Ahmed 2012, 119). In this view, these speech acts intended to assuage community concerns without changing the practices that generated these concerns.

Despite these critiques, CVE practitioner Abdirahman Mahdi viewed Greene as a "genuine leader" and "true partner with the community" as he always "looked out for the community" (informal conversation, April 12, 2017). For some, Greene and other political leaders adequately addressed community concerns by stating their commitment to the Somali community and convening a Somali American Task Force to hold them accountable. For others, high-level CVE practitioners simply disregarded deeper problems that harmed communities, especially Somali youth, through these speech acts.

Through these public statements, CVE actors defended their work as "doing the right thing" for Muslim communities targeted by terrorist recruiters. In this view, CVE could "keep communities safe and healthy" and "defend our democratic society against the civilizational war that violent extremists of all stripes aim to provoke" (Weine 2017, para. 21). Through these speech acts, CVE actors sought to assuage community concerns related to racial and religious profiling. Despite the prominence of these narrative strategies, CVE practitioners and community members differentially responded to these public statements.

"Is That Really CVE?" CVE-Specific vs. CVE-Relevant Programming

Despite these efforts to manage public objections to CVE, some practitioners expressed deep concerns about programs that sought to identify individuals vulnerable to violent extremism. Khoury, for example, reported that "there's a lot of questions in terms of, 'How are you doing *targeting* on who is receiving [CVE] programming?'" Although preventative programs like counter-messaging campaigns could include all youth, more direct interventions identified individuals perceived to be at risk of violent extremism. For Khoury, this identificatory process could "end up being profiling," especially when the "assumption of vulnerability is based on ethnicity, sometimes on religion, and it's unclear if it's based on actual vulnerability. So, the slicing gets done. And how does it end up entering the role of profiling?" Khoury reported that she observed CVE programs "curtail religious freedom" by using religiosity as a proxy for radicalization, even though religiosity "is not the same thing as extremism." Informed by her experiences as a national security practitioner and Muslim woman, Khoury warned that CVE could "end up being profiling" (interview, January 25, 2017, emphasis in original). Even when intentionally focused on addressing all forms of political violence, CVE risked devolving into racial profiling by employing explicitly racialized indicators like increased religiosity or unintentionally using a racialized lens to identify individuals vulnerable to radicalization.

Concerned about how "the slicing gets done," Khoury advocated for prevention programs "for everyone" rather than tailored interventions that targeted specific individuals. To differentiate between these two approaches, CVE practitioners began classifying their work as either "CVE-relevant" or "CVE-specific." These classifications quickly gained currency in the CVE policy world as they effectively differentiated prevention efforts "for everyone" from direct interventions.

CVE-specific "refers to measures designed to prevent violent extremism in a direct, targeted fashion, such as intervening with someone drawn to extremist ideologies" (Green and Proctor 2016, 28). This process involves "getting referrals from the community members, the family members" about "loved ones" vulnerable to radicalization and then developing tailored interventions to "off-ramp" these individuals from the perceived pathway to violent extremism (Khoury, interview, January 25, 2017). CVE practitioners design tailored deradicalization programs for each identified individual, like culturally relevant counseling and religious (re)education.

Some CVE actors objected to both the identification of at-risk individuals using disproven indicators and the effectiveness of CVE-specific interventions. Researcher Ron Stuart reported that "the story nobody wants to tell, but it actually needs to be told, 'cause this is what happens when you do interventions, is it doesn't work. It's not meant to work all the time. Anybody who says intervention is effective any high percentage at a time, I don't know who they're doing interventions with; there's no intervention that I'm aware of that has really high percentages of effectiveness" (interview, February 17, 2017). In this view, CVE-specific interventions experienced a high failure rate and identified individuals using disproven indicators of violent extremism.

CVE-relevant measures "are more general, intending to reduce vulnerability to extremism in an indirect way. CVE-relevant efforts are primarily advanced through education, development, human rights and governance programs, and youth initiatives" (Green and Proctor 2016, 28). From Khoury's perspective, CVE-relevant programs were "open to everyone" and thus did not target "a particular ethnicity, a particular religion, gender, nothing." A local CVE-relevant program related to internet safety, for example, welcomed all community members and taught "the whole spectrum" of online "child predators," such as "pedophiles, cyber-bullies, and extremists." For some practitioners, focusing on CVE-relevant programming eschewed the problems of implicit bias and racial profiling that generated public opposition to their work (interview, January 25, 2017).

Despite her commitment to this work, Khoury cautioned that CVE-relevant programming risked labeling conventional "good governance" initiatives as national security programs. Khoury questioned this approach, asking, "If you're providing services to an underserved community, is that really CVE?" (interview, January 25, 2017). This process securitized the provision of social services by delivering "good governance" initiatives under the banner of countering violent extremism. Given the ongoing disinvestment in immigrant neighborhoods, I observed some community leaders accept CVE funding to provide much-needed social services like culturally responsive counseling and youth sports leagues, even if they did not consider violent extremism to be a significant issue in their communities. Some, however, rejected these funds because they could jeopardize community partnerships and require reporting mechanisms akin to intelligence gathering (Arab American Action Network 2017). Community organizers therefore rejected the premise that they should receive these services as potential security threats, arguing that they deserved these resources as worthy community members.

As these examples illustrate, CVE practitioners, researchers, and communities responded to the charge of racial profiling in different ways, whether by redesigning their CVE programs, dismissing these concerns altogether, making public declarations of their commitment to civil liberties and civil rights, or developing CVE-relevant programs "for everyone." Practitioners reached for different national security vocabularies, logics, and research to justify their work in the face of constant community resistance. Although "policies of the state are enacted amid tension and difference," practitioners often deployed coherent frameworks that reaffirmed a broader commitment to CVE (Mountz 2010, 58).

The different narratives, norms, and logics CVE actors used to make sense of, organize, and justify their work produced different programming across the United States. Although higher-level bureaucrats like Greene worked to establish a coherent narrative about CVE, institutional workers often generated their own understandings of CVE that departed from federal- and state-level practices. Although some public officials minimized the role of racial and religious profiling in the implementation of CVE programs, practitioners like Khoury redesigned their efforts to address the problem of profiling. Despite these efforts, however, federal policymakers sometimes undermined this work by intensifying CVE's focus on Muslim communities, in national security forums, policy directives, and funding opportunities. Rather than conceptualize the security state as a disembodied monolith, these struggles over the meanings and practices of CVE demonstrate how the daily work of institutional workers drove the uneven implementation of national security policy.

Ideologically Ecumenical: Toward Equal Opportunity CVE

As CVE actors labored amid palpable pressures and tensions, some directly addressed the problem of racial and religious profiling by creating more inclusive programming that equally targeted "sovereign citizen extremists," "environmental extremists," "white supremacy extremists," and "militia extremists." Tanvir Rahman, for example, recognized that directing "99.9% of your effort" at "the Muslim and Arab communities, and at ISIS and al-Qaeda-inspired [violence] eviscerates trust" (interview, November 10, 2016). Given this damaging shortcoming, Rahman sought to engage all communities in CVE programming.

The CVE policy world has referred to this inclusive approach as "ideologically ecumenical." According to Adrian Baker, an ideologically ecumenical CVE program "dealt with not just people who are associated with al-Qaeda and ISIS but also violent far-right actors and even violent far-left actors as well" (interview, January 27, 2017). The DHS Homeland Security Academic Advisory Council (HSAAC) (2017) similarly encouraged a "big tent" approach that addressed "all forms of violent extremism, regardless of ideology, focusing not on radical thought or speech, but on preventing violence" (15). Daniel Glickman reported that the "problem set" of violent extremists was "broader than Islamists" and therefore required a more comprehensive "solution set" (participant observation, March 29, 2017). An "ideologically ecumenical" or "big tent" approach intentionally broadened CVE efforts to include all known forms of violent extremism in the United States, from ecoterrorism to white supremacy. In 2019, DHS formally institutionalized this ideologically ecumenical approach by establishing the Office for Targeted Violence and Terrorism Prevention, thereby "expanding the aperture of terrorism prevention" to counter "a broader range of current and emerging threats" (Department of Homeland Security 2019).

Following these logics, DHS representative Amir Samy reported that "radicalization and recruitment have affected all populations of society," including "people who are American-born, white males." This means that "the nature and scope of the threat is diverse." Given this diverse threat, Samy called for a "model of countering and preventing violent extremism" that was "equally diverse and very tailored to a local approach and to local demographics." When asked what a tailored approach might look like, Samy cautioned that "it would be inappropriate for someone who lives and works in Washington, [DC] to opine on" a local issue. Rather than charge federal officials with developing local solutions, Samy urged "local individuals" to "decide how that should be played" (participant observation, August 18, 2016).

As an example of this "equally diverse and very tailored" approach, Samy pointed to how Minneapolis "pioneered" CVE with a "prevention framework" to "inoculate young people from all forms of ideologically-inspired violence." For Samy, preventing the "next generation of recruits" depended on a "tailored" big tent approach to countering violent extremism. To narrow these big tent efforts, CVE practitioners needed to be responsive to "local demographics," like Somali parents in Minneapolis who "have seen incidents of young men and women who have attempted to travel abroad . . . to join Boko Haram or Al-Shabaab." For some federal policymakers like Samy, preventing "the next generation of recruits" among Minneapolis's Somali youth exemplified a tailored big tent approach to countering violent extremism in local communities (participant observation, August 18, 2016).

Samy used the concept of ideologically ecumenical CVE to manage public objections to CVE. This concept framed CVE programs as a "tailored" approach responsive to local needs and threats rather than organized by racialized assumptions about who may be vulnerable to violent extremism. Positioning CVE as an equal opportunity or inclusive national security strategy worked to dispel community concerns about racial profiling, even though CVE continued to target Muslim communities disproportionately (Kundnani 2014; Patel, Lindsay, and DenUyl 2018b). In fact, under the Trump administration, "at least 85% of CVE grants, and over half of CVE programs, now explicitly target minority groups, including Muslims, LGBTQ Americans, Black Lives Matter activists, immigrants, and refugees" (Patel, Lindsay, and DenUyl 2018b). This means that state-sponsored CVE programs increasingly target nondominant communities, including Muslims, immigrants, and refugees.

Despite the DHS HSAAC's call for an ideologically ecumenical approach to CVE, a subsequent U.S. Senate Committee on Homeland Security and Governmental Affairs hearing limited its testimony to the problem of "Islamist" violent extremism. In this hearing, ranking member Claire McCaskill (2017) admitted that "the United States faces threats from a variety of sources including white supremacists, eco-terrorists, and ISIS and al-Qaeda members and sympathizers." Yet, McCaskill then reported that "in the context of Sunni-inspired violent extremism, which is where this hearing appears to be focused based on the witnesses, it's absolutely vital that any effort our government undertakes to counter violent extremism is done in partnership with and with the full engagement of the Muslim community." McCaskill confirmed that expert witnesses would focus on "Sunni-inspired violent extremism" as a "civilizational problem," despite recognizing other security threats. By implying that Sunni Islam can "inspire" terrorism, this narrow scope encouraged the "full engagement of the Muslim community," a demand seldom leveled against white or Christian communities to thwart the threat of white supremacist violence.

Like McCaskill, CVE actors often referenced a "diverse threat" before focusing exclusively on "Sunni-inspired violent extremism." Over time, I observed CVE forums begin including a token practitioner working to end white supremacist violence while largely focusing on "radical Islamic terrorism," "Islamist extremism," or "radical jihadism." CVE actors could point to this practitioner as evidence of their ideologically ecumenical approach.

By focusing on "Sunni-inspired violent extremism," this Senate hearing affirmed the targeting of Muslim communities to "optimally protect ourselves and the world against radical jihadism" (Lenczowski 2017). To do so, national security experts testified that the United States needed to monitor Muslim student groups, schools, and organizations capable of radicalizing youth. These experts also suggested that Muslim advocacy groups fostered terrorist militancy. Asra Nomani (2017), for example, referred to Muslim organizations like the Council on American-Islamic Relations (CAIR) and Muslim Student Associations as "soft propogandists" for Islamist extremists. Ayaan Hirsi Ali (2017) similarly warned that "Islamist groups" like CAIR "have enjoyed not just protection but at times official sponsorship from government agencies duped into regarding them as representative of 'moderate Muslims' simply because they do not engage in violence," despite their putative circulation of "the ideology that justifies, promotes, and celebrates those acts [of violence]." Contrary to this fear-filling framing, CAIR (2015) seeks to "enhance understanding of Islam, encourage dialogue, protect civil liberties, empower American Muslims, and build coalitions that promote justice and mutual understanding." By positioning this mission as allied with "Islamist causes and interests," Nomani (2017) suggested that Muslim civil rights organizations "push Islamist ideas," equating political action with "radical jihad."

In their senate testimony, national security experts concluded that politically active Muslims advanced "Islamist causes and interests." To counteract these "Islamists," John Lenczowski (2017) called on "politically moderate Muslims who do not seek radical Jihadist domination" to deliver messages to "Islamic audiences concerning issues of radical jihad." In addition, Lenczowski (2017) encouraged the Central Intelligence Agency (CIA) to "quietly and covertly" support these moderate Muslim voices by "embark[ing] on a major revival of its covert political influence capabilities." To win this "ideological war," Lenczowski (2017) implored the U.S. security state to give "funding, media assistance, and possibly even physical protection" to "politically moderate Muslims . . . capable of arguing against the killing of innocents." By conflating political activism with violent extremism, Lenczowski (2017) portrayed "politically moderate Muslims" as "good Muslims" and Muslim civil rights advocates as terrorists. In this view, politically moderate Muslims could serve as an antidote to "bad" or "radical" Muslims who pose a national security threat to the United States.

Despite calls for an "ideologically ecumenical" approach to CVE, the trope of the Muslim terrorist seethed below the surface of congressional national security debates and organized CVE practices, which approached politically active Muslims as terrorist threats. Practitioners and community members unintentionally reached for these tropes to make sense of local security threats, evident in Khoury's warning that CVE could devolve into religious profiling and in WORDE's identification of Arab students experiencing "acculturation-related stress" as possibly radicalizing. Although many practitioners rejected these fiercely anti-Muslim interpretations of pressing national security threats and referred to these expert witnesses as "Islamophobes," the circulation of these narratives influenced how individuals differentially enacted CVE programs.

Shortly before the institutionalization of CVE, the trope of the Muslim terrorist coherently crystallized in the emerging term "going Muslim." Hoover Institution fellow Tunku Varadarajan (2009) coined the phrase "going Muslim" to make sense of Major Nidal Hasan's 2009 Fort Hood shooting. For Varadarajan (2009), "going Muslim" signified the "turn of events where a seemingly integrated Muslim-American—a friendly donut vendor in New York, say, or an officer in the U.S. Army at Fort Hood—discards his apparent integration into American society and elects to vindicate his religion in an act of messianic violence against his fellow Americans" (para. 2). The concept of "going Muslim" framed all Muslims as both duplicitously feigning assimilation and always already on the verge of "messianic violence." Such provocative narratives resonate with the U.S. public, who come to fear all Muslims, including their friendly donut vendor.

To stage this argument, Varadarajan (2009) borrowed the phrase "going postal" used to describe a phenomenon whereby overworked U.S. Postal Service workers attacked their managers and coworkers through a series of violent incidents. Varadarajan (2009), however, argued that Hasan did not "go postal"—"snap[] and gun down his colleagues"—and denied a "psychological snapping point" in the case of the "imminent violent Muslim" (para. 1, para. 3). Instead, "going Muslim" referred to the cultural process through which U.S. Muslims reject integration in a fit of murderous rage. "Going Muslim" involves a "calculated discarding of camouflage—the camouflage of integration—in an act of revelatory catharsis" (para. 3).

In this framework, "going Muslim" means "becoming violent," a reductionist conclusion that misses "the racist harassment that Hasan faced in the [U.S.] army [and] the emotionally debilitating pressure of his job as an overworked psychiatrist" (Kumar 2012, 162). In this view, "all Muslim Americans are 'imminently violent,' and while they appear to be integrated into American society, they are in fact ticking time bombs who will inevitably explode into violent murderous rage" (Kumar 2012, 162). This conclusion, however, belies decades of research that "found only a limited likelihood of attacks by home-grown terrorists" and "no evidence that American Muslims were becoming more radical" (Patel 2011, 5–6). Despite the public commitment to "ideologically ecumenical" approaches to countering violent extremism, high-level CVE actors further institutionalized anti-Muslim racism, creating policies, norms, and practices that reasserted the image of the Muslim terrorist, evident in the disproportionate funding of CVE programs in Muslim and other nondominant communities.

Despite the primacy of the "going Muslim" thesis on the national stage, some practitioners emphatically contested the anti-Muslim logics that organized local programs, noting the harm some CVE initiatives inflicted on Muslim communities. Practitioner Bassem Ali, for example, rejected the "going Muslim" thesis, concluding that the perceived problem of "Islamist extremism" was "overstated," especially "compared to the violence of the Klan" (participant observation, November 10, 2016). Ron Stuart similarly worried that the "going Muslim" concept led law enforcement to disproportionately pursue "Islamist extremism" while "neglecting" mounting white supremacist violence. Stuart further reported that "we're focused in on ISIS like a laser beam and we can't look at anything else" even though "local law enforcement consistently ranks far-right extremists at either the top or near the top" of its threat assessment. Although local police "see white supremacy and jihadists as equal threats," federal agents used "rhetoric that's much more focused on the jihadi" (interview, February 17, 2017). Stuart's comments illustrate how local interpretations of pressing security threats often conflicted with national rhetoric that reinforced the "going Muslim" thesis, ultimately creating a demand for "jihadi"-focused CVE programs. As local practitioners like Ali and Rahman developed programs inclusive of all forms of violent extremism, national initiatives and vocabularies often overshadowed these "ideologically ecumenical" efforts.

Responding to growing calls to widen CVE's scope to address white supremacist violence, critics warned against an "ideologically ecumenical" approach. As Fatema Ahmad concluded, "We aren't looking for equal opportunity surveillance," especially given CVE's reliance on "debunked theories of radicalization that end up criminalizing First-Amendment-protected rights" (as quoted in Southorn 2017). A coalition of community organizations similarly argued that the "inclusion of white supremacist-focused groups would not decrease or redistribute the damage done to Muslim communities as a whole through this type of surveillance" ("Statement: AMEMSA Groups Oppose Expansion of the Countering Violent Extremism Program" 2017, para. 2). Critics contested the exploitation of growing concerns about white supremacist violence to justify CVE since this national security approach disproportionately targeted Muslim communities and used scientifically flawed indicators to identify individuals vulnerable to violent extremism.

Some CVE actors, however, used the problem of white supremacy to reframe CVE as an inclusive program that addressed all forms of violent extremism. The 2016 White House Strategic Implementation Plan, for example, announced a partnership with Life After Hate/ ExitUSA to study "the reasons why individuals from the white power movement participated in violent activities" and examine "cases of those who voluntarily choose to leave the movement" (White House 2016, 12). Created by former white supremacists, Life After Hate/ ExitUSA helps white supremacists leave a life of hate by disengaging from the white power movement. To do so, Life After Hate staff work with self-identified white supremacists who reach out for support. This strategy has insulated white supremacists from one of the more controversial aspects of CVE: detecting individuals vulnerable to or in the process of radicalizing using disproven indicators, risk factors, and warning signs.

In 2016, Life After Hate applied for a DHS CVE grant to target both "far-right extremists" and "jihadists." To do so, Life After Hate proposed abandoning its prior practice of working with self-identified white supremacists. Instead, Life After Hate (2016) sought to use Moonshot CVE's Digital Shepherds technology to "automate the process of identifying individuals at risk of radicalization, assessing vulnerability against databases of indicators of risk, and assigning each user a risk score" (2). To do so, Digital Shepherds "uses publicly available data posted on Facebook to identify individuals at risk of falling into the orbit of extremist organizations" and then assigns Facebook users a "risk score based on a unique risk assessment algorithm which weights variables such as identification with violent extremist ideology, frequency and depth of engagement, connectivity and environment of each user" (Life After Hate 2016, 4). Although a "human analyst" later verified Digital Shepherds' findings, the use of "online identifiers" like "keywords, links, images, and groups" to "build a bespoke database of U.S.-specific far-right and Jihadist extremist risk factors online" has never been scientifically proven as effective or accurate (5).

Applying military doctrine to domestic operations, Life After Hate sought to identify people and threats "before their deadly potential [was] realized, at a point when they [were] effectively indistinguishable from the wider urban populace" (S. Graham 2010, xii). The proposed algorithmic assessment framed this identificatory process as an objective science, without questioning the data used to calculate and assign a risk score. In its first known effort to address both far-right extremism and jihadism, Life After Hate proposed undertaking a scientifically disproven task it had never used: identifying individuals vulnerable to radicalization and assigning these individuals a risk score based on their Facebook activity.

Given the concerns about growing white supremacist violence following the election of President Trump, Life After Hate experienced an upsurge of financial, political, and personal support. Critics, however, questioned the use of rising white supremacist violence to justify CVE programs like Life After Hate's, contending, "You can't fight Trump-style hate with the surveillance state" (Southorn 2017). Organizer Debbie Southorn (2017) argued that "by rallying around CVE, some progressives are promoting law enforcement collaborations through a counter-terror lens—thereby undermining anti-racist struggle and the well-being of Muslims across the United States" (para. 4). Despite good intentions, the ongoing support of CVE programs targeting white supremacist violence shores up the very institutions and processes that harm communities of color. Expanding CVE to include white supremacists has not mitigated its impact on Muslim communities or solved its faulty science (Patel, Lindsay, and DenUyl 2018b). As one community organizer concluded, "The path to hell is paved with good intentions."

In addition to strengthening the U.S. security state, this "ideologically ecumenical" approach has equated white supremacist violence with jihadism. This false equivalence erases how whiteness has organized the ideological structures, political processes, and legal frameworks in the United States, including the slave patrols and Indian constables that led to modern-day policing in the United States. Pathologizing individual white supremacists provides an alibi for the embedded societal racism that, by design, produces premature death in communities of color through hyperincarceration, restrictive housing covenants, limited educational and health-care opportunities, and state and vigilante violence. Lumping together ecoterrorists, white supremacists, jihadists, and other nonparallel groups obfuscates the differences in political goals, (state) power, and tactics.

As these examples illustrate, CVE actors struggled to define what constituted an "ideologically ecumenical" approach to CVE. To do so, they reached for dominant narratives, discourses, and tropes like "going Muslim" to make sense of, organize, and justify their daily work. Government forums like the senate hearing provided a platform for some Muslim leaders who sought to narrow CVE's focus on

"Islamist extremism" and urged "politically moderate Muslims" to contribute to CVE efforts. In addition, these federal forums amplified anti-Muslim racism and corresponding national security policies that presumed all Muslims were uniquely susceptible to violence. Local CVE practitioners therefore struggled to differentiate their "ideologically ecumenical" programs from "government-led" initiatives that targeted Muslim communities. Some critics, however, rejected these inclusive programs given the continued use of disproven warning signs to identify individuals vulnerable to violent extremism and disproportionate focus on "Islamist extremism." Despite local debates about CVE, higher-level bureaucrats like David Greene crafted a coherent national security narrative that smoothed over these tensions, clarified the utility of CVE, and performed a commitment to the civil rights of Muslim communities.

Astroturfing: The Conscription of Muslim Leaders into the Domestic War on Terror

In this charged context, some Muslim leaders willingly developed CVE programs to protect their children from terrorist influences, despite fierce opposition. Abdirahman Mahdi, for example, "worked together with the government" because "there are some kids who *are* radicalized, and they are radicalizing fast." Mahdi, however, reported that his own CVE efforts generated derision from community members who told him, "You have no soul. You're selling out our community." Despite constant threats, Mahdi remained committed to CVE, arguing that "it's better off with us at the table than someone else being at the table. . . . Anti-CVE people don't want to engage at the table. If they see you sitting at the table, they ban you." Mahdi referred to these "anti-CVE people" as "ostriches" because "they plant their heads deep in the ground and they don't see reality" of "young people actually planning to join ISIS" (interview, April 13, 2017). Like other Muslim leaders, Mahdi viewed CVE as a progressive national security approach that protected youth from terrorist radicalization without relying on coercive counterterrorism tactics like entrapment. Mahdi's contentious experiences reveal how the perspectives of Muslim leaders could conflict with how their constituents understood CVE, sometimes in ways that could not be managed.

Given these conflicts, some community members accused CVE actors of "astroturfing," a political tactic to "create an impression of widespread grassroots support for a policy, individual, or product, where little such support exists" (Bienkov 2012, para. 2). To create this impression, federal policymakers relied on select Muslim leaders to publicly endorse CVE, even if the broader community rejected this national security approach. As Mahdi explained, "If I'm at the table, that could give a policy a brand of legitimacy that, if I weren't at the table, it wouldn't have" (interview, April 13, 2017). Mahdi understood that his presence in community meetings could legitimize CVE as a community-led national security initiative, particularly in the face of ongoing opposition to it.

In Minneapolis, U.S. Attorney Andrew Luger convened a fifteen-person Somali American Task Force, which contributed to and therefore legitimized local CVE efforts. Minneapolis organizer Bashir Cilmi conceded that "Luger saying that this is what your community wanted is semi-true" because the task force publicly endorsed CVE. From Cilmi's perspective, however, Luger used the task force to exploit community leaders "willing to yield to dictatorship practice and implement programs that single out the Somali community" in exchange for political prestige, career advancement, and financial gain (participant observation, April 21, 2017). Although this hand-selected task force included local leaders, Cilmi argued that it did not represent the many Somali families that objected to CVE. Citing similar concerns, CVE practitioner Aedan Warabe referred to this task force as the "Luger Boys," who worked at the behest of the "top law enforcement official" to gain "money, political power, and clout" often withheld from Muslim, Black, and immigrant communities (interview, April 13, 2017). Yusuf Elmi similarly reported that, although some community leaders said, "No, this is a table we don't want to be at," others "knew the value of the power they may gain by aligning themselves with law enforcement and government affairs" (interview, April 14, 2017). Seeking legitimacy, government officials called on willing Muslim leaders to publicly endorse local programs, even if this meant "pushing what communities don't want and don't need" (participant observation, April 21, 2017). Some Muslim leaders cooperated with the U.S. government to protect their children from terrorist radicalization, rein in the domestic war on terror, and gain access to political power and community resources.

In this context, some CVE critics objected to the U.S. security state's appointment of "Muslim lords" or a "special class of Muslim leaders" to work on its behalf through partnerships like the Somali American Task Force (Muslim Matters 2016; Kazi 2017). In this view, CVE strategically "divide[d] the Muslim community between the 'engagers'—those who will do law enforcement's bidding—and the non-engagers, which comprises of everyone who disagrees with the government's preferred narrative about the Muslim community" (Muslim Matters 2016, para. 10). In addition, "the creation of 'engagers' sometimes involved use of 'astroturfing' by funding 'Muslim leaders' that claimed to be independent, but upon further inspection, turned out not to be" (para. 10). Rather than celebrate the rise of Muslim leaders to key political roles, critics argued that the U.S. security state used these leaders to legitimize and enhance the policing of Muslim communities. "Engagers," however, defended their cooperation as the necessary means to fight the domestic war on terror on the community's own terms.

Referencing U.S. slavery, South African apartheid, and the Israeli occupation of Palestine, Muslim Matters (2016) contends that "all oppressive systems have people from within the targeted group that benefit from the oppression" and that "there are always people from within the targeted group who serve as apologists for the system, justifying the fraudulent frame of dangerousness of their own group and profiting from the popular narrative they help nurture and sustain" (para. 11). To enact CVE, the U.S. security state has relied on Muslim leaders to circulate damaging narratives, policies, and programs, even if these leaders admitted that such practices were "awful" (para. 12). In this way, CVE is "not merely a government program, but a system where newly constituted Muslim nobility [are] deputized by law enforcement to push a harmful narrative of the Muslim community and divide it" (para. 16). Although some Muslim leaders contributed to CVE in exchange for "money, political power, and clout," others viewed their CVE work as "protecting the community" (Mahdi, interview, April 13, 2017). The U.S. security state therefore used community fears of racial profiling, preemptive prosecutions, and FBI stings to advance CVE as a progressive alternative to coercive policing.

Given these complex reasons for participating in CVE programming, critics encouraged Muslim leaders to reject CVE and engage in political resistance in ways that united, rather than divided, their communities. Elmi, for example, advised that to "stop the government, you challenge the government. You don't challenge your own people because the more you challenge your own people, now your own people will organize against you and now you have an internal war. . . . All that would've fed internal destruction" (interview, April 14, 2017). Elmi urged community organizers to resist the government rather than demonize Muslim leaders who endorsed CVE. Instead of blaming Muslim leaders for their participation in CVE programming, Elmi indicted the U.S. security state for creating an impossible dilemma that forced Muslim families to contribute to the domestic war on terror as a way to recuperate their social value and gain access to community resources, human dignity, and political and cultural recognition.

As public objections to CVE intensified, the U.S. security state also has turned to community organizations to legitimize its efforts and mask its involvement in local programming. HSAAC (2017), for example, recommended that DHS distribute CVE grant funds through "third party intermediaries" like community organizations (17). The delivery of DHS funds through "trusted partners in the community" protected recipients from "stigmatization" by concealing their collaboration with DHS (17). In Minneapolis, for example, the U.S. Department of Justice launched its 2014 CVE pilot program in partnership with a local community organization, Youthprise. Youthprise distributed $216,000 to Somali-led community organizations to undertake local CVE programming, making it more difficult for community members to trace these federal funds and their intended purpose.

The Brennan Center for Justice reports that "the actual recipients of [DHS] CVE funds are frequently obscured because about half of the funds allocated are earmarked for pass-through organizations, consultants, or contractors. Just under half of the funds earmarked for these entities (approximately 45 percent) will be distributed to unidentified groups and individuals" (Patel, Lindsay, and DenUyl

2018c). The U.S. security state has used community organizations to endorse, legitimize, and even hide local CVE programming funded through federal grants issued by DHS and DOJ. Critics contested these "astroturf groups" for "claim[ing] they are independent while in fact being severely compromised by financial rewards and government endorsement" (Muslim Matters 2016, para. 11). Aware of these tactics, community organizers devised strategies to follow these complex funding routes and warned anti-CVE community organizations about any possible funding conflicts.

As media began reporting which community organizations received federal CVE funding through Youthprise, targeted youth expressed fear, outrage, and disbelief. For example, when a young person learned that a popular community organization received federal CVE funds through Youthprise, he feared for his own safety, writing on social media: "I'm scared to attend their events. Does this program spy on our community? Will the [community organization] turn over to the FBI sign-in lists or dissenting questions because of their participation in the program?" As news of this funding traveled across Minneapolis, some families refused to use the organization's services.

In an email, a representative from this organization admitted that "the language of CVE is offensive, and any funding attached to the Dept. of Justice is tainted in the eyes of Minnesota's Somali community. Their caution is warranted." The organization's president also conceded that, given the community response to CVE, "the money just was not worth it." As some youth contested local CVE programs, this organization shifted its stance, eventually refusing any involvement in CVE because of its harmful logics and criminalizing impact.

Despite these palpable fears, Youthprise president Wokie Weah defended her acceptance of CVE grants, arguing that such funding could "advance racial equity and youth leadership in Minnesota" (as quoted in Mercer 2016). In May 2016, Youthprise collaborated with the Minnesota legislature to raise an additional $1.45 million for "Somali youth development." Combined with its initial DOJ "pilot city" CVE grant, Youthprise's "Somali Youth Development Fund" swelled to nearly $2 million. Although Youthprise continues to use its Somali Youth Development Fund, it maintained that it "will not seek or accept funding from sources focused on anti-radicalization of Somali youth, including funds attached to CVE" (personal communication, April 13, 2017). Although Youthprise denied any continued involvement in the CVE policy world, it still used funds earmarked for CVE and even applied for a 2016 DHS CVE grant for a proposed $1 million project. Weah viewed these funds as a viable mechanism "to position the Somali community for bigger and better things" (as quoted in Mercer 2016). For Weah, collaborating with the U.S. security state helped ensure that "all youth thrive."

For activist organizations like the Young Muslim Collective, however, Youthprise had colluded with the U.S. security state and harmed Somali youth. If Youthprise wanted to "make meaningful and honest atonement for supporting and profiting from CVE," it needed:

1. Public statement outlining the ways in which you've harmed Somali youth and continue to harm with your affiliation with CVE/CIE in the form of a press conference[2]

2. A detailed outline of the ways YouthPrise seeks to repair and restore relationships broken by participation in CVE/CIE and must be approved by anti-CVE/CIE activists and elders

3. Submit a public letter to the Department of Justice, Trump Administration, and Homeland Security rescinding your support and condemning the program and your previous participation

4. Immediate resignation of President Wokie Weah

5. A full audit of the Somali Youth Development Fund to confirm no other funding from radicalization programs/DOJ/terrorism-related funding

6. Pledge to refuse all future funding aimed at de-radicalization of Somali community

7. Pledge to include community in all future decisions/programs regarding community funding and engagement

8. Public community forum to answer all community grievances about past, current and future

9. Make public how CVE/CIE funds have been/are being allocated within 6 recipient organizations who received it

10. Make public all groups, organizations, individuals and government which you have worked with related to CVE/CIE (Young Muslim Collective, public Facebook post, July 14, 2017)

As these demands indicate, the Young Muslim Collective called on Youthprise to make amends for its past harm and to sever all ties with CVE funding, government organizations, and programs. Although some community leaders viewed CVE as a community-led strategy to protect children from terrorist influences, the Young Muslim Collective argued that CVE reaffirmed harmful anti-Muslim narratives and reinforced the criminalization of Black Muslims.

Although federal policymakers have partnered with Muslim leaders and organizations capable of legitimizing local CVE programming, communities often have contested these collaborations. To incentivize participation in this charged context, federal policymakers have rewarded Muslim leaders with additional funds, job promotions, and public appraisals. Minneapolis CVE practitioner Abdimalik Mohamed, for example, rose from program director of a community organization to community outreach specialist for the U.S. Attorney's Office to community engagement specialist for DHS. Through their public objections, anti-CVE organizers criticized Muslim leaders like Mohamed for collaborating with federal law enforcement officials, advancing the criminalization of their communities, and personally benefiting from these collaborations. Despite these community contestations, federal policymakers used select Muslim leaders and organizations to portray CVE as a "community-led and -sourced" national security strategy. Some Muslim leaders like Mahdi agreed to advance CVE both for personal gains and to protect children from terrorist recruitment.

In this controversial context, Elmi indicted the U.S. security state for stoking social conflict to maintain its power and authority. Rather than contribute to their "internal destruction" that only strengthened the U.S. security state, Elmi urged the Somali community to unite in the fight to "stop the government" and guard against "deceptive solutions." In his own organizing, Elmi sought to reveal how the U.S. security state used community concerns about past abuses to offer CVE as a viable alternative and conscript Muslims into carrying out its daily operations.

Elmi's advice follows previous Muslim civic engagement in the United States, which refused to conform to the prevailing interests of the U.S. political establishment. In the 1990s, for example, Muslim leaders "challenge[d] dominant views seeking to marginalize and stigmatize their constituency and instead assert[ed] counter-narratives that uplift the experiences of an otherwise voiceless minority community" (Al-Arian and Kanjwal 2014, para. 9). This political engagement unfolded in a "piecemeal fashion and largely on the community's own terms, which necessarily meant that certain doors were closed to particular groups who carried the unfortunate baggage of representing a community with policy concerns that often conflicted with the accepted line inside the DC beltway" (para. 9). In this context, Muslim leaders advanced a more progressive political project, sometimes generating fierce opposition from the political establishment.

After September 11, Muslim institutions in the United States "sought to expand their cooperation with the American political establishment, confront the dominant narrative on Islam and Muslims, and build bridges with other communities" (Al-Arian and Kanjwal 2014, para. 11). Because domestic and foreign operations work together to advance U.S. empire, Muslim leaders were "forced to sync with a highly contested set of foreign policy positions while contending with the rise of a new national security culture at home" (para. 11). During this time, the United States outlined a strategic plan to engage "moderate Muslims." In 2007, for example, RAND Corporation published a report, "Building Moderate Muslim Networks," that encouraged U.S. politicians to develop an international database of possible Muslim partners and a plan for developing these partnerships, with an eye toward "moderate Muslims" like secularists, liberals, and moderate Sufis (Rabasa et al. 2007). Like Lenczowski's senate testimony, the RAND report argued that "the creation of moderate Muslim networks would provide moderates with a platform to amplify the message of moderates, as well as some protection from extremists" (Rabasa et al. 2007, xii). Since the U.S. government cannot engage directly in ideological projects, "moderate Muslim networks and institutions" could facilitate the inculcation of moderate views, beliefs, and norms. By conforming to the "moderate Muslim" archetype and allowing the U.S. security state to define the rules of this engagement, these Muslim leaders have become "implicated in the ideology and practices of a U.S. empire that has increasingly set its sights on the world of Muslims during the past two decades" (Al-Arian and Kanjwal 2014, para. 1). The U.S. security state has relied on "moderate Muslims" to legitimize and advance, not soften, its imperial formations, evident in the community endorsements of CVE. Muslim leaders, meanwhile, have engaged the U.S. government in a concerted effort to keep their children safe from terrorist influences and rein in the domestic war on terror.

Abdullah Al-Arian and Hafsa Kanjwal (2014) warn that "while many may consider the increasing involvement of Muslims in the corridors of U.S. empire to be a positive development for American Islam," little has changed for ordinary Muslims across the globe (para. 16). In fact, "cosmetic appearances of acceptance notwithstanding, one can scarcely point to any substantive policy changes over the past decade in relation to foreign or domestic issues that historically have been of importance to Muslim communities" (para. 16). Although CVE actors argued that increasing Muslim cooperation in the domestic war on terror could rein in governmental overreaching, the U.S. security state has continued to use FBI stings, constant surveillance, and other coercive counterterrorism tactics in pursuit of national security. Some Muslim communities therefore rejected CVE and refused to engage governmental agencies that historically have pursued, profiled, and prosecuted their loved ones in the name of national security.

Furthermore, the continued disinvestment in immigrant communities has meant that local leaders have sought political office to garner financial, social, and cultural resources to support young people. Cash-strapped, some local leaders have turned to CVE as a viable mechanism to provide social services, culturally relevant counseling, and educational programming. As Aysha Khoury concluded, the provision of these "good governance" services "had not been done and they're now being done but they're being called CVE" (interview, January 27, 2017). By implementing CVE initiatives, local leaders gained access to financial support and political power otherwise absent in their communities. Muslim leaders used these monies to fund sorely needed programs, like youth soccer leagues and arts education, often provided on the assumption that Muslim children were "ticking time bombs" (participant observation, April 21, 2017). The state thus used its disinvestment to pressure Muslim leaders like the "Luger boys" to pursue CVE funding and related political positions.

Critical of these concessions, CVE practitioner Aedan Warabe concluded that these Muslim leaders were "Luger tools" who served the interests of the anti-Muslim political establishment instead of their own communities (interview, April 13, 2017). Elmi, however, warned that directing outrage and opposition toward Muslim leaders fueled an "internal war" that strengthened the U.S. security state. Organizers thus needed to "challenge the government," which continued to treat Muslim communities as internal threats to U.S. national security. The contestations over the ethics, efficacy, and impact of CVE reflects deeper debates about the best methods to transform systems of oppression and reduce racial profiling, political exclusion, and coercive policing.

The Fourth Way: Community-Led CVE as an Alternative to Coercive Counterterrorism

Given the uneven implementation of CVE, the role of law enforcement in local programming varied across the United States. As Bassem Ali reported, in Chicago, "a young person ended up getting the social services he needed" without "getting referred to law enforcement" at the same time nine Somali youth "got arrested" in Minneapolis on terrorism-related charges (interview, March 16, 2017). As news of these types of arrests circulated, targeted communities worried about how CVE facilitated the surveillance, monitoring, and incarceration of Muslim youth. CVE actors used different strategies to manage these public concerns, like offering conflicting accounts about the role of law enforcement in local CVE efforts, reframing their work as "community-led," and minimizing their collaborations with policing institutions.

In Minneapolis, U.S. Attorney Andrew Luger led a polarizing CVE initiative to "deradicalize" Somali youth after a series of preemptive prosecutions led to the conviction of nine Somali youth for conspiring to provide material support to ISIS and to commit murder abroad. U.S. District Court Judge Michael Davis sentenced three of the young men to thirty or more years, arguing that these long prison sentences would deter future terrorists. Although CVE practitioners used these prosecutions to justify their work as an alternative to these punitive solutions, they generated palpable fears that CVE intensified the criminalization of Somali youth. Given this context, community organizer Absame Omar distrusted Luger, explaining, "Your job is to prosecute crime. You're not going to worry if kids get their juice boxes" (participant observation, April 21, 2017). As a federal prosecutor, Luger struggled to convince Somali families that CVE protected, rather than criminalized, their children.

In response to local resistance to CVE, law enforcement official David Greene traveled across Minnesota to demonstrate his commitment to protecting Somali youth and their civil liberties. As he worked to manage community concerns, Greene offered contradictory narratives about the role of law enforcement in local CVE programming. In an August 2016 speech, for example, Greene reported, "I've been working with other religious and community leaders to build a prevention program that has *absolutely nothing to do with law enforcement* but has to do with building community resilience here in Minnesota against terror recruiting. . . . These are intervention programs that are community-led, not led by the government, and have *nothing to do with law enforcement.*" Yet, Greene also stated that ongoing collaborations between "our civic society, our Somali community, and our law enforcement partners" protected youth from "terror recruiting." Greene suggested that local CVE efforts both had "nothing to do with law enforcement" and involved "law enforcement partners" (participant observation, August 18, 2016, emphasis added). As this speech indicates, Greene offered conflicting accounts about the role of law enforcement in local CVE efforts. Facing mounting resistance, Greene struggled to convince communities that CVE served as an alternative to, rather than a new form of, policing predicated on the assumption that Somalis were uniquely susceptible to violent extremism.

Given the contentious community response to Minneapolis's model, some CVE actors defined their work in direct opposition to efforts that involved law enforcement. To do so, these actors distinguished "community-led" programs from "government-led" ones. For example, when I reported Greene's conflicting comments, Baker responded by saying, "One thing, right off the bat, is that it's David Greene doing that." Given the central role of "the top law enforcement official" in local initiatives, Baker argued that "first and foremost there needs to be recognition between civil society-/community-sourced and -led CVE efforts versus government-led and -sourced CVE." This distinction could help "ameliorate legitimate concerns" about CVE's role in surveilling, monitoring, and arresting youth. The involvement of "the top law enforcement official" acted as a "structural barrier" to solving "legitimate" community concerns about the criminalization of Muslim youth in the United States. Baker concluded that community-led CVE initiatives more effectively addressed "non-state ideologically-motivated violence" without relying on law enforcement (interview, January 27, 2017). In this view, current community-led CVE initiatives had learned from the failures of past government-led projects like Luger's and Greene's.

Aysha Khoury expressed a similar commitment to maintaining a "demilitarized" space for CVE work. From her perspective, instead of "certain types of initiatives being led by military or law enforcement, the civil society should be engaging that space, especially when it comes to dealing with ideas because we do not want the government to be telling people, 'This is the only way you can think or believe, at all'" (interview, January 25, 2017). Given her concerns with police-led CVE, Khoury advocated for "civil society–led" CVE as an effective and ethical alternative. Like the use of the term "CVE-relevant," practitioners used the community- or civil society–led CVE classification to distance themselves from initiatives centered on law enforcement interventions and interdictions.

Given these distinctions, community organizations committed to CVE sought to establish "civil society–led" programs that minimized the role of law enforcement. The Muslim Public Affairs Council (MPAC) (2014), for example, developed its Safe Spaces Initiative "as an alternative to both heavy-handed law enforcement tactics and government-led countering violent extremism (CVE) programs" (7). "Rather than accept the notion that the only way to deal with terrorism is through tactics such as widespread surveillance and the use of informants," the Safe Spaces Initiative "relies on community-led and community-driven programs that communities and mosques will benefit from beyond the national security context" (7). These efforts include "ramping up social media as a vehicle for a counter-message to ideological violence and supporting communities in maintaining our collective security" (7). MPAC (2014), however, also argued that "mosque leaders should build relationships with public officials and law enforcement in order to have a presence and role in the affairs of the broader community" (27). Given these collaborations in pursuit of a more community-driven CVE initiative, Muslim Matters (2017) branded MPAC as a "security contractor acting against the wishes of the Muslim community and at the behest of the DHS, which has awarded it a grant for its services" (para. 11). For some critics, the creation of "community-led" CVE programs still advanced the U.S. security state's agenda, relied on DHS funds, and reaffirmed the dangerous notion that Muslims were uniquely vulnerable to violent extremism. Others, however, viewed such work as a welcomed alternative to government-led programming by reducing, though not eliminating, the role of law enforcement.

At the federal level, CVE actors developed new practices and narratives to minimize the actual and perceived role of law enforcement. Daniel Glickman, for example, defined CVE as "the fourth way," offering an alternative to three options: FBI sting operations, labor-intensive surveillance, and "doing nothing." As "the fourth way," CVE supported community engagement efforts that addressed the "pre-criminal dilemma," whereby individuals have radicalized but have not yet committed a crime. Because "being radical isn't a crime," the United States could not "arrest people for their thoughts." By engaging "relevant communities" in deradicalization efforts, CVE offered an alternative, nonpunitive approach to the "problem set" of violent extremism (participant observation, March 29, 2017).

In offering an example of this nonpunitive approach, Glickman pointed to a "big data" CVE method that did not involve the U.S. government or local police. In this example, video-sharing website YouTube, technology incubator Jigsaw, and technology startup Moonshot CVE collaboratively developed the Redirect Method to counter online extremist content. The Redirect Method deployed algorithms to determine when internet browsers selected ISIS videos on YouTube. As with many YouTube videos, this new technology redirected viewers to watch an advertisement before their selected ISIS videos. The Redirect Method forced YouTube viewers to watch an anti-ISIS advertisement with an "ISIS feel to it" before their selected ISIS video. This technological approach sought to reduce the power of ISIS recruiters by offering antiterrorism video content.[3] For Susan Bailey, the Redirect Method was one "fourth way" strategy to fight ISIS, as it did not involve law enforcement in any capacity (participant observation, March 29, 2017). This approach, however, assumed that consuming and subscribing to radical ideas could lead to violence.

Even though the Redirect Method distanced itself from the U.S. government, some warned that it normalized the practice of using money and influence to determine, monitor, and police the online content internet users encountered. Although Bailey viewed the Redirect Method as "making the internet safer," Kieron O'Hara (2016) asked if "putting people off ISIS" through this technique could "be done without undermining the other important tenets about how we live together and organize ourselves, including free expression and access to information?" (para. 11). Worried about increased internet surveillance, one college student posted a photo of an internet search for "ISIS (but chill this is for class)" with the caption: "When you're doing research for your 'radical Islam class' but don't want to be on a FBI watch list." Given the U.S. government's use of "tangible things" like internet browsing patterns in the prosecution of terrorism cases, targeted youth feared that their internet searches could lead to their arrest (Martin 2013). Other critics worried that managing Google searches and YouTube viewership introduced another set of ethical, practical, and political questions related to ideological policing, freedom of expression, and open access to information. The Redirect Method, however, was markedly different from other CVE programs that relied on community-police relationships to identify, report, and work with individuals perceived to be vulnerable to violence.

In response to these concerns, some federal policymakers argued that only independent companies like Google could undertake these projects without violating the constitution. DHS policy advisor Jaylani Darden and FBI senior advisor Matt Rogers both noted that the U.S. government cannot "directly" engage CVE because "that's an ideological project." Given constitutional protections like freedoms of speech, religion, and association, the U.S. government could not undertake ideological campaigns that directed people on how or what to think (participant observation, October 7, 2016). These constitutional limitations compelled the U.S. government to offload the ideological project of countering violent extremism onto community organizations, corporations, and schools. From this perspective, constitutional concerns partially drove the shift from government-led to community-led CVE, meaning "third-party intermediaries" took on the ideological work the U.S. government could not.

Given both the use of "third-party intermediaries" to distribute CVE funds and conscription of other organizations into CVE work, some community organizers argued that "all groups with Muslim constituencies should disclose all contracts with the government, their application with the narrative for why they asked for the money, as well as the proposed budget. They should also disclose all correspondence with the government, including emails" (Muslim Matters 2017, para. 18). Because targeted communities worried that organizations hid their relationships with the U.S. government in their implementation of "community-led" CVE initiatives, constituents demanded transparency. Even though community organizers demanded more transparency in CVE programming, they also called on the U.S. government to provide resources that support healthy communities without applying an antiterrorism lens and without collaborating with law enforcement.

In response to these demands, some CVE practitioners readily announced their relationship with law enforcement. In Maryland, WORDE publicized its ongoing partnership with local law enforcement to address the problem of violent extremism. This partnership facilitated the creation of WORDE's Building Resilience Against Violent Extremism (BRAVE) initiative, "a *community-led* public safety model" used to "generate[] public awareness about the risk factors of violent extremism and empower[] the appropriate figures to intervene with vulnerable individuals before they choose a path of violence" (World Organization for Resource Development and Education 2017b, para. 1, emphasis in original). Despite the centrality of "community-led prevention programs" in "building resilience against violent extremism," WORDE employee Nazanin Zaghari advised:

> We shouldn't delude ourselves into thinking it could be done without the support of law enforcement. [This] program would *never* have been possible without the Montgomery County

Police Department. The limited number of terrorist attacks in the United States are owed in part to the brave men and women who protect this nation. The American people, our government officials have a zero tolerance for terrorism. And programs for radicalized persons who present a threat to public safety will require even more law enforcement matter and involvement than those in the prevention space. (participant observation, August 18, 2016, emphasis in original)

For Zaghari, law enforcement officials were central to the BRAVE initiative, which was branded as the quintessential community-led program. In fact, I observed local, state, and federal leaders herald BRAVE as an exemplar that could serve as a blueprint for "community-led" programs nationwide. Initiatives like BRAVE therefore could include law enforcement while still maintaining the "community-led" label.

Like Zaghari, some CVE practitioners announced the role of law enforcement in their local efforts to manage community concerns. Tanvir Rahman reported that he was "very transparent about who I am, what I do, my associations." He regularly updated his social media accounts to communicate his latest meetings, especially when they involved law enforcement: "I posted on my Facebook page: I was at the NCTC today. You know, today I was at the FBI office. Tomorrow I'm at this church." Rahman also encouraged community members to record him and file Freedom of Information Act (FOIA) requests, insisting that these actions could hold him accountable. Given these efforts, Rahman proffered that "I'm not aware of anything else that I could do, other than to be as transparent as possible" to address concerns related to policing, surveillance, and intelligence gathering. If these measures did not "assuage concerns," Rahman concluded, then "there's nothing anybody can do to overcome that level of fear" (interview, November 10, 2016). Through these communications, Rahman sought to minimize community concerns about his relationship with law enforcement and their role in local CVE programming. As these examples illustrate, some CVE practitioners like Rahman tried to be transparent about their work with law enforcement officials.

Although CVE practitioners offered strong statements about their collaborations with law enforcement, they sometimes held conflicting opinions about the role of law enforcement in countering violent extremism. Rahman, for example, objected to the FBI sting operation that led to the arrest of Adel Daoud in Illinois, arguing, "I can't believe that the *only* solution is to use a sting operation: go ahead and take him from Point A to Point B, and then arrest him, and then put him in jail. There's got to be a better way." Rahman also reported that a father had "reached out to the FBI and said, 'Hey, my son is saying things that I'm really concerned about.' I mean, the man turned his son in and said, 'Help me!' And what did they do? They conducted a sting operation, and now he's in jail. I think all that is what has created that toxic nature, or that toxicity to the term CVE." Despite his concerns with these FBI stings, Rahman asked, "If your kid is doing something to get the attention of the FBI, like tweeting nonsense stuff or going along with the informant, aren't they doing something at least a little bit wrong?" Rahman also argued that FBI stings were successful because they "get people susceptible to violence" and "send a signal to people not to do violent extremism." Given these conflicting accounts, Rahman pursued a "better way" to address the problem of violent extremism by collaborating with law enforcement officials willing to facilitate community-led alternatives to coercive policing (interview, November 10, 2016). As an employee of a state law enforcement agency and recipient of a DHS grant to educate communities on the warning signs of radicalization, Rahman struggled to distinguish his work from other DHS-funded initiatives exclusively targeting Muslim communities.

Abdirahman Mahdi similarly offered conflicting analyses, arguing that "if the DOJ is willing to fund afterschool programs, welcome them! Basically, welcome them! If they ask us for surveillance and they say, 'We need you to do this—x, y, z,' we'll tell them point blank, 'We are Americans just like everyone else so bullshit. Get out.'" Yet, Mahdi also asked, "Is there a better tool" for terrorism prevention than FBI stings and entrapment? "No, seriously," Mahdi implored, "if you have a better tool, now is the time to come up with an answer. And that's the problem I have with anti-CVE people. They don't have any!" (interview, April 13, 2017). "Anti-CVE people," however, worked to build alternative forms of safety and security independent of the institutions that historically have criminalized communities of color. As these statements indicate, CVE actors held sometimes contradictory understandings about the role, utility, and impact of local, state, and federal police in preventing violent extremism.

Because "the term CVE itself has become polarizing and automatically associated with certain practices and behaviors with law enforcement," some practitioners rebranded local initiatives (Baker, interview, January 27, 2017). CVE practitioner Masoud Kaleel, for example, reported that it was "well-known" that "people do not want to hear CVE, even just the acronym." Rather than discuss CVE, Kaleel talked to community members about "building resilience against the lure of violent extremism" (participant observation, November 10, 2016). Similarly, Boston renamed CVE as "Promoting Engagement, Acceptance, and Community Empowerment" (PEACE) while Minneapolis traded CVE for "Building Community Resilience." For some CVE practitioners, rebranding their programs resolved the issue of toxicity and distanced their work from "certain practices and behaviors with law enforcement."[4]

Legal scholars, however, warned that CVE programs "change their names regularly, often in the face of community opposition or other public criticism, which thwarts accountability and obscures the nature and purpose of renamed programs" (Patel, Lindsay, and DenUyl 2018d, 1). Bashir Cilmi similarly cautioned that "CVE by any other name is still CVE" (participant observation, April 21, 2017). For critics, this rebranding offered mere window dressing, rather than more substantive changes, to CVE programs and policies.

Despite clear evidence to support community concerns related to racial profiling and police surveillance (Patel and Koushik 2017), some CVE actors rejected these analyses as "unintelligent," "misinformed," and "basic." For example, when I relayed Somali concerns about CVE's role in intelligence gathering outlined in the FBI's own documents, Rahman declared this a "not smart" and "conspiracy theorist" analysis. Baker similarly was exasperated that "people are talking about this issue and don't even have a baseline understanding of what are the stats and how to come up with definitions and basic standards." Although Baker affirmed that "there are some very, very genuine concerns that people have about their liberties, about their privacy, about their civil rights," he also proffered:

In my opinion, the narratives and the descriptions of what
people—especially a lot of CVE critics—have described as
CVE . . . they're tantamount to alternative facts. And I don't
like saying that, though, Dr. Nguyen. I'm serious. I really, really
don't, because a lot of the folks who are saying these things
are former colleagues of mine from advocacy. And I'm a little
bit, sort of, astonished at times because these are people who I
would think otherwise know better, and I would think that, as
leaders, they would help to direct the conversation in a more
productive manner. But they don't. (interview, January 27,
2017)

In this instance, Baker described CVE critiques as "alternative facts"
so divorced from reality that it "astonished" him. Rather than engage
these critiques as serious appraisals, Baker reduced community concerns to "hyperbolic rhetoric," forgoing any reflexive recalibration or
dismantling of CVE. These charged responses illustrate the intensity
of CVE debates, which often generated hostility and conflict in local
communities.

Although these CVE actors sometimes relied on a painfully de-
meaning tone, I do not dismiss their analyses, interpretations, and
concerns as nefarious. They clearly demonstrated a commitment to
solving the perceived problem of violent extremism while addressing
community concerns related to the abrogation of civil rights and civil
liberties. Alejandro Beutel, for example, offered that while "some of
my fellow community members may completely disagree with my
analysis and takeaways," he could "at least take personal comfort in
knowing that communities are making better informed decisions by
hearing from more than one particular narrative" (public Facebook
post, May 23, 2017). Instead of only engaging in heated debates, CVE
practitioners like Beutel sought to better inform local communities
through formal presentations, informal conversations, and policy
briefs. In this view, CVE offered a viable alternative to coercive counterterrorism by increasing community oversight and decreasing the
role of law enforcement.

In addition, I recognize that the role of law enforcement in CVE
programming varied across contexts; not all initiatives relied on the
police in the same way. In Minnesota, local police, FBI agents, and

the U.S. Attorney were central in executing CVE policies. Bassem Ali, however, noted that his own work in Illinois to deradicalize youth through religious training never involved the police. Because CVE actors differentially engaged law enforcement, those who sought to minimize police collaborations struggled to distinguish their work from "government-led" programs and faced similar public opposition.

Given the variable role of law enforcement, grant reporting mechanisms, and history of anti-Muslim surveillance, community members often met CVE actors with suspicion, distrust, and even hostility. In this context, Muslim leaders have pursued what they viewed as ethical programs responsive to community concerns, even amid accusations of astroturfing, racial profiling, and criminalizing their own communities. They have managed these community concerns using different strategies, like refusing to work with police, making their work with law enforcement transparent, developing "ideologically ecumenical" programs, and/or dismissing these concerns as "unintelligent" or "basic." Some Muslim leaders have welcomed the opportunity to engage CVE as an alternative to conventional counterterrorism tactics while others have viewed "community-led" CVE as a perceptively liberal but equally damaging national security strategy by calling on social service providers to act as terrorist watchdogs using disproven indicators, risk factors, and warning signs of violent extremism. As these examples illustrate, CVE actors offered competing understandings, practices, and justifications for their work.

Rejected: Trump and the Drive to Counter Radical Islamic Extremism

The 2016 election of President Trump challenged the very strategies CVE actors had used to manage public objections to their work. Shortly after the 2017 presidential inauguration, for example, the Trump administration suggested it would rebrand Countering Violent Extremism as Countering Violent Islam (CVI) or Countering Radical Islamic Extremism (CRIE) (Ainsley, Volz, and Cooke 2017). Such a rebranding would fulfill a campaign promise to address "Islamic extremism." Trump's proposal generated fierce debates across the political spectrum about the legitimacy, legality, and constitutionality of such a rebranding. Struggling to gain community trust, CVE actors responded to Trump's plan in different ways, from refusing to engage CVE, to waiting to see if Trump executed this plan, to welcoming the rebranding. Like the concept of "ideologically ecumenical" CVE, these strategies sought to manage public objections that threatened the vitality of CVE under a Trump administration both praised and criticized for its targeting of Muslim communities in its antiterrorism efforts.

Given these debates, researcher Ron Stuart held conflicting opinions about Trump's desire to rebrand CVE as CVI or CRIE. On the one hand, the proposed rebranding would make the anti-Muslim impetus behind CVE programming "more honest." On the other hand, a "countering violent Islam" initiative would further "neglect" the "problem of white supremacist violence." For Stuart

> The situation remains kind of optimistic in the sense of, well, now DHS will be, if this ends up happening, they'll be doing what they're already doing, but it'll be more honest. Because it's already totally slanted, right? But they just say it's not, you know? And there are people, well-intentioned people in DHS that want to more broadly attack the problem and all that, and we can certainly recognize that. But clearly, there's a bias already. And so now you say, "Well, at least it's transparent, the bias!" Right? Nobody can argue it's not biased. But on the other hand, obviously, it's outrageous and it's going to really potentially do some detriment. We're already neglecting the problem of white supremacist violence, and now it'll just guarantee that neglect continues and even get worse, which now it's really striking, given the extent of the problem and the long-standing nature of the problem. (interview, February 17, 2017)

Although Stuart viewed the "CVI" label as a "more honest" description of a "totally slanted" policy framework, he worried that this renaming would continue to direct attention away from the "long-standing" problem of white supremacist violence and reaffirm the concept of radical Islamic extremism. Raising these concerns, however, required admitting that CVE was "totally slanted" and "biased," a concession that ruptured prior framings of CVE as "ideologically ecumenical."

Researcher Adrian Baker also expressed concern that Trump's

proposed rebranding would intensify CVE's focus on Muslim communities and, more sinisterly, "revert back to counterterrorism" and "double-down on that." Because he understood CVE as "not CT," Baker warned that CVI could renew a commitment to coercive policing practices like FBI stings, preemptive prosecutions, and entrapment, although these practices did not stop with the formal introduction of CVE into the domestic war on terror. Baker worried that this approach would refuse any efforts to collaborate with Muslim communities (interview, January 27, 2017). Unlike Stuart's assessment, Baker's commentary reaffirmed CVE as an alternative to counterterrorism with a more "ideologically ecumenical" approach.

Despite these concerns, Rahman refused to worry about Trump's proposal, even after a "community effort to lobby [him] to reject the money" he received from DHS under the Trump administration. Instead of rejecting these CVE funds, Rahman wrote an executive summary of his grant proposal to detail "here's what we plan to do with the money." By making his plans transparent, Rahman sought to assuage concerns about the Trump administration's control over local CVE programming and its impact on targeted communities. In this justificatory statement, Rahman explained that he "recognized that extremism comes in many different forms including the extremist right." He also indicated plans to "build a training to address all of those forms" of violent extremism through ongoing collaborations with community organizations and "different faith communities." "Muslims," Rahman concluded, "are just one piece of it." Given this personal autonomy over local efforts, Rahman reported that "until the government tells us, 'Here's the money but you can only focus on Muslims,' we're not going to take any steps to preemptively reject the money. We're a state agency that looks to help the community. . . . It would be irresponsible to reject that. But I'm not going to do anything that stigmatizes the Muslim community" (interview, November 10, 2016; informal conversation to correct research findings, March 20, 2017).

From Rahman's perspective, he had a duty to accept all government funds that could "help the community." He even questioned how "reasonable people" disagreed with him for taking money from DHS since organizations also "take money for Medicaid or disaster relief that come[s] from the state and DHS." For Rahman, the funding source did not contribute to his decision-making process, in part because he felt communities would accept funding from DHS for other forms of support like disaster relief. By positioning himself as autonomous from the dictates of federal funders, Rahman remained unfazed by the Trump administration's approach to terrorism, dehumanization of Muslim communities, and support for institutions that have treated Muslims as incipient terrorists. He also sidestepped community concerns related to the role of law enforcement in the design and implementation of local programming and the continued application of an antiterrorism lens to their constituents.

CVE practitioner Yasir Ahmed optimistically hoped that the Trump administration would rectify "what went wrong under the Obama administration" in Minneapolis. Ahmed saw possibility in the introduction of "new players" into the CVE policy environment who could "cultivate new relationships with the community." "If they have a new Somali liaison," Ahmed explained, "they could have trust, with credibility, and that can be fair and neutral." Through these new partnerships, "CVE can be successful" (informal conversation, April 12, 2017). For Ahmed, Trump's inauguration ushered in an opportunity to reevaluate the current state of CVE in Minneapolis, which could guide future programming and regain community trust. To do so, Ahmed encouraged federal and local actors to include new community leaders in the CVE process, rather than rely on "old players" with no credibility in the Somali community. Ahmed's commentary fueled common assertations that the new generation of CVE programs could "learn from past mistakes."

Contravening some CVE actors, four community organizations rejected their 2016 DHS CVE grants, citing the Trump administration's proposed rebranding as a key factor in their decision.[5] These organizations still supported CVE, but worried that Trump's focus and rhetoric could harm their community constituents and jeopardize the integrity of their work. In Minneapolis, Somali youth empowerment organization Ka Joog rejected its $499,998 DHS CVE grant, explaining, "Our nation's new administration and their policies . . . promote hate, fear, uncertainty, and even worse, an unofficial war on Muslim-Americans and immigrants" (Abdollah 2017). As an early CVE participant and advocate, Ka Joog's refusal indicated intense concerns about the Trump administration's approach to countering violent extremism.

In Michigan, Leaders Advancing and Helping Communities (LAHC) also declined a $500,000 DHS CVE grant, citing the "current political climate" (Abdollah 2017). In California, the Claremont School of Theology rejected its $800,000 DHS CVE grant after a 7–1 board vote. Claremont president Jihad Turk reported that while the decision was difficult, "the context is too acrimonious now, and the rhetoric against Muslims too alarming to work with this administration" (Ali 2017). In Virginia, Unity Productions Foundation of Potomac Falls rejected its $396,585 DHS CVE grant "due to the changes brought by the new administration" (Abdollah 2017). Although these organizations contributed to CVE programming during Obama's tenure, they worried that the Trump administration would require increased collaboration with law enforcement and a narrowed focus on Muslim communities, conditions that compelled them to reject highly coveted resources. By exceptionalizing the Trump administration, these rejections treated CVE as a viable national security strategy under more progressive leadership rather than an anti-Muslim initiative always already imbued with and institutionalizing anti-Muslim racism.

Given their prior commitments to CVE, community organizations that rejected this specific DHS grant did not always regain community trust, despite Ahmed's optimism. Minneapolis residents speculated that political goals, rather than concerns about Trump's "unofficial war on Muslim-Americans and immigrants," fueled Ka Joog's rejection. One community leader surmised that Ka Joog returned the money because families had boycotted the organization, meaning Ka Joog "didn't have any kids" and "if you don't have the kids, you don't need the money." In addition, executive director Mohamed Farah was considering a run for city council at the time Ka Joog rejected its CVE grant, a political move met with suspicion.

Referencing the rapid political ascendency of Farah and his colleague Abdimalik Mohamed, college student Axado Isnino concluded that the "Islamophobic and anti-Black push [for CVE] helps make political careers and non-profits." Isnino argued that rejecting federal funds could not make amends for Farah's role in introducing CVE to Minneapolis and pushing racist narratives about Somali youth radicalization. Absame Omar also criticized Ka Joog, noting that "when shootings happened in Cedar-Riverside, Ka Joog wasn't around. When we needed money for basketball, Ka Joog wasn't there." For some critics, Ka Joog's fluctuating commitment to CVE reflected a deeper desire to gain political power and prestige rather than address the pressing concerns raised by the Somali community. Some Somali community members thus viewed Ka Joog's rejection of its DHS CVE grant as a political, rather than ethical, move. Because Minneapolis's Somali community "became starkly divided over CVE," the rejection of federal grants aroused suspicion among critics who distrusted local leaders who previously contributed to CVE programming (Hirsi 2017, para. 31).

Despite these four rejections of the DHS CVE grant, Baker's concerns about an intensified focus on Muslim communities and "doubling-down" on conventional counterterrorism efforts came to fruition in June 2017. Although the Obama administration announced the 2016 DHS CVE recipients on January 13, 2017, President Trump immediately froze the funds after his January 20 presidential inauguration. After reevaluating grant applications, Secretary of Homeland Security John Kelly announced a revised list of recipients who subsequently were required to "affirm acceptance of the grants and agree to terms and conditions, such as providing performance data" (Department of Homeland Security 2017). This reallocation of grant funds "nearly tripled the amount of CVE funding that flows to law enforcement agencies (from approximately $764,000 to $2,340,000)" (Patel, Lindsay, and DenUyl 2018c). Furthermore, 85 percent of the funded projects "explicitly target minority groups," including Muslims (Patel, Lindsay, and DenUyl 2018b).

As a part of this reallocation, the Trump administration increased funding for police departments in Denver, Boston, Las Vegas, Los Angeles, and Houston. It also awarded additional law enforcement applicants, including police departments in California, Minnesota, and Massachusetts. To provide funding for these new grant recipients, the Trump administration cut initial grantees like Music in Common, Coptic Orthodox Charities, Project Help Nevada, the University of North Carolina at Chapel Hill, Life After Hate, and the Muslim American Leadership Alliance (Department of Homeland Security 2017). The redistribution of funds revealed the Trump administration's preference for CVE programs that collaborated with law enforcement and that focused primarily on "Islamist extremism."

Departing from a language of countering violent extremism, Secretary Kelly described this grant program as an effort to "advance America's capacity to counter terrorist recruitment and radicalization in the United States through community-driven solutions" (Department of Homeland Security 2017). Secretary Kelly further explained that "grantees were selected in part because of their potential to support law enforcement and other frontline defenders, to demonstrate programmatic effectiveness, and to use taxpayer resources efficiently to create independently sustainable programs." As an original grant awardee removed from the revised list, for example, the Muslim Public Affairs Council (2017) reported it "was excluded because we did not meet the criteria of working with law enforcement to counter violent extremism" (para. 7). Despite its grant rejection, MPAC (2017) reaffirmed its commitment to confronting "all forms of domestic terror" through "community-led" interventions "without law enforcement involvement" (para. 6). As these statements illustrate, Secretary Kelly centered the support of "law enforcement and other frontline defenders" in evaluating the provision of DHS CVE grant money. By privileging the support of law enforcement in evaluating CVE grant applications, the Trump administration affirmed its commitment to "government-led" initiatives willing to engage in conventional counterterrorism methods, intensifying community fears of anti-Muslim surveillance, entrapment, and arrests under the banner of "community-driven solutions."

Policymakers, practitioners, and researchers differentially made sense of and responded to the Trump administration's approach to CVE. For some practitioners like Yasir Ahmed, Trump's inauguration ushered in the opportunity to learn from the grave mistakes of President Obama's approach to countering violent extremism. Others welcomed Trump's proposed rebranding of CVE, arguing that "Countering Radical Islamic Extremism" was a "more honest" representation of this national security work. CVE practitioner Tyler Mathers, for example, reported that his trips to Washington, D.C., revealed "it's Islam all the time," meaning the CVE policy framework always had minimized white supremacist violence in favor of "radical Islamic extremism" (interview, December 27, 2016). The name "Countering Radical Islamic Extremism" more accurately characterized this national security approach. In addition, some practitioners

like Amy Kerns worried that Trump's election handed white supremacists a "mainstream platform" as the new administration "skated
over domestic extremism" by white supremacist groups in its proposed Countering Radical Islamic Extremism approach (interview,
January 5, 2017). These variable conclusions demonstrate how CVE
actors differentially interpreted and enacted CVE policies, practices,
and politics under the new administration.

The inauguration of President Trump initiated a series of changes
that disrupted the carefully crafted narratives used by CVE actors to
manage public objections to their work. In response, CVE actors developed new methods to respond to community concerns, whether
by rejecting grants under the Trump administration, arguing that the
new administration offered the opportunity to "learn from past mistakes," calling attention to CVE's "bias," and warning that new priorities could "double down" on counterterrorism. Through these methods, CVE actors positioned their work as a progressive alternative to
past practices and as a viable way to keep their children safe from terrorist influences, even under the Trump administration. Like my own
family's patriot acts, cooperating with the U.S. security state—to
"deal more effectively with the threat of violent extremism emanat-
ing from within" by "teach[ing] Muslim children that being a good
Muslim and being a patriotic American go hand in hand"—militated
against popular images of the Muslim as an impossible subject, perpetual foreigner, or incipient terrorist (Afeef 2015, paras. 7–8).

Refusing a Politics of Representation: Toward Alternative Forms of National Security

To protect their children and gain political power, some Muslim leaders diligently cooperated with the U.S. security state to reform the
domestic war on terror through increased community control and
oversight. Junaid Afeef and Alejandro Beutel (2015), for example, applauded "community-driven" CVE as an effective strategy for "preventing targeted violence on the community's own terms" (para. 7).[6]
DHS senior policy analyst Jaylani Darden similarly supported CVE,
arguing that this initiative was in "Muslim, Middle Eastern, and
South Asian communities" because "there's a willing community"
that "wants to do something about the issue" and "will step forward

and do whatever they can to make sure that they create resilience against violent extremism" (participant observation, October 7, 2016). Darden explained that CVE flourished because communities wanted to gain local control over domestic security practices, protect their children from terrorist radicalization, and defend their civil liberties and civil rights.

For Darden and other CVE actors, the shift to community-led CVE achieved "affirmative recognition and institutional accommodation of societal and cultural differences" (Coulthard 2014, 3). After decades of political marginalization, community-led CVE recognized Muslims as a partner in the domestic war on terror rather than a threat to be excluded. Through CVE, Muslim leaders had a "seat at the table" and could direct domestic security initiatives "on the community's own terms."

College student Hodan Hassan, however, argued that "CVE is the politics of representation that presents a face that looks like you but is a mouthpiece for the government" (participant observation, April 21, 2017). In this critical view, the incorporation of Muslims into the domestic war on terror through community-led CVE initiatives has shored up support for the very security agencies that historically have criminalized communities of color and deputized social service providers as the police through their new role in identifying, reporting, and off-ramping individuals perceived to be at risk of violent extremism. Furthermore, CVE policies have conscripted Muslims as terrorist watchdogs without attenuating the use of "government-led" anti-terrorism programs like FBI stings, which continue today through increased cooperation between communities and law enforcement. By complementing and enhancing hard and soft technologies of control, CVE has strengthened, not reined in, the domestic war on terror, while appearing to address governmental overreaching, racial profiling, and coercive policing (participant observation, April 21, 2017).

Given these debates, Coulthard (2014) reminds us that "when delegated exchanges occur in real world contexts of domination, the terms of accommodation usually end up being determined by and in the interests of the hegemonic partner in the relationship" (17). This means that the colonized must reject the "objectifying gaze and assimilative lure of colonial recognition" by "turning away" from the discourses and structures of state power through the refusal of "greater inclusion into the institutional matrix of the larger settler state and society" (45, 99). In their call to "turn away" from the anti-Muslim discourses and structures advanced by the U.S. security state, community organizers framed CVE as a colonial venture done in "the furtherance of the American project, which is violence." One organizer, for example, warned that "CVE is the head of the spear"—the beginning of new forms of anti-Muslim violence carried out by community leaders on behalf of the U.S. security state (participant observation, April 21, 2017). Rather than seek greater inclusion into the political establishment through their participation in the domestic war on terror like their elders, young adults refused to capitulate to the U.S. security state and pursued alternative forms of safety that did not depend on the very structures and institutions—including community organizations conscripted into CVE work—that have criminalized their communities for decades.

To protect their peers from the "assimilative lure" of colonial recognition, community organizers created political education forums to discuss and debate CVE and its organizing logics. At one forum, for example, college students introduced the public audience to the work of local CVE practitioner Mohamed Ahmed (known as "Average Mo"), a Minneapolis gas station manager who produced animated videos to counter terrorist recruitment. Before viewing one such video, one organizer described Average Mo as "an example of internalized colonialism," as he came to identify with and adopt the colonial narratives that position Muslim youth as a civilizational threat and therefore in need to CVE programming to "civilize your savage." In this forum, Average Mo served as an instructive case study to understand the assimilative lure of CVE projects and the need to resist the "colonial discourses that creep into people's minds" (participant observation, April 21, 2017). The "long-term stability of a colonial system of governance," after all, "relies as much on the 'internalization' of the forms of racist recognition imposed or bestowed on the Indigenous population by the colonial state and society as it does on brute force" (Coulthard 2014, 31). Rather than embrace the political recognition conferred through their participation in the domestic war on terror and collaboration with the U.S. security state, community organizers took on the challenge of imagining and creating alternative forms of public safety "on their own terms, without sanction, permission, or engagement of the state" (Simpson 2011, 17).

To incubate these freedom dreams, community organizers studied the internalized colonial logics that organized the technologies of control employed by their own elders in the name of national security. To demonstrate the "utter garbage" of CVE narratives and learn more about internalized colonialism, for example, organizers screened Average Mo's "The Bullet or the Ballot" video. In this one-minute video, Average Mo (2015) asked Muslim youth, "the bullet, the bomb, the knife, or the ballot, which do you prefer?" To encourage youth to reject violence, Average Mo (2015) taught "all you young Muslims" that "we have a choice. It is the ballot. Democracy. We are not a bullet. Not a bomb. Nor a knife. We are Muslims, not fools."[7] The organizers rejected this reductive narrative that assumed Muslim youth needed to be taught to prefer the ballot rather than bullet. Given his internalization of racialized tropes, Average Mo created videos premised on the belief that his own community was uniquely vulnerable to violent extremism and needed to learn to embrace Western democratic practices.

Average Mo's "A Muslim in the West" video similarly implored young Muslims to "walk in both worlds," following both the "traditions of Islam" and the culture of the "new world." Rather than follow ISIS's demand to "reject the new world," Average Mo encouraged young Muslims to "straddle" both cultures. In doing so, Average Mo endorsed and acted on radicalization theories that framed Muslims in the United States as imminently violent because of these cultural negotiations (Patel, Lindsay, and DenUyl 2018b).

In this video, Average Mo assumed that young people straddle "incompatible cultural divides," an approach that "risks reinforcing notions of a fundamental clash between cultural systems" (Abu El-Haj and Bonet 2011, 35). Instead, viewers must "resist a picture of Muslim and American . . . identities as existing on two ends of a continuum rather than thinking of them as overlapping fields within which young people position themselves differently, at different moments in time" (Abu El-Haj and Bonet 2011, 40). Average Mo's description of "walking in both worlds" reinforced the clash of civilizations thesis and ignored how young people actively construct transnational iden-

Screenshot of "The Bullet or the Ballot" video created by Mohamed Ahmed.

tities that defy binaries. Although Average Mo did not collaborate with law enforcement in the making of these videos, community organizers rejected this approach because it recited familiar narratives that justified the global war on terror and positioned Muslim youth as ticking time bombs.

The assumption that youth "walk in two worlds" organized many CVE programs, especially school-based projects like "global citizenship education." Through the social construction of Muslim youth as a "generational threat," CVE actors have ushered in a new set of educational policies and programs to discipline children as "good Muslims" and "deserving citizens" willing to comply with, not turn away from, the U.S. security state. It is to these educational initiatives, and their chilling effects, to which I now turn.

CHAPTER 5

THE GENERATIONAL THREAT
Youth Radicalization and the Domestic War on Terror

On July 7, 2016, U.S. media reported that twenty-five-year-old military veteran Micah Johnson opened fire in downtown Dallas, Texas, tragically killing five police officers. After hours of negotiation, Dallas Police Chief David Brown detonated a "bomb robot" in the evacuated building where Johnson had taken refuge. The blast killed Johnson. As news of the bomb robot spread, legal scholars raised concerns about the increased militarization of the police, denial of due process, and abrogation of constitutional rights and international law. Community organizers compared the police killing of Johnson to the calm arrest of Dylann Roof.

Reporting on the Dallas shooting, CNN cited Johnson's internet browsing history, which included "dozens of sites that focused on injustices committed on the Black community," as evidence of his rapid online radicalization. Friends and acquaintances pointed to Johnson's expertise on "the history of the Martin Luther King assassination" and study of Malcolm X as additional signs of radicalization (Griffin, Fitzpatrick, and Devine 2016, para. 5). Soon after, the FBI (2017a) established a new terrorist category known as the "Black Identity Extremist" (BIE). With the rise of the nonviolent Movement for Black Lives, the FBI argued that "perceptions of police brutality against African Americans spurred an increase in premeditated, retaliatory lethal violence against law enforcement" by "Black Identity Extremists" like Johnson (2). In its report, the FBI blamed "BIE ideology" for propelling Johnson toward violence, although security experts worried that this conclusion simply reinvigorated the

FBI's "decades-long targeting of Black activists as potential radicals" (Winter and Weinberger 2017, para. 20). In the FBI's view, the online radicalization of Johnson signaled a broader domestic terrorist threat that needed to be managed by the U.S. security state.

The Black Identity Extremist label aligns with popular psychiatric practices advanced in the 1960s by Walter Bromberg and Frank Simon, who described schizophrenia as a type of "protest psychosis" that afflicted Black men. According to these psychiatrists, protest psychosis generated "hostile and aggressive feelings" in Black men who listened to Malcolm X's speeches on Black liberation or joined organizing groups like the Black Panthers (Metzl 2009, xiv). In this clinical approach, Black men who "espoused African or Islamic" ideologies or adopted "Islamic names" demonstrated a "delusional anti-whiteness" that required psychiatric intervention to protect the United States from homicidal violence (Metzl 2009). The racist concept of protest psychosis continues to inform the coercive policing of community organizers of color as threats to national security, especially Black Muslims policed both as Blacks and as Muslims.

Drawing from these logics, the FBI (2017a) argued that "BIE violence peaked in the 1960s and 1970s" during the civil rights movement, thereby equating Black political dissidence with terrorism (6). Exploiting Johnson's violence, the 2017 BIE designation renews these early efforts to represent and police Black and Muslim organizing as a threat to U.S. security, liberal democracy, and national unity. Anchored by this history of pathologizing Black and Muslim organizers and criminalizing psychiatric disabilities, the contemporary interpretation of what counts as "terrorism," the dominant narrative that Johnson radicalized through his online study of Black liberation, and the deadly militarized police actions to prevent "Black Identity Extremism" reveal the discursive, political, and material responses to the perceived rise in homegrown terrorism by nonwhite actors.

Referred to by the U.S. Homeland Security Advisory Council as the "generational threat," young adults like Johnson increasingly have been at the center of debates about violent extremism in the United States. The FBI (2016c), for example, reported that "violent extremists of all kinds [are] attempting to radicalize and mobilize the youth of America and even lure them overseas" (para. 1). Clinical psychologist Saher Fatima more specifically warned that Muslim youth have struggled to "reconcile home values with the values of larger society," a developmental conflict that has led to a "crisis of who I am" conducive to terrorist recruitment (participant observation, November 10, 2016). Subscribing to traditional understandings of youth development, this approach views youth as uniquely vulnerable to "ideological influences" and therefore susceptible to "predatory" recruitment by extremist groups (Aly 2014, 373).

Like the "Black Identity Extremist" designation, the concept of the "Islamic terrorist" has generated policies and practices presuming that Muslim youth are more vulnerable to violent extremism than white children. A Texas substitute teacher, for example, called the police because she believed her six-year-old student, Mohammad Suleiman, was a terrorist. Although the teacher insisted that Suleiman repeatedly said "Allah" and "boom," Suleiman's parents reported that their son was nonverbal (Wallace 2017). Using racial clues to conduct an extemporaneous threat assessment, this teacher interpreted the six-year-old student as a national security risk. Given these racialized assumptions about Muslim youth, many CVE programs specifically have targeted Muslims, Somalis, refugees and immigrants, diasporic communities, and others "facing disenfranchisement by society" (Denver Police Department 2016). In this context, some CVE actors mobilized local educational resources to protect disenfranchised youth from terrorist influences and enhance "homeland and hometown security" (Dearborn Police Department 2016). Prefigured in contemporary U.S. society as a "threat to the moral and social order" of the nation (Patterson 1985, 103), disenfranchised youth differentially have participated in, and contributed to, these educational programs.

In this chapter, I examine the strategic efforts to "inoculate young people from the ideology of violence" and how targeted youth experienced, interpreted, and responded to these efforts. As President Obama (2015a) explained, to prevent violent extremism, "the world has to offer today's youth something better," particularly through "economic, educational, and entrepreneurial development" (para. 10). Following counterinsurgency's population-centric approach to fighting the global war on terror, CVE-oriented educational services have contributed to the "campaign to prevent people around the world from being radicalized to violence," which is "ultimately a battle for hearts and minds" (para. 14). To examine this domestic battle for hearts and minds, I investigate (1) global citizenship education programs that supplemented traditional public schooling to prevent violent extremism, (2) school-based CVE initiatives, and (3) a higher education program to produce the next generation of CVE workers and digital innovations.

Through this analysis, I argue that although educational initiatives have worked to protect youth from predatory recruitment, these efforts have subjected targeted youth to constant criminalization, surveillance, and cultural erasure. Drawing from literatures on the securitization of humanitarian aid, I also contend that these practices have further politicized and securitized the provision of social services like public education and culturally responsive counseling. Youth spaces like schools therefore have served as key geopolitical sites through which the U.S. security state has intervened to advance its global war on terror agenda.

Building Resilience: Global Citizenship Education

The urgent national narrative of a "generational threat" provoked local demands to shield youth from terrorist radicalization. Community leader Masoud Kaleel, for example, described how "young people get these messages and they get confused when they're asked to join" terrorist groups. Given his concerns about youth radicalization, Kaleel always asked, "What can we do to protect young people?" Kaleel's desire to "help the community" and "protect young people" drove his participation in and commitment to CVE (informal conversation, January 20, 2017). Like the concept of the "coming of the superpredator" that amplified the criminalization of "frightening" youth of color (DiIulio 1995), the narrative of the "generational threat" marshalled a series of CVE programs to deter Muslim youth from terrorist radicalization in the name of public safety. Community leaders like Kaleel engaged these CVE programs to protect their children.

Given this understanding of the generational threat, CVE actors viewed education as a key tool to "build resilience" to radicalization and reduce violent extremism. According to this paradigm, "quality education in itself can play a critical role in helping young people distance themselves from extremism and resist the 'pull factors' that may drive them to recruitment" through "awareness raising, generating respect for others, and creating and maintaining cultures of peace and dialogue" (Center on Global Counterterrorism Cooperation and Hedayah Center 2013, 1). Educational initiatives also can minimize cultural isolation and alienation, additional factors believed to "push" young people toward violent extremism. Concerned about the perceived rise of youth terrorists, CVE actors developed a portfolio of educational programs to buffer Muslim youth from the push and pull factors that could draw them closer to violent extremism (see also Moffett and Sgro 2016).

As a part of this educational portfolio, CVE actors established global citizenship education programs to "socially engineer a more integrated identity like the global citizen" resilient to violent extremism (participant observation, October 8, 2016). In a workshop, CVE practitioner Petra Kovac defined global citizenship education as a "human security approach" and a "defensive measure" organized around sociologist Ulrich Beck's cosmopolitan theory. In his scholarship, Beck (2011) argues that the "global other is in our midst" because "everybody is connected and confronted with everybody—even if global risks afflict different countries, states, and cultures very differently" (1348). Shared global risks—nuclear, ecological, human, territorial, technological, and economic—formulate the basis of newly emerging imagined cosmopolitan communities that "break[] up and overcome[] the container conception of the national" in the service of warding off global threats (1355). In the presence of global risks like economic crises and terrorist attacks, "the imagined community of cosmopolitanism becomes essential to survival" (1349). Global risks demand cosmopolitan solutions, including cosmopolitan communities, global identities, and global governance. Global citizenship education could contribute to the development of cosmopolitan solutions to the perceived global yet intimately local problem of violent extremism.

Guided by Beck's cosmopolitan theory, Kovac argued that a "global citizen mindset . . . surpasses national identities, surpasses any of these smaller pieces of clearly identified identities and so global citizenship education must induce a transformative process in students." For Kovac, this "cognitive, behavioral, and emotional development of young people as global citizens" effectively prevented violent extremism by "rebuilding individual and group resilience through this process."[1] By fostering the "integrated identity" of the global citizen, global citizenship education created more flexible spaces of belonging and counteracted identity-based groups like Muslim Student Associations (MSAs).

This approach views the accommodation of cultural differences and the drive for pluralism as "contributing to social division" and therefore incompatible with social cohesion (Keddie 2014). The cultivation of cultural identities through educational venues like Muslim Student Associations generates deep cultural divides between students, thereby eliminating the possibility of developing a sense of common humanity and cross-cultural solidarity useful for fighting homegrown terrorism and fostering peace. Instead, global citizenship education programs have promoted global identities that transcend cultural, religious, and racial affiliations believed to be exploited by terrorist recruiters. As a CVE tool, global citizenship education has encouraged young people to subordinate their racial, cultural, and national differences to an identification with the global (or cosmopolitan). From the perspective of CVE advocates like Kovac, this transformative process militates against social exclusion, alienation, and bullying that could facilitate the turn to violent extremism.[2] This approach, however, stigmatizes cultural institutions like MSAs developed in response to ongoing cultural erasure and state-sponsored violence.

A Center for Strategic and International Studies report on CVE similarly urged the United States to "work with likeminded countries and the United Nations to advance initiatives, like global citizenship education, that encourage governments to revise curricula, textbooks, and other instructional materials to reflect the diverse experiences, backgrounds, and composition of society itself" (Green and Proctor 2016, 34). Such collaborations could "stem the spread of extremist ideologies and intolerance in education systems" and cultivate global identities resilient to terrorist recruitment (34). UNESCO's *Teacher's Guide on the Prevention of Violent Extremism* also called for an investment in Global Citizenship Education (GCED) programs to strengthen the education sector's response to violent extremism. Similar to Kovac, UNESCO (2016) argued that GCED could "nurture a sense of belonging to a common humanity," which can "help raise the defenses of peace against violent extremism" (15). In this view, global citizenship education programs could safeguard children from terrorist influences.

Informed by these recommendations, community organizations have developed global citizenship education programs to prevent violent extremism. In Maryland, WORDE's Global Citizen Forum trained Muslim students "on recognizing and assisting peers who might be experiencing isolation, personal crisis, or bullying" (Williams, Horgan, and Evans 2016, 17). By teaching Muslim students to recognize and use the "early warning signs of distress or crisis," the Global Citizen Forum worked to "empower youth" to "assist vulnerable individuals in seeking support services," thereby developing their global leadership skills like cross-cultural communication, peer intervention, and conflict resolution (World Organization for Resource Development and Education 2017a, para. 3). As a "peer gatekeeper program designed to improve youth's help seeking behaviors to overcome challenges they may experience in their lives," the Global Citizen Forum approached Muslim youth as susceptible to "destructive and violent behaviors" and therefore in need of positive youth development programming (para. 1). In doing so, the forum approached peer intervention—the identification and reporting of vulnerable individuals—as an inarguable feature of global citizenship.

As the Global Citizen Forum example demonstrates, the concept of global citizenship is understood to be universal and shared. However, utilitarian simplifications—"dismembering an exceptionally complex and poorly understood set of relations and processes in order to isolate a single element of instrumental value"—cannot be made universal and therefore imposed uniformly everywhere (Scott 1998, 21). In this case, "global citizenship" is a utilitarian simplification, not a universally shared construct. Global citizenship therefore is "a challenging concept in that it demands both understanding of the interconnectedness of life on a finite planet while at the same time accepting that this interconnection cannot be based on a universalism that *denies and denigrates difference*" (Abdi, Shultz, and Pillay 2015, 1, emphasis added). Typically imposed rather than developed multidirectionally, this view assumes a universal consensus about the rights, duties, norms, and obligations that constitute global citizenship, even though "there is by no means agreement about what these should be" (Dower and Williams 2002, 5).

Global citizenship education programs unilaterally can determine which epistemic, ethical, and moral paradigms should organize teaching and learning in school contexts that typically prioritize dominant cultures that "do[] not work for everyone" (Abdi 2015, 18). Although global citizenship education can nurture youth as social actors with a sense of global rights, responsibilities, and social justice, it also can impose a Western-centric schooling that erases and denigrates local cultures, knowledges, and practices. When placed in a CVE context, global citizenship education programs approach cultural, religious, racial, and religious differences as threats to social cohesion and therefore drivers of violent extremism. To enhance both local and global security, communities must work to eliminate these forms of difference and encourage children to report peers who appear vulnerable to terrorist influences. Global citizenship education therefore can be, and has been, used to induce a "transformative process in students" that cultivates a "global citizen mindset" that "surpasses national identities."

CVE advocates have argued that global citizenship education initiatives "can be models for promoting social cohesion in diverse communities," particularly among learners perceived to be "poorly connected to, or misinformed about, international events" (Green and Proctor 2016, 32; UNESCO 2016, 16). Education therefore could serve as a viable antidote to the "paucity of knowledge and understanding about other faiths and cultures" in "some Muslim-majority countries and communities" where "religious education promotes the idea that all nonbelievers are infidels" and "legitimizes violence against non-Muslims or Muslims from different sects" (32). CVE actors have suggested that education programs can counteract divisive religious education and "paucity of knowledge" in Muslim communities that have fostered social conflict, a "leading indicator of whether violent extremists will be able to find traction" (32). Research studies, however, demonstrate that there are no scientifically proven indicators of violent extremism and that Islamic schools are not "incubators of violent extremism," "Taliban factories," or "ticking bombs" (Brennan Center for Justice at New York University School of Law 2015; Patel 2011; Kundnani 2014; Horgan 2008). Instead, the representation of religious schools as terror factories works to "advance and rationalize the imposition of state-funded, NGO-run programs" that complement U.S. military drone strikes on schools (N. Nguyen 2014, 17). In this way, education operates as geopolitical and ideological tools through the inculcation of Western epistemologies and the discursive construction of Islamic schools as hotbeds of extremism, thereby authorizing military, humanitarian, and educational interventions that advance Western interests.

Although UNESCO framed youth as misinformed, one college student reminded me that "there's a war going on," a necessary context to understand why a small number of U.S.-based youth sought to travel to Syria to "take out" Bashar al-Assad, a "bad guy" (informal conversation, December 2, 2017). Rather than assume youth were misinformed or duped into terrorism, this young person encouraged me to view these "foreign fighters" as political actors with a firm understanding of the interplay between global and local social forces.

Although nurturing "a sense of belonging to a common humanity as well as respect for all" is a worthwhile goal for educators, this process must not facilitate the criminalization or elimination of cultures distinct from Judeo-Christian, Anglo-Saxon, and/or European traditions in the name of national security (UNESCO 2016, 15). As observed in Kovac's comments, the cultural narratives that have driven CVE-oriented global citizenship education evoke the colonizing logics that justified Indigenous boarding schools across North America. Throughout the nineteenth and twentieth centuries, these boarding schools acted as "an agent for Indigenous social engineering and cultural transformation," thereby protecting settlers from Indigenous attacks (de Leeuw 2007, 342). By framing Indigenous resistance to colonization as evidence of inherent barbarity, European settlers sought to civilize, pacify, and control Indigenous populations. In this context, Indigenous boarding schools worked to eliminate Indigenous cultures perceived to threaten national security.

Across North America, Indigenous boarding schools functioned as "confined and specific sites" used to "transmit and enact" colonial ideologies believed to be both universal and superior (de Leeuw 2007, 342). Directed by federal legislation, government officials forced Indigenous children to attend residential schools away from their homes with the expressed goal of "assimilating" and "civilizing" putatively "savage" youth. To do so, residential schools destroyed children's connections to their homes, transmitted stories of Indigenous inferiority, conditioned children's bodies to European cuisine through imposed diets, replaced Indigenous dress with European clothing, sexually assaulted girls, and scrubbed clean children's dark skin. This "intimately corporeal" colonial project of cultural genocide pressed upon Indigenous children so that they would "come to embody the expectations of colonial expectations" (de Leeuw 2007, 347). Although young people continually resisted the colonial project of residential schools, studies of Indigenous experiences register a slow violence at work in and through these schools and youth cultures, bodies, and psyches in the name of national security.

The logics that compelled the creation, implementation, and persistence of Indigenous boarding schools endure today, generating new demands for educational arrangements that diffuse the threat of difference through cultural assimilation and elimination by "socially engineering a more integrated identity like the global citizen." As Ann Stoler (2016) instructs, "Colonial pasts, the narratives recounted about them, the unspoken distinctions they continue to 'cue,' the affective charges they reactivate, and the implicit 'lessons' they are mobilized to impart are sometimes so ineffably threaded through the fabric of contemporary life forms they seem indiscernible as distinct effects, as if everywhere and nowhere at all" (5). These colonial connectivities bear on the present, cuing racialized tropes of the dangerous Other to be controlled by eliminating social difference through the production of the "global citizen." Like Indigenous boarding schools, some CVE-infused global citizenship education programs have worked to subordinate cultural, racial, and religious differences for an identification with the global in the name of national security.

By "socially engineering a more integrated identity like the global citizen," CVE practitioners have sought to develop social cohesion resistant to terrorist influences. Although CVE programs have invoked a liberal language of child protection, they also have instantiated an illiberal impulse to pacify, discipline, and regulate Muslim youth through educational programming that can counteract the role of cultural institutions like Muslim Student Associations. Global citizenship education programs certainly can, and have, promoted cultural sensitivity, mutual respect, and shared understandings. When applied to antiterrorism agendas, however, these programs risk denigrating difference in the name of national security.

Educators must be aware of and guard against the cooptation of their work in ways that harm rather than support nondominant communities, particularly in times of war. *Critical* global citizenship education, for example, challenges the concept of universality, questions the meanings associated with the global, and offers "something better than monocultural knowledge categories" to promote the "sharing of socially more inclusive ideas and multi-locational perspectives which should facilitate our humanist desires to live together, learn from one another, and from there, co-construct new possibilities of redeemable and viable citizenships that indemnify the lot of both the individual and the community" (Abdi 2015, 20). Rather than demonize difference as a driver of violent extremism, these decolonizing approaches value epistemic pluralism and polycentric knowledge construction as the foundation of global citizenship education, questioning the very concept of "the global."

#ThinkAgainTurnAway: Tweeting at Terrorists

Despite the growing popularity of global citizenship education programs, some CVE actors worried that this approach was too "resource- and time-intensive" and suggested that social media campaigns could amplify the reach of these efforts while reducing local costs (participant observation, October 8, 2016). Other CVE actors argued that social media campaigns amounted to "tweeting at terrorists," an unproductive use of time and resources, especially in local communities (participant observation, May 16, 2017). The debates about the role of social media in countering violent extremism reveal how CVE actors struggled to define "best practices," diffuse the "generational threat," resolve the disconnect between national demands and local needs, and gain political prestige and resources useful to their communities.

Initial CVE social media campaigns floundered, causing practitioners to rethink their approach to combatting terrorism online. The U.S. State Department, for example, launched Think Again, Turn Away, a social media initiative to "expose the facts about terrorists and their propaganda" through Facebook and Twitter. Because terrorists increasingly recruited online, the State Department tasked its analysts with "post[ing] messages on English-language websites that jihadists use to recruit, raise money, and promote their cause" (Schmitt 2013). To do so, analysts shared counter-messaging articles and directly interacted with prominent terrorist accounts using the hashtag #ThinkAgainTurnAway.

Shortly after #ThinkAgainTurnAway's 2013 English-language launch, the State Department admitted that the campaign failed. *Foreign Policy* reported that "not only was the campaign ineffective, but it actually became a platform for different extremist groups promoting violence to engage each other" (Omar 2015). Through the initiative, "groups were able to reach out to a new target audience of youth as well as improve and build on shared rhetoric" (Omar 2015). Given these flaws, *TIME* magazine dubbed the campaign to "tweet[] counter messaging material and address[] prominent jihadist accounts" an "embarrassing" venture (R. Katz 2014). State Department representative Tom Williams admitted that #ThinkAgainTurnAway failed, in part, because it was not a "research-based or evidence-based campaign" (participant observation, October 8, 2016).

Aysha Khoury urged me to "dismiss" social media campaigns as ineffective. From her perspective, "you can't just throw a message at someone and that'll be done with it. Humans don't work that way. They want to talk about things. It's an easy checkmark. You use social media and [organizations] can say, 'Yes, this was done'" (interview, January 25, 2017). Nazanin Zaghari also admitted that she was "not really a believer" of social media's role in refuting the high volume of ISIS content (participant observation, August 18, 2016). Despite increasing federal, state, and local social media campaigns to counter terrorist propaganda and stymie terrorist recruitment, some local CVE practitioners questioned the utility of such cursory interactions with people online.

To supplement these digital efforts, the United States has engaged in social media "takedowns" to combat terrorist recruitment and protect vulnerable youth. Social media platforms like Facebook and Twitter have established standards to identify, evaluate, and remove accounts that engage in terrorist activity, thereby reducing the influence of terrorist recruiters. These platforms also have blocked user content if they promote or encourage terrorism.

CVE practitioners and critics alike have questioned the efficacy and ethics of the takedown approach. The Brookings Institution, for example, reported that "while the suspensions raise the barrier to joining the social network—in the sense that they reduce the number of invitations ISIS can successfully broadcast—they do not by any means make joining impossible. The interior of this network is changing as a result of the suspensions, making it a much louder echo chamber" (Berger and Morgan 2015, 58). Although account suspensions may "discourage some new members of the network from remaining," there also "is a risk that the more focused and coherent group dynamic could speed and intensify the radicalization process" (58). In addition to these concerns, the Brookings Institution asked: "Is it ethical to suppress political speech, even when such speech is repugnant? Do suspensions destroy valuable resources of intelligence? Do suspensions have a detrimental effect on targeted networks?" (53). Despite increasing calls for social media takedowns, the Brookings Institution raised serious questions about the ethics of silencing repugnant speech and the effectiveness of these tactics in dismantling terrorist networks.

Today, U.S. schools increasingly rely on software to monitor students' internet activity, drawing directly from earlier iterations of CVE social media campaigns and gang suppression tactics. Impero Software, for instance, piloted "anti-radicalization" software to monitor the internet activity of students in five U.S. schools. An Impero spokesperson explained that "the system may help teachers confirm identification of vulnerable children, or act as an early warning system to help identify children that may be at risk in [the] future. It also provides evidence for teachers and child protection officers to use in order to intervene and support a child in a timely and appropriate manner" (as quoted in D. Taylor 2015). To identify vulnerable children, Impero's (2016) software used an "anti-radicalization keyword library" to detect students who used search terms like "jihadi bride," "war on Islam," and "Message to America" (an ISIS propaganda video) (para. 5). Once Impero's software detected the use of flagged keywords, it "alerted those responsible for 'safeguarding' issues within the school such as counselors and captured a screenshot or short video to provide context," enabling those alerted to "analyze the activity and determine if it is a true threat or if there is another explanation (such as suicide research for a class assignment on *Romeo and Juliet*)" (Impero Software 2016, para. 5). In addition to the detection of these keywords, Impero's software could "block students from accessing the internet or certain websites and view screenshots and timelines of student activity. Administrators can create reports and export data on student or class activity, or on trending phrases" (para. 6). By using Impero's software, schools sought to identify students vulnerable to radicalization and reduce violent extremism.

Despite these aims, communications expert Pam Cowburn warned that "teachers should not be expected to spy on their pupils but to encourage them to learn about, discuss, and challenge different ideas" (as quoted in Burgess 2015). Given the increased criminalization of Muslim youth, Cowburn argued that "we need to be careful that these measures aren't counter-productive, making some children feel stigmatized, alienated, and that they are being watched" (as quoted in Burgess 2015). Although Impero Software emphasized its role in "safeguarding," not spying on, children, critics worried that these practices amounted to ideological surveillance, which can chill intellectual exploration, classroom conversation, and political debate.

Like their critics, CVE practitioners worried about the impact and implications of these surveillance practices in schools, especially when "61 percent of Americans [have] expressed unfavorable views of Islam" (Telhami 2015, para. 5). Khoury detailed how U.K. "security agents" questioned a Muslim first-grade student for "hours" after he mentioned that some people used the label "ecoterrorist" to describe individuals who use violence to protect the environment. This example illustrates how these monitoring practices can criminalize curiosity and limit student learning. From Khoury's perspective, "if you make it part of the responsibility of schools or educators to do that monitoring, without training, it can be very problematic." Given the difficulty in discerning between signs of "struggling with life" and signs of radicalization, Khoury worried about tasking "quite influential teachers" with monitoring student behaviors in this way (interview, January 25, 2017). Arun Kundnani similarly warned that "the great risk" of CVE programming has been "creating an atmosphere of self-censorship, where young people don't feel free to express themselves in schools, or youth clubs, or at the mosque" (as quoted in Khaleeli 2015). Constant surveillance through internet tracking software and teacher monitoring has generated deep fears such that children have refrained from discussing political issues in the classroom and conducting online searches about terrorist radicalization (Abu El-Haj 2015). This self-censorship inhibits classroom debate and eliminates safe spaces for youth to test out new ideas and learn from past mistakes.

Critics also reported that such ideological monitoring and reporting ineffectively targeted Muslim students, noting that 80 percent of referrals in the United Kingdom were rejected as unsubstantiated and that 90 percent involved Muslim youth (R. Price 2016). Moreover, scientific studies demonstrate that "the majority of people holding extreme views never commit violent acts and many who engaged in terrorism did not previously demonstrate strong ideological attachments" (German 2016, para. 3). This means that policing extremist thought is insufficient in preventing violent extremism. In fact, "even with all of the FBI's investigative tools and intelligence capabilities, it cannot reliably predict who might be violent in the future, as much as we may wish otherwise" (para. 3). Given the FBI's repeated failure to detect violent actors like Omar Mateen, CVE critics questioned the capacity of teachers to undertake this work and the potential harm of deputizing teachers as law enforcement agents who come to view their students through an antiterrorism lens. From racial profiling to chilling political discussion, these school surveillance practices have criminalized, demonized, and alienated Muslim students while calling on teachers to monitor and report their students if they express extreme views or use vocabularies that arouse suspicion, whether mispronouncing "cucumber" or Googling "ISIS." Despite stated intentions to protect children from terrorist influences, these tactics have intensified the school-prison nexus rather than provided alternatives to it.

"Not Bombs, Bullets, and Drones": Securitizing Universities to Counter Violent Extremism

Given the limitations and possibilities of these digital approaches, Tom Williams viewed the merging of social media campaigns and global citizenship education programs as the "next frontier of CVE." This merging took advantage of social media's reach and global citizenship education's depth. Williams pointed to the Peer 2 Peer: Challenging Extremism (P2P) program as a leading example of how CVE partners have combined the cumulative potential of both social media and global citizenship education while avoiding the flaws of each approach. Through P2P, university students worldwide have competed to develop the next generation of innovative CVE approaches by harnessing the power of social media, youth activism, and millennial sensibilities (participant observation, October 8, 2016).

To develop the P2P program, the White House National Security Council and State Department approached EdVenture Partners (EVP), a company that established student opportunities to solve local business problems. After the BP oil spill, for example, EVP explored the development of a "social media strategy to educate millennials about energy realities in America." To solve these business problems, EVP brought its clients to university classes, "providing genuine learning opportunities for [students] while they're *in* the university environment, so basically bringing the experience into the classroom, where students have a *real* client, who has real problems, who gives the students real money to spend but also says, 'Hey, I expect some results'" (Scott Sacco, interview, February 17, 2017). Rather than send students to EVP for internships, university professors integrated clients into their classrooms.

As a part of their classroom learning, students worked with these clients to meet their business needs, whether related to marketing, branding, or employee recruitment. Following this model, the National Security Council approached EVP in 2014 as a client wanting students to "develop a campaign against ISIL and extremism." From EVP employee Scott Sacco's perspective, "Government clearly is not the most credible messenger with developing a counternarrative to these guys. . . . Who better to create the counter-message to counter extremism and hate speech than the very same audience extremists are trying to recruit?" (interview, February 17, 2017). As a client, the National Security Council sought to collaborate with EVP so students could develop effective counter-messaging campaigns to combat violent extremism. These efforts coalesced into the Peer 2 Peer: Challenging Extremism initiative, initially funded by the U.S. government and later Facebook.

The White House (2016) reported that "the objective of P2P is to engage university students, who earn academic credit, to create authentic narratives on social media that challenge violent extremist recruitment" (14). Following this objective, P2P students "develop a social and digital media initiative, product, or tool to push back on extremism. They get to decide what extremism means to them on their campus, their community, their state, their country, globally. We don't put any parameters or boundaries on how they interpret *how* they want to develop the initiative, product, or tool." Students also "get to decide one of four target audiences: (1) the at-risk, (2) the silent majority (typically Muslims who don't speak out against extremism), (3) the uncommitted population that research indicates have a higher propensity to radicalize as they go through that searching phase, or (4) the civil-minded students who create movements and mobilize over social issues of the day." EdVenture Partners viewed this P2P approach as "hyper-localized problem-solving" that called on nearby university students to "dismantle violent ideologies by creating these positive counter-narratives" (Scott Sacco, interview, February 17, 2017).

To minimize constitutional concerns related to the government's role in shaping ideology, the State Department slowly distanced itself from P2P by publicizing Facebook's role in the initiative and dividing the competition into two: one for U.S. participants and one for international participants. As a part of this process, the State Department rebranded the international competition as P2P: Facebook Global Digital Challenge. As one P2P participant explained, "Facebook picked up the international teams and it's the sponsor for the international program and that's why the competition is now split. The name Facebook just translates better for international teams. It's a little dicey when you're talking about international teams working on a project for the U.S. government" (Sarah Hughes, interview, January 31, 2017). EdVenture Partners took the "U.S. government brand off of Peer 2 Peer" because "a lot of countries were mighty skeptical of the U.S. government" (interview, February 17, 2017). To minimize the perceived role of the U.S. government in this ideological project, the State Department reorganized and renamed the P2P competitions. Critics, however, worried that this rebranding strategically concealed, rather than addressed, the U.S. government's role in the P2P competition.

204 THE GENERATIONAL THREAT

At the time of my fieldwork, EdVenture Partners involved more than 10,000 students from 100 universities across the United States and 250 universities in 70 other countries. As a key tool in the "CVE industry," P2P "introduced *legions* of young people to the possibility that they can actually make a living and change the world at the same time" (interview, February 17, 2017, emphasis in original). In this way, P2P combined the power of global citizenship education with the reach of social media campaigns.

Several CVE actors applauded P2P's "education-CVE nexus," especially because the initiative brought social media into the classroom to address terrorist recruitment. Sacco viewed P2P as "the best program the government has ever created, and it is absolutely not bombs, bullets, and drones. This is soft power, changing hearts and minds. It's credible because it's developed by young people. It's the platform that people use to get information and build communities" (interview, February 17, 2017). Given these affirmations, the U.S. government continues to funnel resources to the program, amplifying the role of students and social media in fighting terrorism without "bombs, bullets, and drones."

To support university professors in implementing the P2P program, the National Counterterrorism Center provided participants with "a *ton* of secondary resources from around the world." "If your students don't know anything about extremism," Sacco explained, "we have some very select documents that we say, 'Read this and you're gonna pretty much know what you need to know to do a good job with this project.'" These materials explored "different kinds of extremism," including "white supremacists, nationalists, and sovereign citizens in the U.S." P2P participant Sarah Hughes, however, reported that "it was an easy direction to decide on [ISIS]," figuring "that's the direction we were supposed to go anyways because a lot of the research that we were provided with was research on ISIS" (interview, January 31, 2017). P2P professor April Brewer also confirmed that "the brief tells you that you have to go pretty much in the direction of violent extremism perpetuated by ISIS. . . . The brief says violent extremism, but I know the research papers that you get are ISIS-oriented" (interview, February 14, 2017). The research briefs developed by the State Department directed student teams toward anti-ISIS projects.

Despite these ISIS-related materials, Sacco reported an increasing student focus on white supremacy. In addition, two schools "pulled out of *this current* [2017] semester because of the direction the new [Trump] administration might go," like exclusively targeting Muslim communities for CVE programming (interview, February 17, 2017). By selecting and distributing student materials, the State Department managed how students thought about and responded to the perceived problem of violent extremism, effectively erasing other threats to public safety, like ongoing war, economic displacement, and state violence. The selected focus on ISIS narrowed classroom debates in ways that legitimized the U.S. security state. These materials, however, were not overdetermining as some students created projects to combat white supremacy and some schools stopped participating in the program because of their concerns about a disproportionate focus on Muslim communities.

Working with a group of her peers, Hughes developed an anti-ISIS social media campaign targeting the "silent majority," meaning "people who kind of know extremism's wrong but don't really know what to do or how to help, or maybe they just don't know *enough* about it." In the process, students developed a clear set of principles, emphasizing that they "did not want to use fear as a motivator" and "thought that just preaching to people about the dangers of ISIS would push people away and turn them off because it's a very uncomfortable thing for a lot of people to talk about. It's very scary." Instead, her team created "positive counter-messaging" that sought to raise awareness about violent extremism as well as the experiences of Muslims in the United States (interview, January 31, 2017).

As they developed their project, Hughes and her team recognized that "being Americans, we didn't really feel as though we had the first-hand knowledge [of violent extremism], so we wanted to go find those people that do and find the people that are experiencing this and suffering this. So, we conducted interviews with people that were best involved in this topic," including refugees and U.S.-born Muslims (participant observation, October 8, 2016). Students assumed that their status as "Americans"—meaning white and non-Muslim citizens—distanced themselves from the problem of violent extremism so they consulted with Muslims and refugees perceived to have more "first-hand knowledge."

With an operating budget of $2,000 sponsored by the Department of Homeland Security and $400 in Facebook ad credits, Hughes's team used this "first-hand knowledge" about what targeted communities "are experiencing and suffering from" to develop a social media campaign to raise awareness about "ISIL, Islam, refugees, and how ISIL uses social media." In the process, students interpreted the provided informational resources on violent extremism and acted on them in their own ways, rejecting demands to use fear or rely only on secondary materials to develop their CVE project.

Like other P2P projects, Hughes's team developed an innovative social media campaign that informed the "silent majority" about the problem of violent extremism and increased public awareness about the difference between Islam and extremism. Viewing her work as a type of public education, Hughes reported that the social media projects developed through P2P have "reached over twenty million people since it started in 2015," making it "the largest collective surge on extremism that the world has ever seen." Another P2P participant described the program as "letting a thousand flowers bloom" (participant observation, August 18, 2016). In this view, P2P amplified the reach of time- and resource-intensive education initiatives like global citizenship education.

Hughes also reported that even after the competition's conclusion, "our campaign essentially becomes the Department of State, so they can take it and use it as examples, so we're always tied to them." In the P2P model, the State Department was Hughes's client, meaning she designed a CVE product for use by the State Department. As both State Department products and social media campaigns, P2P projects continued to reach young people after the competition's conclusion.

Despite state pressure to focus on ISIS, Hughes and other participants heralded P2P as a necessary program to "empower the next generation" and "do good for the world as a whole" through "the most amazing and innovative campaigns and tools." In the process, students "got that experience in the marketing field" and created "an actual product" useful for the job market (interview, February 17, 2017). As a marketing professor, Brewer viewed P2P as an important "digital marketing internship" opportunity for her undergraduate students in her social media marketing class. For students seeking a job in digital marketing, P2P was a "hot thing" that gave students a "leg-up over students that have not done internships or anything in digital media" (interview, February 14, 2017). Like other CVE actors, students engaged P2P in search of career advancement, prestige, and political power while "doing good."

Popular media and university partners often praised P2P for its commitment to countering violent extremism through innovative technologies. In its review of P2P, the *New York Times* declared that "students are the newest U.S. weapon against terrorist recruitment," noting that "the Department of Homeland Security is enlisting American college students in its efforts to stop the radicalization and recruitment of young people, mostly immigrants, by foreign terrorist groups" (Ron Nixon 2017, para. 1). This review portrayed "American college students" as the solution to the radicalization of immigrant youth.

Celebrating its third-place team, the University of Massachusetts at Lowell similarly affirmed how the P2P competition "tap[ped] college students' social media skills to counter the influence of extremists and terrorists in their own communities, from white supremacists in the U.S. to ISIS and homegrown terrorist cells in troubled countries" (Ryan 2016, para. 2). Its students developed Operation250, a "website showing preteens and teenagers how extremist organizations—in particular the Islamic State (also known as ISIS, ISIL, or DAESH)—use social media to find, befriend, convert, and isolate young people, and then recruit them as members" (Webster 2017, para. 6). As a third-place finisher, this student team received a $1,000 award in addition to two angel investors, including former National Security Council member and counterterrorism expert Roger Cressey. With these investors, Operation250 developed a robust portfolio of materials to "educate children, parents, and teachers about online safety and how to most effectively protect themselves from coming into contact with online violent extremist material and individuals."[3] Targeting ISIS-inspired terrorism, Operation250 also began offering classroom visits and presentations, seminars for parents and teachers, and reading materials to encourage "critical thinking within children around the topics of terrorism, online safety, and radicalization." As Operation250 indicates, P2P projects sometimes turned into full-scale campaigns that advanced CVE programming across the United States.

As the "next CVE frontier," politicians, universities, and popular media applauded P2P's youth-oriented social media campaigns. In fact, Senator Cory Booker sought to further institutionalize the P2P model through his proposed (but unpassed) Countering Online Recruitment of Violent Extremists Act of 2016, which would "authorize the Secretary of Homeland Security to establish university labs for student-developed technology-based solutions for countering online recruitment of violent extremists" (S. 2418, 114th Cong. [2015]). As this bipartisan bill indicates, both liberal and conservative politicians heralded "technology-based CVE solutions" led by university students.

Despite the overall praise for P2P's approach, some have expressed concern that these practices have militarized and securitized schools. U.S. military and intelligence agencies historically have "funneled large sums of money into universities to advance their interests," thereby incentivizing militarized research projects (Gonzalez 2010, 37). Following World War I, for example, the 1916 National Defense Act initiated the Junior Reserve Officer Training Corps (JROTC) to develop the next generation of military recruits and to "train[] the popular public mind to the necessity and needs of defense" through the U.S. public school system (Coe 1927). Prompted by the Soviet launch of *Sputnik* during the Cold War, Congress also passed the 1958 National Defense Education Act that funded college students in the areas of foreign languages, regional studies, and science, arguing that "the defense of this Nation depends upon the mastery of modern techniques developed from complex scientific principles." These initiatives worked to gain public support for military action and to train students to contribute to different war efforts, whether as soldiers, scientists committed to advancing nuclear weaponry, or linguists capable of espionage. State-sponsored initiatives to combat violent extremism in and through universities reactivate these Cold War institutional arrangements that effectively securitized U.S. schools.

In this historical context, the P2P program directed faculty expertise and classroom resources toward countering violent extremism, a transformative process that has enhanced the university's role in the global war on terror. To entice faculty to participate in and support the P2P program, the State Department provided ready-made curricula while the Department of Homeland Security supported student projects. When military and intelligence agencies fund teaching and learning, however, "knowledge is subtly militarized and bent in the way a tree is bent by a prevailing wind. The public comes to accept that basic academic research on religion and violence 'belongs' to the military; scholars who never saw themselves as doing military research now do," like Brewer (Gusterson 2008, para. 12). In addition, academics may "wonder if their access to future funding is best secured by not criticizing U.S. foreign policy," stymieing "the kind of critical thinking a democracy needs" as "the priorities of the military further define the basic terms of public and academic debate" (para. 12). This securitizing process limits classroom debate, chills dissent, normalizes dominant understandings of violent extremism, and rewards faculty for aligning their teaching and research with the demands of the war on terror. Although EdVenture Partners and P2P faculty expressed a commitment to combatting homegrown terrorism, the introduction of P2P into universities also synchronized classroom learning with the needs of the U.S. security state.

Uh-Oh Feelings: Gut Reactions as Force Multipliers

Although social media campaigns reached large audiences, CVE actors have established more holistic practices by calling on teachers, guidance counselors, mental health professionals, and other social service providers to take an active role in preventing violent extremism in their own communities. As a part of this work, CVE actors have trained social service providers to identify youth vulnerable to terrorist radicalization and to refer these children to various intervention services, including culturally responsive counseling, religious training, and after-school programming. Through this process, CVE actors have sought to deradicalize youth and minimize the risk factors "associated with" violent extremism, like disaffection and alienation.

Reinforcing the notion of a generational threat, the FBI (2016d) argued that as violent extremism "evolves and more youth embrace extremist ideologies, it places a growing burden on our educational system to provide appropriate services to students who view hatred or targeted violence as acceptable outlets for their grievances. To complicate matters, youth possess inherent risk factors making them susceptible to violent extremist ideologies or possible recruitment" (3).

From the FBI's perspective, "countering these prevailing dynamics requires a fresh approach that focuses on education and enhancing public safety" (3). Given the perceived threat of violent extremism and the unique vulnerabilities of youth, the FBI suggested that "our educators are in a unique position to [e]ffect change, impart affirmative messaging, or facilitate intervention activities due to their daily interactions with students" (3). The FBI's 2016 findings generated a new commitment to establishing new CVE practices in schools to identify youth vulnerable to violent extremism, address the perceived risk factors that facilitate the radicalization process, and counter terrorist propaganda.

To conscript teachers and schools into the CVE industry, the FBI (2016d) and other national security agencies developed training materials to "educate school personnel about at-risk behaviors and activities that assist students with reducing social and psychological commitment to violence as a method of resolving a grievance" (4). Responding to these demands, the Rochester Institute of Technology's (2016) DHS CVE grant application proposed workshops for educators "to learn more about violent extremism and how to help students combat it" (3). The City of Los Angeles Mayor's Office of Public Safety (2016) similarly sought to build a "referral system" so that teachers and other social service providers could conduct "field assessments" to identify individuals who may be radicalizing and then refer these individuals to specific services "needed for positive social outcomes" (5). In Maryland, the Building Resilience Against Violent Extremism (BRAVE) model focused on "generating public awareness about the risk factors of violent extremism and empowering the appropriate figures to intervene with vulnerable individuals before they choose a path of violence" (World Organization for Resource Development and Education 2014, 2). Through BRAVE, teachers, youth workers, and school resource officers could refer an individual to the local police department's Crisis Intervention Team, which then directed the individual "to the community partner best suited to counsel him or her away from the path of violence" (2). These different CVE programs centered on training social service providers like teachers to identify and then report youth perceived to be vulnerable to radicalization to the local police department.

Like BRAVE, the FBI (2016d) recommended that schools develop crisis intervention teams, pointing to Virginia's 2013 House Bill 2344, which "mandate[s] the creation of threat assessment teams and procedures for intervention with students whose behavior poses a threat to the safety of school staff or students" (25). To support these efforts, the FBI encouraged states to "consider legislative action or similar measures to curb the spread of extremism within their local communities" in ways "consistent with constitutional rights and freedoms" (25). In addition, the FBI planned to develop teacher trainings to "educate[] school staff on the intervention process and its role in disengagement" (25). The FBI justified these trainings by framing teachers as "crucial partners in identifying at-risk youth and initiating the disengagement process" (25). Guided by the FBI, this CVE approach has deputized teachers as law enforcement officials who identify "pre-criminal" students exhibiting concerning behaviors before they commit a crime or act of violence.

The FBI's school guidelines to identify and report vulnerable youth have supported longstanding behavioral threat assessment processes used to detect early warning signs of violence or other criminal activity in U.S. schools. Some states, for example, require colleges and universities to participate in behavioral threat assessments trainings. My own academic institution maintains an Office of Preparedness and Response, which regularly conducts a "campus risk assessment" to evaluate any possible "threat events." These offices, assessments, and associated trainings increasingly have incorporated CVE initiatives or logics to combat all mass casualty threats.

Given the growing fears of a terrorist attack targeting children, school districts, local departments of homeland security, and law enforcement agencies have provided behavioral threat assessment trainings for teachers and school administrators. One institute's training manual argued that "schools have an obligation to provide a safe environment for learning," including "the ability to prevent violence by evaluating potentially violent students." Given this obligation, the manual supported "strategies for improving planning, preparedness, and violence prevention capacity of schools." To do so, the institute's trainings helped "increase the capacity of schools to identify students with concerning behaviors and intervene before an attack or act of violence occurs." Through these trainings, participants learned to identify threatening students, develop appropriate interventions to reduce the risk of violence, and create mechanisms to circumvent student privacy laws like the Family Educational Rights and Privacy Act (FERPA) in the service of school safety (participant observation, February 9, 2017, and March 20, 2017).

Consistent with the FBI's guidelines, several behavioral threat assessment trainers explained that they taught participants to focus on behaviors, not profiles. Kyle Eagan, for example, acknowledged that "there is no accurate or useful profile of a 'school shooter.'" In the absence of this school shooter profile, Eagan encouraged participants to "focus on behavior that suggests potential for harm or need for assistance." With this focus on behaviors, co-trainer Robert Edwards argued that "the single best predictor of violence" is disciplinary records. Edwards suggested that using disciplinary records "is *not* profiling because we're looking at behaviors" (participant observation, February 9, 2017). The FBI (2017b) also encouraged behavioral threat assessment teams to use school records, which can provide "clues to targeting, research and planning, preparation, emotional leakage, and more" (46). According to the FBI, "patterns of emotional decline or improvement over time can be observed via performance, attendance, or behavioral changes if records are available for a lengthy period" (46). From the perspective of these trainers, threat assessments focused on behaviors eschewed the racial and religious profiling of students. School records therefore could provide objective insight into these behaviors as well as changes in behavior over time.

This approach, however, ignores growing academic studies that demonstrate that students of color, students with disabilities, and queer students are more likely to be disciplined than their white, heteronormative, and able-bodied peers for the same behaviors.[4] School discipline records thus reflect racialized, gendered, and ableist practices that disproportionately punish nondominant students. Relying on these discipline records as "the single best predictor of violence" reinforces these inequitable practices. The shift to "behaviors not profiles" does not eliminate racial profiling in schools; it merely masks these racialized practices.

A two-year ethnographic study at a public middle school, for example, revealed that Black girls were more likely than their white or Latina peers to be punished for acting "unladylike" or being loud while in school, even though few "created disruptions in classrooms"

(E. W. Morris 2007, 506). One teacher referred to Black girls as "loud-ies," effectively punishing their Black femininity by castigating their behavior (being loud). A Government Accountability Office (2018) report similarly determined that teacher discretion "can result in certain groups of students being more harshly disciplined than others" (4). One case study revealed that "Black girls were disproportionately disciplined for subjective interpretations of behaviors, such as disobedience and disruptive behavior" (4). Another study used eye-tracking software "to show, among other things, teachers gazed longer at Black boys than other children when asked to look for challenging behaviors based on video clips" (4–5). In this way, using behaviors or behavioral records as "clues" about a propensity for violence is always already a racialized and racializing process that unevenly marks certain bodies as defiant or deviant. Trainers even admitted that despite their focus on "problematic behaviors" rather than "profiles or stereotypes," they tended to treat violent extremism as a "Muslim problem." Despite individual efforts to minimize racial profiling, a "Muslim bias" often inflected the practice of identifying potential threats (Elliot Adams, informal conversation, November 8, 2016). Race functions as a proxy, or shorthand, for risk and therefore a sufficient trigger for suspicion.

Threat assessment trainers also conceded that "there's always a first time," meaning some school shooters had no recorded incidents of misbehavior. Furthermore, there are "no data on all the cases where friends or family members noticed something 'off' about someone but no violence resulted (i.e., there is no control group)" (Patel and Koushik 2017, 17). This means that it is only in retrospect that school officials assign meaning to past behaviors, suggesting but not knowing if certain behaviors indicated, or contributed to, an imminent threat. Despite these limitations, trainers insisted that using discipline records and monitoring behaviors offered a more liberal and less racist approach to threat assessments.

To support these behavioral threat assessment efforts, trainers called on school staff to "look out for" early warning signs of violence. Edwards encouraged school administrators to "put your English and art teachers on alert" because several mass shooters reportedly wrote poems or drew pictures that indicated an imminent attack. This approach aligns with radicalization research, which suggests that violent extremists "leak" information regarding a planned attack. Given this perceived practice, the FBI (2016d) urged school staff to look for "leakage," a "common warning behavior for students advocating violence" that "occurs when a student intentionally or unintentionally reveals clues to feelings, thoughts, fantasies, attitudes, or intentions that signal an impending act" (17). These clues "emerge as subtle threats, boasts, innuendos, predictions, or ultimatums and are conveyed in numerous forms (e.g., stories, diaries, journals, essays, poems, manifestos, letters, songs, drawings, and videos)" (17). The FBI concluded that "leakage is one of the strongest clues prefacing a violent act" (17). Given these guidelines, one teacher admitted that her school administrator checked Facebook every day, a process through which the school "gathered a lot of intelligence, a lot of information." Under these logics, school staff like English teachers were well-positioned to encounter and identify such leakage in their classrooms.

As a part of these efforts, schools developed campus behavioral threat assessment teams (TATs) to identify and monitor potential security risks. Given the controversial nature of these threat assessment teams, one school sponsored dances and passed out brochures about its TAT to garner support. Other schools established a Youth Taskforce or Students of Concern Committee to brand their TATs as a friendly alternative to coercive policing (participant observation, March 20, 2017). These threat assessment teams evaluated students and determined who could be at risk of harming themself or others using a checklist of "warning signs (indicators and red flags) associated with school shootings in the United States" (Depue, n.d.). Through these outreach efforts, behavioral threat assessment teams sought to frame their work as a liberal mechanism to prevent violence without racially profiling students.

To assist communities in these efforts, CVE actors, think tanks, and federal agencies have developed protocols to evaluate potentially vulnerable individuals. In a 2014 guide for practitioners, the National Counterterrorism Center (NCTC) asked communities to "rate risk and resilience factors" and "assess balance of risk and protective factors" to evaluate an individual's vulnerability to violent extremism. To do so, the NCTC (2014) provided a rating rubric that allowed community members to tally a numeric score used to produce a graph that "present[s] a picture of the balance between risk and protective factors" (18). Communities then used this graph to "identify community resources that could be applied to mitigate risk and bolster resilience based on the ratings for risk and protective factors, as well as gaps in community resources and possible options to address the gaps" (18). As a part of the public health model of CVE, the NCTC assessment provided a tool for communities to determine local risk factors and the resources that could mitigate these risk factors.

Using a 1–5 Likert scale, the NCTC risk and resilience assessment rated indicators like "trust in institutions and law enforcement," "discrimination," "neighborhood safety," "experiences of trauma," "parental involvement in child's education," "family connection to identity group," and access to health care, social services, educational resources, and recreational resources. A calculated score ranging from zero to twenty-four indicated "high risk," meaning an individual in need of interventions to reduce risk factors and increase protective factors.

The NCTC presented this approach as an objective way to assess an individual's "risk and resilience" to violent extremism by focusing on behaviors rather than profiles. These indicators, however, affected a broad range of young people, especially in poor neighborhoods of color subjected to police violence, discrimination, and limited access to health care and educational opportunities. Although these anticipatory risk assessments appear to be race-neutral, these indicators automatically register poor youth of color as more prone to violence than their white counterparts because of the social and economic conditions that shape their everyday lives. Framed as an objective science, these risk assessments deputize community members as national security workers who can identify possible future threats and intervene accordingly.

Political scientist Mark Salter (2008) argues that "risk management has been adopted by a host of state agencies and private corporations as the gold standard in dealing with the new terrorist threat" by "focusing on a pragmatic assessment of the possible and likely sources of danger for an organization" (233). Through these pragmatic assessments, risk management is "offered to civil liberties groups as being more objective, neutral, and expert-led than the potentially discriminatory and prejudicial decisions" typically deployed by law enforcement (Amoore and de Goede 2008, 8). According to these logics, the use of a mathematical risk assessment sidesteps the "discriminatory and prejudicial" problems that have defined previous attempts to identify violent extremists before they commit a crime. Framing these risk assessments as an objective science, however, misses the use of racialized indices as well as the racialized logics used to interpret these data (S. Ahmed 2000; Lyon 2003; Browne 2015). By positioning threat assessments as objective, rather than interpretive, instruments, CVE actors have justified their work as race-neutral, eschewing prior problems of racial and religious profiling. "Channeling law enforcement resources into investigating people based on a potpourri of unproven indicators," however, "isn't likely to snare criminals, but rather to draw scrutiny to individuals whose speech or beliefs are outside the mainstream" (Patel and Koushik 2017, 2–3). By deputizing teachers as proxy national security agents who look for students at risk of terrorist radicalization, CVE has intensified the school-prison nexus.

Despite a commitment to using observable behaviors to identify potential violent extremists in schools, trainers also suggested that teachers could rely on their gut instincts. Sarah Earhart, for example, encouraged participants to use "our heads and our hearts" as a guide to screen potential threats. Earhart explained that "I believe every one of you seated here can feel it in your gut. You know when you meet someone. It's the same thing that we tell little people: It's that *uh-oh feeling!* Ladies and gentlemen, this is not complicated! We all know and perceive when behavior changes." From Earhart's perspective, our gut instincts were useful in the behavioral threat assessment process. As an example, Earhart described how she recently looked in a colleague's eyes and noticed "something's different." She approached her colleague who explained that he was a new father adjusting to a new sleep schedule. Earhart concluded that we can "know and recognize there's changes in people. Sometimes it's how they look. Sometimes it's different behavior. But what we're talking about here, ladies and gentlemen, is a collection of changes of behavior over time. It is not profiling." For Earhart, our uh-oh feeling could guide our extemporaneous threat assessments (participant observation, February 9, 2017, emphasis in original). Prevailing racial formations, cultural histories, and social memories, however, calibrate our "uh-oh feeling" to certain racialized, gendered, and ableist cues that signal an imminent threat and stimulate fear.

Even though Earhart encouraged participants to use our uh-oh feeling to identify potential threats, she also suggested that teachers "aren't good to have on the threat assessment team." Earhart warned that teachers' "bias" and "closeness of relationships" meant that they "don't believe the facts" and "have blinders on." Given these limitations, Earhart urged teachers to enlist an "unskewed eye" that could "seriously look for threats," like police officers. From her perspective, law enforcement "is the golden nugget in our backpack" for educators. By working with law enforcement officials, teachers could minimize their bias and amplify their school's capacity to identify imminent threats by using their uh-oh feeling.

These contradictory logics that both used "gut instincts" as a resource and as an indication of "bias" ignore the cultural histories that shape the social perception of danger. Prevailing social, cultural, and political contexts, after all, calibrate "our eyes and ears" to recognize certain signs, behaviors, and bodies as threats. David Campbell (1992) explains that "those events or factors that we identify as dangerous come to be ascribed as such only through an interpretation of their various dimensions of dangerousness" rather than objective risk assessments (2). A former FBI agent, for example, described how the U.S. government portrayed ISIS as "so great at recruitment" with an active online presence on social media platforms like Twitter. White supremacist websites, however, enjoyed larger audiences that the FBI simply "did not monitor or care about." According to this agent, "contrary to public perception, terrorist deaths are much lower than the 1970s and 1980s and extremist violence does not come close to 1% of overall violence." As an interpretive process, threat assessments privilege some risks like "ISIS-inspired terrorism" over others like homicide and white supremacist violence, irrespective of their actual rate of occurrence. Informed by enduring social, cultural, and political histories, these interpretations calibrate our eyes to identify Muslims and Muslim-looking populations as potential terrorist threats.

Furthermore, the differential valuing of racialized lives means that the U.S. public reads the bodies it encounters for terrorism clues and even uses the body as a sign of imminent violence. Mimi Thi Nguyen (2015) explains that "locating the apprehension of criminality in clothes"—from the hoodie to the hijab—"does not constitute any sort of departure from racial optics that target the body as a contiguous surface of legible information about capacity and pathology" (799).

In this way, "profiles that include these other surfaces—clothes, and also tattoos, hairstyles—teach us how to see race both with and without skin as an anchor" (799). In fact, most anti-gang laws profile gang members though such signs and symbols. CVE similarly targets these racialized indicators, whether "growing facial hair" or wearing "traditional Muslim attire." Through these identificatory practices, "racial optics conceive the profile through the abstraction of contiguous surfaces blurring the distinction between surplus (the tattoo or hoodie as detail) and the ontological (the flesh as essence) that in turn teaches us to see in racial others the unseen truth of criminality" (800). Posed as an objective science, these racial optics generate an "ontological confusion between subject and object" such that the hijab "provides cover for racism's slide into lethal structures that claim to assess and predict threat with disinterest" (800). Although trainers like Earhart suggested that they policed "behaviors not profiles," the terrorist is "rendered knowable though visible signs and screens *fully schematized by racism*" (801). Rather than standing outside of power relations, the early warning signs of a vulnerability to violent extremism are always already rooted in racial hierarchies that direct the eye to recognize certain bodies, and the contiguous surfaces of "traditional clothing" and political thought, as dangerous.

Shared Responsibility Committees: Securitizing Social Services

After the identification of vulnerable youth, CVE actors encouraged communities to develop "multidisciplinary committees" that could "off-ramp" young people from the perceived pathways to violent extremism. Adrian Baker, for example, explained that rather than "reinvent the wheel," CVE practitioners could turn to the "lessons learned" from other violence prevention practices, including the "very, very promising approach" of "multidisciplinary teams" (interview, January 27, 2017). In the CVE policy world, a multidisciplinary team convened a "culturally-competent but trauma-informed group of trained professionals" who provide "wraparound services for those vulnerable individuals" (Zaghari, participant observation, August 18, 2016). Rather than rely only on law enforcement, these multidisciplinary teams have included social workers, teachers, guidance counselors, religious leaders, and community members, who can identify, report, and work with youth perceived to be vulnerable to terrorist radicalization.

From Zaghari's perspective, these multidisciplinary teams engaged a "whole of society approach" by "bringing together people of diverse backgrounds purposefully and strategically." Community leader Masoud Kaleel similarly affirmed multidisciplinary teams as an alternative to punitive counterterrorism approaches by involving "people who felt obligated to help the community" and "expressed concern about what was happening in terms of young people potentially radicalizing in the community" (informal conversation, January 20, 2017). CVE actors framed multidisciplinary teams as an effective community-driven tactic to reduce radicalization without stigmatizing Muslim communities or relying on law enforcement.

Despite these affirmations, some Somali youth in Minneapolis perceived these committees as "outsiders" to their community, even if they were composed of Somali elders. Reflecting on his own experiences in high school, community organizer Absame Omar concluded that these committee members "know nothing about us. And they want to come to our school and tell us how to walk and talk and what to do. America wants you to act a certain way and if you don't, they're not having it" (participant observation, April 21, 2017). Although CVE actors viewed the use of multidisciplinary teams as a way to empower local communities, some community organizers questioned the intentions and motives of these "outsiders" who encouraged them to assimilate to dominant U.S. norms.

Critics also warned that these multidisciplinary teams facilitated intelligence-gathering practices in Muslim and other diasporic communities. In 2016, the *Intercept* obtained a letter that described the FBI's clandestine use of "Shared Responsibility Committees" (SRCs), secret multidisciplinary teams tasked with deradicalizing individuals perceived to be on the path toward violent extremism. These SRCs facilitated the "social and psychological process whereby an individual's commitment to violence is reduced to such an extent that he/she is no longer at risk of using violence as a solution to a grievance" (Federal Bureau of Investigation n.d., 1). To do so, the SRCs "enlist[ed] counselors, social workers, religious figures, and other community members to intervene with people the FBI thinks are in danger of radicalizing—the sort of alternative to prosecution and jail time many experts have been clamoring for" (Currier and Hussain 2016, para. 2). This approach assumes that psychological pathologies drive the turn to political violence and that mental health interventions can correct these pathologies.

To carry out this initiative, the FBI (n.d.) referred individuals to a "voluntarily formed" local SRC, which then designed and implemented an individualized intervention plan (1). Intervention plans included "mentoring support, life skills, anger management, cognitive or behavioral therapies, constructive pursuits, education skills, career building and support, family support, health awareness, housing support, drug and alcohol awareness and treatment, engagement and exposure with perceived adversaries, and mental health care" (1). The FBI pitched this SRC approach as an alternative to conventional counterterrorism measures, noting that it would not "use the SRC as a means to gather intelligence on the subject or his/her potential connections to terrorism" (1). The FBI, however, retained the right to "share any information the SRC provides with other law enforcement agencies, members of the U.S. intelligence community, and foreign government agencies as needed" (2). In addition, federal, state, and local law enforcement agencies could "use their law enforcement and prosecutorial authorities in appropriate circumstances without prior notification to the SRC" (1).

Even though the FBI could report and act on the intelligence it received from an SRC, the FBI required SRC members to sign confidentiality agreements that forbid them from "disclosing information regarding referred individuals outside of the SRC" and "consulting with outside experts regarding an intervention plan on behalf of the SRC for an FBI-referred individual without written permission from the FBI" (2). Despite the FBI's claim that it would not use the SRCs to collect intelligence, it could use information SRCs gathered to take prosecutorial action while limiting public oversight of the SRCs' activities.

Pointing to the recent prosecution of Somali youth on terrorism-related charges, law enforcement official David Greene applauded local multidisciplinary teams in their collaborative efforts to combat terrorist recruitment and radicalization. More specifically, Greene called on Minneapolis's Somali community to "work[] with community leaders—imams and experts—who can help at-risk youth."

Greene affirmed the mobilization of these multidisciplinary teams for the purposes of countering violent extremism, noting that "a network of community resources built by community leaders is now available to assist friends and family members who are concerned about someone who's going down the wrong path toward radicalization" (participant observation, August 18, 2016). In this discussion, Greene suggested that CVE could stop violent extremism "*before* it becomes a criminal matter," thereby protecting youth from prosecution and defending the community from the "generational threat."

To organize their work on these multidisciplinary teams, CVE actors turned to the "theory of community resilience and protective resources," which suggests that "in the face of adversity, social and psychosocial factors at the level of a community can inhibit, stop, delay, or diminish negative outcomes" (Weine, Younis, and Polutnik 2017, 27). CVE actors argued that multidisciplinary teams like SRCs could amplify these protective factors and help individuals "who might be in crisis or otherwise experiencing isolation, discrimination, or bullying" (Williams, Horgan, and Evans 2016, 68). SRCs deployed protective, not punitive, resources to support positive youth development, a process that arguably could prevent violent extremism.

Despite the growing use of multidisciplinary teams, CVE actors offered conflicting and sometimes contradictory understandings about the relationship between mental health and mass violence. Daniel Glickman affirmed the inclusion of "mental health professionals" in CVE programming while explaining that "terrorists have a lower rate of being 'mentally ill' than the general population" and that terrorists "are not likely to be mentally ill." Still, Glickman encouraged communities to develop multidisciplinary teams staffed with "psychologists, counselors, and sometimes police" as an "alternative to police" (participant observation, March 29, 2017). Zaghari also concluded that "there's no evidence to suggest that terrorists have higher levels of severe mental illness in the general population." Yet, she also reported that "psychological conditions, such as cognitive, mental, or emotional disorders, can also contribute to one's propensity to violent extremism. In addition, mental illnesses, in particular post-traumatic stress disorder, are posited as another major factor" (participant observation, August 18, 2016). Rahman similarly surmised that although people with "mental illnesses" were "not necessarily violent," mental illness was an "underlying cause" of violence (informal conversation, November 28, 2016). Even though "the state of the evidence on radicalization and on the interaction with mental health problems is undeveloped," CVE actors suggested that "psychological conditions" could contribute to the radicalization process (Weine, Eisenman, Jackson et al. 2017, 335). By associating mental health with violent extremism, CVE logics criminalized psychiatric disabilities, particularly in Muslim communities.

Contrary to public perception, "mass shootings by people with serious mental illness represent less than 1% of all yearly gun-related homicides. In contrast, deaths by suicide using firearms account for the majority of yearly gun-related deaths" (Knoll and Annas 2016, 81). Moreover, "perpetrators of mass shootings are unlikely to have a history of involuntary psychiatric hospitalization" and thus "databases intended to restrict access to guns and established by gun laws that broadly target people with mental illness will not capture this group of individuals" (82). Even though "mass shootings cause endless public speculation regarding causes and motives," these rare cases "are the result of many complex factors," irreducible to simplified explanations like a "mad or bad" shooter (83). Although mass shootings are "extremely rare events," the constant "outpourings of public horror and outrage" through media generate ineffective public safety approaches and apply scarce resources to infrequent yet highly charged sources of insecurity (82). According to this research, criminalizing mental health ineffectively addresses the problem of mass violence in the United States and harms individuals with psychiatric disability labels.

In addition to clarifying these misconceptions about the relationship between psychiatric disability labels and the production of violence, some mental health professionals have questioned the increasing use of social service providers for national security purposes. Psychologists Alice LoCicero and J. Wesley Boyd (2016), for example, defined CVE as "the new COINTELPRO," a contemporary counterterrorism program that called on mental health professionals to report to law enforcement "on kids who they just think (note, without any knowledge of what the actual signs are) might be on a path toward extremism" (para. 5). Rejecting the conscription of mental health professionals into the domestic war on terror, LoCicero and Boyd declared in *Psychology Today*:

We will not be participating in any CVE programs, and we strongly encourage other mental health professionals to also refuse for the following reasons: We will not spy on our patients. We do not read minds, and we know that none of us can predict the future. We know of several non-punitive approaches to helping ALL kids resist ALL recruitment to violence. They are not high tech and they do not involve the FBI. They involve listening and talking to kids, mentoring kids, educating kids and helping them find paths to meaningful lives, honoring their communities here and any communities they are connected within the US or elsewhere, and taking their grievances seriously. (paras. 11–14)

In this public statement, LoCicero and Boyd refuted the assumption that "would-be terrorists" shared a "psychological profile of someone who might ultimately commit violent acts" and questioned the use of psychologists to identify and report these "would-be terrorists" (para. 7). Whether practitioners applied the CVE label to these efforts, LoCicero and Boyd warned that deputizing psychologists in this way "turn[ed] health care professionals into government informants" (para. 15). Rather than provide an alternative to coercive policing, the integration of mental health treatment and monitoring into CVE efforts could lead to arrest, prosecution, and incarceration. Psychologists therefore refused to apply an antiterrorism lens to their clients and, instead, provided resources that support healthy individuals and communities independent of law enforcement logics and interventions.

The inclusion of mental health professionals into CVE programming can compromise patients' right to privacy through the disclosure of confidential information to law enforcement. For example, when "mental health professionals refer patients deemed 'vulnerable to radicalization' to multidisciplinary teams involving law enforcement, they may disclose information obtained in confidential mental health treatment settings" (Morgan 2018, 804). Furthermore, the use of multidisciplinary teams can "erode confidentiality protections, particularly when law enforcement officials inject themselves into a patient's mental health treatment" (804). CAIR-LA director Hussam Ayloush more directly stated, "We are extremely offended by this program that says American Muslims should get mental health services through the Department of Homeland Security's counterterrorism program, like we are criminals or potential terrorists" (as quoted in Bharath 2018). Some critics objected to the securitization of mental health professionals through their inclusion in CVE programming. Others demanded access to culturally relevant counseling as deserving citizens rather than as ticking time bombs.

In 2016, for example, eighteen-year-old Mahin Khan was arrested and charged with plotting to commit terrorism in support of the Taliban and ISIS after receiving mental health services through the FBI for three years. The FBI first contacted Khan after he sent a threatening letter to a teacher, which prompted a forty-five-day evaluation at an inpatient psychiatric facility "under the directive and supervision of the FBI" (Khan's parents, as quoted in Truelsen 2016). Over the next three years, the FBI reportedly met with Khan "every few months under the pretense of mentoring him and coordinating his mental health care" (Morgan 2018, 791). Struggling to meet Khan's needs, his parents consented to this health-care arrangement with the FBI.

Given his developmental disabilities, Khan's parents reported that they "didn't let him have a phone" because they "didn't trust him with one." Yet, after Khan's arrest, his parents learned that "he had been using a phone given to him by the FBI," which he allegedly used to communicate with an undercover informant, indicating a willingness to commit terrorism (as quoted in Hussain 2016). While offering Khan mental health services, the FBI sent an undercover informant to encourage Khan to plan and conduct a terrorist attack.

Although Khan's parents demonstrated their son's inability to plan, finance, and commit an act of terrorism, Khan currently is serving an eight-year sentence in an Arizona state prison. Given this and similar arrests, CVE critics have worried that the cooptation of mental health services to monitor and report "suspicious" youth was "an affront to the basic tenets of professional ethics, threatening privacy and exacerbating health disparities" (Morgan 2018, 815). Rather than serve as an alternative to conventional FBI stings, the integration of mental health professionals into the management of Khan led to his contact with an undercover informant, arrest, and incarceration.

Given academic, professional, and community concerns related to securitizing social services, spying on youth, and stigmatizing mental health, the FBI announced the suspension of SRCs in October 2016. Some CVE critics, however, questioned if the FBI's intervention program was "really cancelled" (McCarthy 2016). One community member, for example, admitted to serving on an SRC after the 2016 suspension. Others pointed to the FBI sting arrest of Khan as evidence that the FBI had not "effectively implemented" the cancellation of the SRCs in local communities (McCarthy 2016, para. 9). Prior to his arrest, Khan had met with "the FBI, mental health professionals, academic tutors, and community mentors for years," intervention methods the SRCs "sought to formalize" (para. 7). CVE critics worried that, like other rebranding strategies, the U.S. government simply initiated new interventions by another name. Even if the FBI suspended its SRC initiative, its ideas, infrastructure, and tools continued to inform public health approaches to CVE that sometimes relied on multidisciplinary teams.

Despite the reported suspension of SRCs, the ongoing securitization of social services impeded community efforts to support young people. Communities, however, developed strategies to provide social services without the intrusion of security agencies. As a community organizer in Minneapolis, Axado Isnino sought to provide "mentoring and money to counter the organizations taking CVE money." Given CVE's stronghold on the Somali community, Isnino struggled to "figure out how to provide the services that had been securitized under CVE, with no attachments to CVE" (participant observation, August 20, 2017). Because CVE had infiltrated local funding streams, community organizers like Isnino diligently worked to provide social services and other resources disconnected from CVE.

Another college student questioned the use of social service providers to determine if a student poses an "imminent threat" to a school or community, asking:

> Who is making those decisions? I cannot emphasize enough how many teachers I have had—counselors, various leaders who were supposed to help me—who looked at me as a potential threat or someone who needed to be saved or educated, someone who needed to be Americanized. So, I'm sorry, but I'm tired of jumping through the hoops that other people have

set for us to prove that we're worthy of these social services.
(participant observation, August 20, 2017)

Rather than celebrate the mobilization of community resources to fight violent extremism in collaboration with the FBI, critics warned that these multidisciplinary teams deputized mental health professionals as the police who look for, report, and work with youth perceived to be vulnerable to violent extremism. In this view, this approach encouraged targeted youth in disinvested communities to participate in these CVE programs to receive social services and used mental health professionals to enhance police power, fortify racialized hierarchies, and legitimize this national security initiative. Even though social service providers like teachers engage in social control as a part of their daily work, deputizing trusted adults in this way has compelled them to view their clients, students, and patients as potential terrorist threats, reaffirming the carceral logics that organize the school-prison nexus and the use of caring institutions to advance policing in the United States.

Like other forms of carceral care work, psychosocial CVE programs have contributed to the U.S. security state's "therapeutic governance," a form of governance rooted in social risk management that "makes the link between psychological well-being and security" (Pupavac 2005, 161). This type of governance is organized by the assumptions that "humans have a psychological nature, that this psychological state can be more or less 'healthy,' that particular ('therapeutic') methods can improve psychological dysfunction, and that it is in society's best interest to encourage and protect psychological well-being" (Rehberg 2014, 7). In this view, managing psychological health is a matter of good governance and national security rather than a private concern. Therapeutics therefore "manage psychological and emotional conduct in ways that align with the aims of the government" (Haney 2010, 117). Through anticipatory, probabilistic, and preventative interventions organized by white cultural norms, the U.S. security state governs through the management of individual psychology by offering "therapeutic corrections" informed by radicalization research that indicts psychological pathologies in the turn to violence (116).

Through CVE programs, mental health professionals and other

social service providers treat deviations from dominant norms as threats to national security and therefore provide therapeutic interventions to prevent violent extremism. To do so, social service providers use mental health as a proxy for risk and as a means to reprogram youth according to dominant psychological, cultural, and social norms conducive to state governance. Through this purposeful patrolling and psychosocial programming that require "non-state actors to play a much more proactive role in citizens' lives," CVE practitioners and their community collaborators have contributed to the therapeutic governance of their communities, offering new forms of control with a softer, friendlier face (Pupavac 2001, 361).

Learning to Resist the Temptations of Extremism: CVE Curriculum in Schools

In addition to monitoring and reporting student behavior, the FBI (2016b) urged schools to "initiate disengagement activities or craft affirmative messages that dissuade[] youth from dangerous paths" (25). More specifically, the FBI called on high schools to "incorporate a two-hour block of violent extremism awareness training as part of their core curriculums for grades 9–12" to educate youth on "the perils of violent extremism and the effect on their lives, families, and communities" (216). UNESCO's *A Teacher's Guide on the Prevention of Violent Extremism* provided direction on how to manage classroom discussions on violent extremism, noting that "young people need relevant and timely learning opportunities to develop the knowledge, skills, and attitudes that can help them build their resilience to such propaganda" (2016, 9). Although UNESCO encouraged a global citizenship education approach to countering violent extremism, it also recommended classroom discussions that investigate "local manifestations of violent extremism," explore how young people "can make a difference if they make the right choices within their immediate context," and examine the "real risks and consequences of violent extremism" (16). Before discussing these controversial issues, teachers must "connect[] the issue of violent extremism to content in the local curriculum"; "understand[] the social, cultural, ethnic, and religious diversity of the local context"; "include[] minority-group perspectives in the discussions"; and "identify[] the right timing, since controversial issues should not be discussed haphazardly" (16). This approach has strengthened the education sector's response to the problem of violent extremism, working to diffuse the perceived factors the drive terrorist recruitment and radicalization through classroom teachings.

To support these efforts, the FBI (2016d) suggested that schools could mobilize high school alumni as role models who "impart[] affirmative messaging to the student body" and discuss "best practices for coping with the daily stressors from high school while promoting cognitive and physical development" (27). Such efforts could "help students resist the temptations of extremist messages and their violent agendas" and "diminish the likelihood of schools becoming potential nodes of radicalization or recruitment hubs for violent extremists" (25, 4). In this approach, school alumni played a central role in preventing violent extremism.

To complement these classroom activities, the FBI encouraged schools to establish a holistic approach to combating violent extremism. The FBI (2016d), for example, called on schools to cultivate positive student development through "extensive afterschool programming such as sports or club activities" (25). In this view, "what happens after school hours can be critical to sustaining the lessons taught in the classroom" and so teachers should develop "educational programming that goes beyond the school day to teach and involve families and communities" (Center on Global Counterterrorism Cooperation and Hedayah Center 2013, 7). Communities therefore invested in athletics programs as "an important positive outlet for youths as it fosters teamwork, social, and leadership skills, and promotes goal-setting and instills a sense of identity and belonging— many of the factors that violent extremists prey on to recruit youths into their organizations" (5). One CVE practitioner pointed to his own soccer league as an example of how his community protected youth from radicalization, noting that "playing soccer and getting strong" ensured local Somali boys did not engage in "bad things" and helped improve their academic progress (Aeden Warabe, informal conversation, April 13, 2017). Rather than "paying attention to social media" where terrorist recruiters lurked, the boys focused on playing soccer with their friends. After-school programming like soccer leagues or arts classes supplemented in-school CVE activities.

Despite the popularity of these rare sports programs in diasporic communities, some young adults lamented that law enforcement "co-opted" their after-school sports programs in the service of "the CVE industry." For example, college student Bashir Cilmi described how an Ohio basketball tournament "got re-coded as a CVE effort as the media began reporting that people who put this together did this to stop terrorism and gangs." Echoing Cilmi, Absame Omar criticized the continual "branding of sports as CVE" for political gain. From his perspective, "Sports is a part of our culture. Ball is life. They use that as a taken: 'He's not going to be a terrorist because I gave him a 5x5 tournament every Sunday.' Now they're flagging kids who don't want to play soccer. That has nothing to do with terrorism." By positioning soccer programs as central to achieving antiterrorism goals, the introduction of CVE in Minneapolis "securitized social service providers the way we securitized humanitarian aid": To distribute resources like "coaches and equipment" typically denied to disinvested diasporic communities, CVE practitioners relied on "gatekeepers" like local law enforcement who "decided who gets the aid and who participates and what the participation requires" (participant observation, April 21, 2017). By tying much-needed resources like sports programs to CVE, national security practitioners incentivized community participation, including collaborating with local law enforcement.

Since September 11, 2001, local law enforcement agencies have relied on police-sponsored sports leagues to facilitate community policing practices. The New York City Police Department (NYPD), for example, created the NYPD Cricket Cup for South Asian youth. NYPD deputy inspector Amin Kosseim explained that, through community outreach efforts like the cricket league, "you're going to be able to counter radicalization, counter extremism. You want [community members] to come to you with information, and that's not going to happen unless you have that rapport" (as quoted in Tharoor 2013). The NYPD applied a community policing approach to the problem of violent extremism, fostering relationships with communities to gather information on Arabs and South Asians.

As a part of this community policing project, NYPD officers "were encouraged to join adult soccer and cricket leagues as players. They kept lists of places where Arabs and South Asians gathered to play and watch sports" (Tharoor 2013, para. 17). Using this human intelligence, the NYPD Demographics Unit authored a "Sports Venue Report," which listed the "eighteen cricket fields and forty other venues where South Asians congregate in New York" (para. 17). After mapping these sites, the NYPD "conducted fieldwork, in the form of visits, to these locations to ascertain the required information" (New York City Police Department n.d., 2). Under the guise of community outreach, the NYPD used its participation in soccer and cricket leagues to map Arab and South Asian communities and gather information on popular sports venues, without ever informing its participants. These secretive intelligence-gathering practices led organizations like the Arab American Association of New York to withdraw their sponsorship of various sports leagues across the city (Zirin 2013). Given the NYPD's record, young adults like Cilmi and Omar questioned all CVE-related sports programs, fearing surveillance, monitoring, and intelligence-gathering practices. They also challenged gaining access to these resources as potential terrorists rather than as deserving citizens.

Although practitioners viewed this approach as a way to protect youth from terrorist recruitment without law enforcement, young people worried that these sports programs could facilitate the identification and reporting of individuals perceived to be vulnerable to violent extremism. One athletics center, for example, provided Somali youth with free passes to use its facilities. These youth "played soccer three times a week," "went to the gym four days a week," and attended "arts programming." To develop a social network map of their associates, the center gave youth guest passes. Through these guest passes, CVE practitioners "knew who their friends [were]" and collected "good data," including their progress in school, how often they visited the center, and "which friends they bring with them." This athletics center provided its typical social services while also developing practices to gather "good data" useful in preventing terrorist radicalization and recruitment (Aedan Warabe, informal conversation, April 13, 2017). Youth organizers challenged the co-optation of their sports leagues on the assumption that Muslim children were incipient terrorists who needed additional support to diffuse this generational threat as well as the required reporting of program participants to federal funders like DHS (Arab American Action Network 2017).

Given their experiences with CVE, youth felt under constant surveillance by adults who came to view them through a radicalization lens.

The surveillance function of these youth-oriented CVE practices calls into question the purpose of education, the role of teachers, and the ethics of incentivizing research, teaching, and after-school programming aligned with the needs of the U.S. security state. Increasingly concerned about the "generational threat," communities reconfigured their schools and curricula to address the perceived problem of violent extremism, often through community-police partnerships. By reorganizing to meet the state's prevailing geopolitical goals, public schools actively contributed to the domestic war on terror.

Although some youth rejected these tactics, many community members viewed this approach as an effective intervention and alternative to conventional counterterrorism methods. Given these contravening conclusions, CVE often divided communities, instigating intense debates about how to protect youth and from what. These contestations strategically narrowed the terms of debate, forgoing other ways of radically reimagining public safety and national security.

"A Liberal, Fascist Program": The Slow Violence of CVE Programming in Minneapolis

Although politicians and practitioners like Scott Sacco framed CVE as an alternative to "bombs, bullets, and drones," some young people experienced CVE as a deeply violent intervention. Throughout my fieldwork, I observed some college students describe CVE as a policy framework that intensified, not mitigated, the constant criminalization of their communities, political organizing, and religious practices. From their perspective, the liberal language of CVE masked the illiberal practices that defined this national security approach. In this view, struggles to bring liberalism to domestic antiterrorism regimes through CVE has increased the surveillance, monitoring, and criminalization of Muslims in the United States through teachers, mental health professionals, and schools. Rather than usher in new ways of supporting racialized communities and destabilizing the organizing logics of conventional counterterrorism, CVE actors rehearsed familiar narratives that have framed Muslim youth as more vulnerable to terrorism and deputized social service providers as the police who identified, reported, and worked with individuals vulnerable to violent extremism.

In Minneapolis, community organizers reported that the introduction of CVE into their city heightened surveillance, suspicion, and policing in their neighborhoods, schools, and mosques. In 2015, for example, Minneapolis Public Schools (MPS) announced a new DOJ initiative that hired "experienced youth workers" to monitor school cafeterias and non-classroom settings where they could "spot identity issues and disaffection" perceived to be "root causes of radicalization" (Kiernat 2015). Although significant research studies by both CVE proponents and critics demonstrate that there is no single profile of a violent extremist, no single pathway toward violent extremism, and no portfolio of "root causes" of violent extremism, MPS promised "intervention teams" staffed by youth workers, mental health professionals, and parents who could address "identity issues and disaffection," particularly among Somali youth (Kundnani 2014; Shah 2014b; Schanzer 2012; Denoeux and Carter 2009; Sageman 2015; Chang and Kim 2016; Obama 2015b; Bjørgo 2011; Horgan 2008). Although MPS officials and local politicians applauded these efforts as an alternative to coercive policing, critics viewed these efforts as intensifying anti-Black and anti-Muslim surveillance by deputizing school staff as the police. Experiencing "identity issues and disaffection"—common among youth in the United States—marked Somali students as potential future terrorists. These critiques also surfaced in Illinois where community organizers questioned efforts to educate communities in identifying and working with individuals exhibiting "warning signs of radicalization to violence." Although CVE practitioners viewed this approach as a progressive alternative to FBI stings, community organizers rejected all programs that relied on disproven social science, collaborated with law enforcement agencies, and provided social services on the presumption that disenfranchised youth were vulnerable to terrorist influences.

Given the conflicting assessments of CVE's harms and benefits, Minneapolis politicians, practitioners, and youth struggled to gain narrative authority in describing CVE's impact on their communities. David Greene and other officials managed the image of CVE by fram-

ing this national security approach as an alternative to law enforcement. Some youth, however, contested this image by educating their
peers about how CVE intensified criminalizing practices already un-
derway in their communities. These competing narratives generated
distrust, confusion, and anger across Minneapolis. Given the credibility, power, and prestige of key CVE advocates like Greene, media
often ignored youth or minimized their concerns, despite a cogent
analysis anchored by empirical evidence.

Given this silencing, in this section I explore how some targeted
youth understood and experienced CVE firsthand, defining for themselves what constituted ethical national security, public safety, and
community-building practices in Minneapolis. I examine how youth
came to view CVE as a "liberal, fascist program" that demonized and
harmed their communities, despite its humanitarian facade. Lastly, I
consider how the implementation of CVE in schools and other youth
spaces has securitized the provision of social services to advance U.S.
interests, much like the securitization of humanitarian aid to achieve
geopolitical goals. Although this analysis looks specifically at CVE
in the Twin Cities, it is instructive for thinking through how CVE
programs can be designed as, or devolve into, intelligence-gathering
activities.

In 2017, community organizers hosted a panel aimed at "decoding
radicalization policy." By convening Somali families and allies, the
panelists sought to inform their communities about CVE practices in
their schools and communities, provide an analysis of these practices,
and develop strategies to protect each other from CVE programming.
As a part of this political education session, the community organizers distributed information cards that defined CVE as "an insidious
surveillance program that seeks to incriminate, surveil[ ], and alienate young Muslims under the guise of social service." This information card also noted that CVE "exists to create a system that funnels
Muslims into the prison industrial complex" and "is based on the
belief system that there are indicators that distinguish who is prone
to 'terrorism' or 'terrorist' reqruitment [sic]" even though "there is
nothing to prove that such [indicators] exist." Organized by Somali
college students, this panel worked from the premise that CVE criminalized Black, Muslim, and diasporic communities using scientifically disproven indicators of violent extremism. Unlike other events

I observed in Minneapolis, this panel offered Somali students a space to critique CVE and organize proactive responses to this national security approach. The community organizers therefore livestreamed and archived this event for public viewing online.

Community organizers identified serious flaws with CVE, sometimes calling for a complete withdrawal of CVE programs from their schools and neighborhoods. Absame Omar, for instance, described the introduction of CVE into his Minneapolis public high school as "adding to the barriers we're already facing" as Black Muslim youth. He also reported that CVE practitioners attended Jummah (Friday prayer) "to see who is going and who is not," a type of surveillance that "made it hard to get things done" and eventually led some young men to stop frequenting the mosque because they felt criminalized when they worshipped. Other former students worried that Minneapolis Public Schools curated an "internal database of students who were concerning." Some MPS graduates therefore viewed CVE actors as "coming after our safe spaces we've created for ourselves." In practice, CVE generated deep fears among Somali youth in Minneapolis, who experienced intensified criminalization in their everyday lives, whether in their schools, mosques, or neighborhoods.

Although some local practitioners often reduced these concerns to the panicky paranoia of young people, obtained documents support student concerns related to racial profiling and intensified police surveillance. In 2009, for example, the Saint Paul Police Department (SPPD) (2009) launched a new initiative called the African Immigrant Muslim Coordinated Outreach Program (AIMCOP), funded by the U.S. Recovery Act Grant Program and U.S. Department of Justice (1). Citing the "particular concern" of "the demonstrated radicalization of 20 youth from our area who have left for Somalia to fight for the terrorist organization Al-Shabaab," AIMCOP sought to reduce violent crime through "community outreach" (1). AIMCOP forged strategic partnerships between the FBI, U.S. Attorney, Ramsey County Sheriff's Office, Muslim American Society, St. Paul Intervention Project, Somali Community Council, St. Paul Young Women's Christian Association (YWCA), and SPPD. These partners worked to "gain the trust of Somali immigrants" by "attend[ing] community meetings in targeted areas and refer[ring] youth to the [Police Activity League] and YWCA programs" (4). By building a strong relationship with the community, the AIMCOP team planned to "use[ ] established criteria that will stand up to public and legal scrutiny" to "establish a list that identifies radicalized youth, gang members, and violent offenders" (4). Using disproven indicators of violent extremism, the AIMCOP strategy required team members who interacted with identified youth to "submit a contact report" that would be stored in a database shared with AIMCOP partners (4). As these documents demonstrate, AIMCOP exploited community outreach to gather intelligence on the Somali community in the Twin Cities under the banner of national security.

The AIMCOP grant proposal revealed that "the effort of identifying the targets" helped "increase law enforcement's ability to maintain up-to-date intelligence on these offenders, alert team members to persons who are deserving of additional investigative efforts" and "serve[d] as an enhanced intelligence system to alert team members to the fact that they are interacting with an individual who poses a greater risk to personal and public safety" (Saint Paul Police Department 2009, 4). After this intelligence-gathering phase, SPPD officers "move[d] to the enforcement mode using the information they gained from the prevention period as well as automated intelligence and reporting systems already in place to identify 'hotspots' for crime" (5). By developing community relationships, the AIMCOP team sought to gather actionable intelligence to enhance its policing functions under the rubric of countering violent extremism.

To address these concerns, St. Paul Police spokesperson Steve Linders claimed that "the intelligence aspect never came to fruition. The program evolved away from that" (as quoted in Currier 2015). Muslim American Society of Minnesota executive director Asad Zaman, however, reported that his organization hired a police liaison using AIMCOP funds. The police department asked Zaman to "turn over a list of people at the programs," but Zaman refused (as quoted in Currier 2015). The intelligence aspect "never came to fruition" because of community resistance. AIMCOP, however, had established other avenues for intelligence gathering through its community outreach and contact reports.

Initiated in 2009, AIMCOP worked to combat radicalization in Minnesota five years before the Obama administration launched CVE pilot programs in Minneapolis, Los Angeles, and Boston.

AIMCOP departed from previous community outreach activities conducted by the St. Paul Police Department that "allowed the development of credible training and afforded previously unavailable access to sensitivity trainers" without engaging in deradicalization or intelligence gathering (Jensen 2006, 81). Increasing concerns about homegrown terrorism shifted the SPPD's tactics, leading to new efforts to gather intelligence through community outreach activities (M. Price 2015). Set in motion by new terrorism studies research, fears of radicalizing youth fueled a paradigm shift in local policing. The AIMCOP initiative paved the way for additional CVE programming, with an emphasis on identifying and off-ramping radicalizing Somali youth across the Twin Cities.[5]

In 2015, the St. Paul Police Department applied for, and received, a State Department of Homeland Security Law Enforcement Terrorism Prevention (LETP) grant for $100,000 to fund the overtime pay of SPPD officers working on the "Countering Violent Extremism program" (Saint Paul Police Department 2015, 7). In its grant application, the SPPD (2015) reported that after its AIMCOP grant funding ended in 2012, it "has continued to do outreach in the East and West African community with on-duty personnel" and "would like to enhance what we started in the original AIMCOP by focusing on outreach programs for East & West African youth and engagement programs for East & West African elders" (1). Citing a "whole of community approach," the SPPD (2015) continued to refer youth to the YWCA, 180 Degrees, Neighborhood House, and St. Paul Parks and Recreation for "needed services" (1). In addition to these community organizations, the SPPD (2015) outlined several mosques as "partners in our community outreach," including Masjid Al-Ihsan Islamic Center, Minnesota Da'wah Institute, Somali American Center, Prayer Center on Pedersen Street, and Prayer Center on McKnight Road. AIMCOP therefore served as an early blueprint for police-led CVE initiatives across the Twin Cities, particularly in "East and West African" neighborhoods.

Through these community collaborations that target "East and West African youth" as uniquely susceptible to terrorist radicalization, SPPD's "outreach strategies" have included: a junior police academy to foster interest in law enforcement careers and build trust between youth and police, summits to promote wellness and teach social media safety, community forums to establish positive community relations, and recreational and tutoring services to develop positive police/youth community relations (2015, 1–2). The SPPD (2015) argued that these community programs could "reduce and/ or prevent our youth from disenfranchisement which can lead to radicalization into terror groups like ISIS and al Shabab," "increase[] access to and use of the criminal justice system," "improve perceptions of law enforcement within East African communities," and "develop individual relationships between immigrant youth, their families, the community and law enforcement" (2). The SPPD therefore framed its community engagement as a way to protect youth and increase public safety. In this view, enhancing community-police relationships through community outreach programs has facilitated information sharing useful in addressing local problems.

Despite the ongoing expansion of community outreach initiatives, student organizers rejected these efforts, labeling them a "liberal, fascist program inaugurated under Obama." Because they experienced CVE as a criminalizing project that enhanced coercive policing in their community, some Somali organizers framed CVE as a form of violence that denied them their humanity and blamed them for their "Muslim problem." They rejected police-led "community outreach" programs as seductive tools to gather information on community members and therefore facilitate preemptive arrests. Although they lived in a disinvested community, Somali organizers objected to the provision of social services on the premise that they were "ticking time bombs" rather than community members deserving of resources, support, and political power (participant observation, April 21, 2017).

Even though local practitioners conceptualized CVE as an alternative to conventional counterterrorism measures, the AIMCOP initiative reveals how federal, state, and local law enforcement agencies have gathered actionable intelligence through community engagement. An FBI (2015b) memorandum summarizing the 2015 White House Summit on CVE, for example, reported that "countering violent extremism (CVE) has been a centerpiece of this Administration's counterterrorism strategy" (1). In 2015, the FBI Office of Partner Engagement convened a Countering Violent Extremism Conference for agents and analysts "who have oversight of or involvement in counterterrorism matters" (2015, 1). In a summary of its conference objectives, the FBI stated that its CVE efforts "strengthen our investigative, intelligence gathering, and collaborative abilities to be proactive in countering violent extremism by addressing catalysts leading to radicalization and mobilization" (2). For the FBI, the "four pillars of the CVE paradigm" consisted of "Partnerships, Engagement, Prevention, and Intervention" (2). Organized around these pillars, the FBI CVE strategy "buil[t] on existing, and increasingly new, trusted partnerships with law enforcement and community organizations" (2). The FBI also described intentions to "develop a community-led committee who will share the responsibility to provide an off ramp in order to discourage individuals from going down the path of targeted violence" (3). The conference training sought to "inform field office management about how to set up, resource, and conduct intervention teams with their communities" (3). Contrary to how local practitioners conceptualized CVE, these federal memoranda and convenings clearly positioned CVE as an intelligence-gathering project involving FBI agents.

As CVE practitioners sought to distance themselves from police-led initiatives, these federal commitments and local community-policing practices cast suspicion on all CVE programs, regardless of their actual relationship with law enforcement. In this charged context, CVE practitioners like Junaid Afeef struggled to demonstrate how their own efforts to train mental health professionals to identify and work with individuals vulnerable to violence had learned from these toxic practices. The Arab American Action Network (AAAN) (2017), for example, warned that local communities should "not be deceived by a softer, gentler CVE" offered by Afeef (para. 1). More specifically, AAAN explained that "the problem for members of our communities is not that we are becoming radicalized; the problem is that we are victims of hyper-surveillance, of being constantly marked as the embodiment of the enemy of the United States, of rampant harassment and entrapment" (para. 7). Although Afeef (2018) argued that cooperating with the U.S. security state to address "all forms of targeted violence" could safeguard civil liberties, reduce the criminalization of Muslim communities, and protect youth from terrorist influences, organizations like AAAN refused to engage with local CVE efforts, even the new generation of programs that sought to remedy past mistakes. Instead, AAAN rejected CVE's organizing logics and sought to protect children from the U.S. security state.

Like AAAN, some community organizers argued that CVE unfairly criminalized Muslim youth, denied them their humanity, and demolished their "safe spaces." In a public statement, Muslim college students across the United States affirmed that they "completely condemn the CVE program," citing how it "has marginalized and Otherized the Muslim community," "assumes that we as Muslims are inherently criminals," and "tries to infiltrate our communities." A Somali community organizer similarly criticized his elders for participating in the "CVE industry," warning that "the fire lit by hypocrites will burn the believer too" (participant observation, April 21, 2017). Informed by their experiences with local programming, some youth rejected CVE's organizing assumptions and the policing practices these assumptions authorized.

Other youth organizers placed CVE within a broader framework of colonial conquest and enduring colonial narratives that have justified U.S. empire as a humanitarian project. College student Hodan Hassan, for example, credited CVE's popularity with the strategic advancement of a "colonial discourse" that suggests that CVE can "civilize the savage" and that Somali youth should gratefully say, "Thank you for bringing us to America and civilizing us and putting pants on us." Rather than "venerate whiteness," Hassan encouraged her peers to recognize that they were "fully human" by rejecting CVE and its organizing logics that positioned Muslim youth as ticking time bombs, only deserving of social services to enhance national security.

Through these critiques, youth organizers revealed how CVE articulated with global operations of U.S. empire by conflating internal and external enemies and rehearsing colonial narratives of the "civilizational threat" putatively posed by Muslims. In this view, CVE itself was organized around damaging assumptions about political violence that harmed targeted communities. As Cilmi reported, CVE logics influenced local social service providers who came to view Somali through a radicalization lens. Regardless of the role of law enforcement in local CVE programming, youth organizers challenged the concept of violent extremism and the use of social service providers to identify, report, and work with youth perceived to be vulnerable to violent extremism.

Rather than conceptualize CVE as a more humane global war on terror strategy, some youth organizers experienced (and resisted) CVE as a type of social death, the systematic process by which individuals are denied their humanity. Although CVE did not always produce the spectacular violence of FBI stings or police killings, CVE inflicted a slow violence on "Muslim-looking" youth through constant criminalization, surveillance, and monitoring. These practices have intensified police power, both its mundane and spectacular expressions.

Mothers and Sisters: The First Line of Defense

This "whole of community" CVE approach also mobilized women, using feminist discourses to position "mothers and sisters" as both agents of change and victims of violent extremism. Zaghari, for example, explained that "it's important to see women as change agents and heroes, not just victims. So, women and mothers and sisters and family members may be that first line of defense. In other words, in this country and in other countries, while fathers are out earning a living and may not be home as often, it is the mother that would first recognize those warning signs [of violent extremism]." From Zaghari's perspective, women served as "an accompaniment to the male aspect of [CVE]" and "important leaders and change agents in radicalization and countering violent extremism" (participant observation, August 18, 2016). Drawing from dominant gender norms, CVE practitioners affirmed women's role as protectors and caregivers in the fight against homegrown terrorism.

Mustafa Hawari also affirmed that, in the CVE context, "family is really the central focus" and that "the mother is even more important than the father because the kids listen to their mother while they obey their father." Because "Arab and Muslim children obey their father, but they listen to their mother about almost everything, the mother plays a bigger role in this society." Given this domestic role, Hawari argued that "giving support to the mother is perhaps more helpful and more powerful than, say, to the father. It's just something to put some emphasis on the mother and give her the kind of support she needs" like "social services and anything you can give to the mother" (participant observation, October 7, 2016). By framing the "family context" as the woman's domain, CVE actors charged women with preventing violent extremism, thereby securitizing their homes.

Following these heteropatriarchal norms, some CVE practitioners developed programs explicitly aimed at mobilizing women to combat violent extremism. The organization Sisters Against Violent Extremism (SAVE), for example, "designed and implemented a locally-tailored [set] of what are called Mothers Schools." Through the Mothers Schools, SAVE "identified a group of key women influencers in the community and trained them in how to, in a family context, recognize possible signs of radicalization and be able to give them culturally-appropriate, locally-resonant techniques for how to deal with that. Again, from a family context." SAVE schooled mothers in how to identify the warning signs of radicalization and to "deal with" the problem of violent extremism in their homes (Williams, participant observation, October 7, 2016).

To conscript women into this gendered national security work in the United States, CVE actors circulated tragic narratives about children who joined terrorist groups. In 2013, the Midaynta Community Services and the Somali Action Alliance Education Fund began an initiative called the Broken Dreams Project. The Broken Dreams Project involved "mothers who came together and said, 'We want to talk [to] the community about what we felt when our children left to join a terrorist organization.'" Through this narrative campaign, mothers retold the devastating details of losing their children to terrorist recruiters. One mother detailed "how she found out about the death of her child" by watching CNN. She also evocatively described the "pain of losing him" (Emily Evans, participant observation, October 7, 2016). The resultant *Broken Dreams* documentary "showcases the plight of families whose sons had joined Al-Shabaab" (Jama, Niyozov, and Yusuf 2015, 3). After screening the film, researchers reported that "the stories of the grieving Somali mothers and fathers" effectively "moved community members in our audience" and "awoke many to the grim reality of violent extremist groups preying on our youth" (4).

By exploiting the pain and loss of mothers, the Broken Dreams Project convinced its viewing audience of the urgency behind countering violent extremism and reaffirmed that terrorists "preyed" on youth. In doing so, the Broken Dreams Project sought to mobilize "programs and groups that will come out of the community and give that space to be creative" and to establish "proper outreach" (Evans, participant observation, October 7, 2016). Yusuf Elmi similarly reported that U.S. Attorney Andrew Luger "took the mother of one of the kids who was arrested all over [Minnesota] to preach the message that my kid was a terrorist . . . so we have to work with the law enforcement" to prevent future arrests (interview, April 14, 2017). These provocative narratives have justified CVE as a necessary project to protect youth from the tragedies exacted through terrorist recruitment. Mothers' grief both justified and advanced the CVE policy framework, turning the home into a key battleground in the fight against terrorism.

The cinematic memorialization of Somali youth fused individual losses with collective grief. These stories, however, articulated with a "hierarchy of the dead" such that these painful losses were important insomuch as they could set in motion a national security response to protect deserving lives (Sturken 2002, 383). Individual losses evoke collective grief because the dead signal the acute insecurity that blankets the United States and stir the emotional demand to prevent future losses. By coupling grief with national security, "national civic identity has been experienced as a trauma that conflates patriotism, suffering, and abhorrence for what is construed as oppositional to 'America'" (Berlant 1997, 1). These governing narratives of a "traumatized identity" have "dramatically reshaped the dominant account of U.S. citizenship," such that the "good citizen" both mourns those who "go missing" and militates against those who could inflict such trauma in the future (1). It is not an individual loss of a Somali child that stirs the United States to action; it is the fear of what could be lost—our own corporeal vulnerability—that mobilizes the U.S. public to action, participating in racialized efforts to reduce the social conditions that generate violence and to punish those who threaten the nation. These grief-stricken narratives render a "cartography designed to bring relief to 'us' while bringing 'them' *into* relief; at once a therapeutic and a vengeful gesture, its object was to reveal the face of the other *as* other" (Gregory 2004, 49). This affective campaign both denied Somali youth of their humanity and exploited their deaths to justify CVE programming in local communities.

The stories of heroic and traumatized "mothers and sisters" articulate with other feminist narratives mobilized in the service of the global war on terror. As pictures of burqa-clad Afghan women circulated in U.S. media immediately following 9/11, "the task of liberating Afghan women was . . . conveniently grafted onto the war agenda" (Chishti and Farhoumand-Sims 2011, 122). This epistemic project engages "colonial feminism," a feminism "used against other cultures in the service of colonialism . . . tailored to fit the particular culture that was the immediate target of domination" (L. Ahmed 1992, 151). First Lady Laura Bush (2001), for instance, argued that U.S. "military gains" across Afghanistan helped "fight against terrorism" and "fight for the rights and dignity of women." Given the perceived success of U.S. military operations, Bush concluded that Afghan women were "no longer imprisoned in their homes. They can listen to music and teach their daughters without fear of punishment." Bush thus humanized war by framing it as a feminist mechanism to secure the rights of dispossessed Muslim women and creating a "gendered imperative" that produces a "greater rationale for war" (M. J. Alexander 2005, 98). CVE actors have extracted these colonial feminist narratives and applied them to domestic communities by positioning CVE as a feminist national security approach that both protected U.S.-based Muslim women from future trauma and called on them as "heroic women" who could undertake this work from their homes. By activating feminist discourses, CVE actors framed this gendered work as a culturally responsive and progressive retooling of the war on terror. This is how "CVE is done in the furtherance of the American project, which is violence" (Axado Isnino, participant observation, April 21, 2017).

Slow Violence: New Forms of Shock and Awe

Isnino's analysis of CVE points to a deeper set of imperial power relations that generate daily violence through the ongoing surveillance, monitoring, and policing of Muslim communities as internal threats to national security. Despite the intensified focus on FBI stings or police killings, political geographer Simon Springer (2012) explains that "the material 'act' of violence itself is merely a nodal point, a snapshot of oppressive social relations" (138). Rather than register violence only in its spectacular forms, social scientists must examine the banal, embodied, and visceral geographies of war that exact a gradual and incremental violence on targeted populations. Such an approach captures the multiple specters that targeted youth like Isnino have confronted, rendering a more complex analysis of state violence.

Indigenous scholars have centered these slow violences in their study of and resistance to settler colonialism. Drawing from her study of child welfare policies that disrupt Indigenous homescapes, political geographer Sarah de Leeuw (2016) maps the "biopolitics of colonialism acting through legal mechanisms that are used by government representatives such as social workers, police officers, and judges to enact this slow and everyday violence of Indigenous erasure" (20). Through child welfare policies, for example, the state removes Indigenous children from their homes, an unspectacular form of violence that "slowly but very surely" kills Indigenous cultures, families, and their relationship with land (21). These "quotidian defamations of personhood inflected at an insistent pace" inflict a slow and steady violence on Indigenous communities (Stoler 2016, 8). Rather than only focus on the deaths of Indigenous children under the care of the state, we must register how child removal policies exact a slow violence aimed at eliminating Indigenous cultures, families, and peoples.

Calling attention to these gradual and attritional forms of violence, Robert Nixon (2011) contends that violence is not always "spectacular nor instantaneous" but instead "incremental and accretive" (2). Reversing Clausewitz's famous dictum that "war is politics by other means," Colleen Bell (2011) argues that "civilian interventions integral to counterinsurgency render *policy as a war by other means*" (311–12, emphasis added). This reversal "accounts for the way in which civilian power relations—and in this context, those power relations at play within the institutions of liberal modernity—are themselves invested in the forces of war" (312). By complementing calibrated violence, counterinsurgent tactics, like racialized surveillance and the strategic provision of social services, have inflicted a slow violence on targeted populations.

Through the recasting of community spaces like schools and mosques as critical national security sites to thwart the "generational threat," Muslim youth came of age under constant surveillance. Community organizers like Isnino described these criminalizing experiences as a type of social death slowly inflicted on their communities. One community organizer, for example, reported that "as a Muslim American," CVE "makes me feel criminalized. It makes me feel like because of my religious identity, I will be viewed through the lens of national security. It makes me feel like I am viewed as a potential terrorist first, a counterterrorism tool second, and an everyday, normal American citizen entitled to their constitutional freedoms last" (participant observation, August 20, 2017). For young adults like Isnino, CVE worked from the premise that their "humanity is subpar" and that Muslims were "savage," racist discourses that authorized the "civilizing" of Muslim communities through psychosocial, religious, and cultural reprogramming. Cilmi rejected educational initiatives that contributed to cultural genocide and epistemicide, asking, "How can I assimilate into a racist culture?" By calling attention to these "quotidian defamations of personhood inflected at an insistent pace," targeted youth framed CVE as a type of violence aimed at Muslim erasure.

In response to these dehumanizing processes, youth of color sometimes acted as "subversive beings" who contested the policies and programs that criminalized their bodies, religions, beliefs, thoughts, imaginations, and cultures (paperson 2017, xiii). Community organizers, for example, questioned the use of social services funded by CVE, noting that "the money is coming from the same police that racially profile us on the streets." Another organizer asked:

> When we say that we're trying to identify who is susceptible to violence before they commit anything, who is it that's deciding who those people are that are susceptible? Is it the same police who decide to shoot Black people who are selling a cigarette or a young Black child who has a toy gun in a park? 'Cause if you're working with those same institutions, I don't trust that they are able to identify who is susceptible to violence when time and time again we have said that these theories have been debunked. (participant observation, August 20, 2017)

Rather than rely on "the same institutions" that criminalize, brutalize, and murder Black children, these community organizers began developing structures and supports independent of the U.S. security state, ultimately redefining the concept of security.

By placing CVE in relationship to anti-Black and anti-immigrant

policing, Muslim youth began forging alternative futures that radically reimagined prevailing notions of public safety, national security,
and freedom. As one organizer concluded, "true power—and where
justice will come from and where freedom will come from—is the
power of people. It's not going to be based on money that is coming
from a government that we have seen oppress people through various
methods" (participant observation, August 20, 2017). It is to these
co-constitutive power relations and the freedom dreams they have
inspired that I now turn.

CONCLUSION
Reimagining National Security

The fake road, its cruel deception, is what we have to abandon.
—Adrienne Rich, *The School among Ruins*

In 2017, a former gang-involved student reported that U.S. Immigration and Customs Enforcement (ICE) agents raided his Chicago home in search of an undocumented immigrant. During the raid, the agents showed the student a picture of their suspect, describing him as a Muslim man and imminent national security threat. When the student commented that the person "looked Mexican not Muslim," the agents argued that Muslims "hide out" in Mexican neighborhoods because "they can blend in." After searching the student's home, the agents left. A few days later, another ICE agent called the student to report that he was "all clear" and then demanded the names of any undocumented immigrants living nearby (personal communication).

By insisting that Muslims hid in Mexican neighborhoods and confirming that a person could "look Muslim," ICE agents mapped the "terrorist/criminal" label onto a strategically ambiguous Brown body to justify their raid under the rubric of national security. The process of re-racializing Mexicans as Muslim criminalizes all Brown bodies as potential criminals and possible terrorists. These messy interactions create a malleable category of "terrorist/criminal" that can be deployed to target Brown bodies as threats to both public safety and national security. This example illustrates how the national security drive to police "Muslim-looking" populations has enhanced the U.S.

security state and its targeting of Black, Brown, and immigrant bodies and communities.

This terrifying act of state-sponsored violence also reveals how technologies of control traffic across time, space, and contexts, transmuting policing practices that reaffirm racial hierarchies. la paperson (2017) similarly reports how "technologies of antiblackness circulate onto non-Black bodies. In a U.S.-Mexican borderland context, for example, we see the condensation of anti-Black and anti-Indigenous technologies to dispose of brown bodies and to create frontier space—a militarized zone of policing and death" (12). Documenting similar transpositions, one community organizer argued, "When we talk about the war on terror and how Muslims have been criminalized, we have to make the connection to the war on drugs and the way that Black people have been criminalized for years" (participant observation, August 20, 2017). This organizer argued that CVE has drawn from and intensified coercive policing practices that have criminalized, enclosed, and eliminated Black bodies. In this view, CVE programs have strengthened anti-Muslim racism and reinforced the policing of Black, Brown, and immigrant communities through the application of similar technologies of control, ontological illegality, and lethal geographies. CVE thus is an instructive case as it illuminates the technological transits of racial hierarchies and associated policing practices used to control, assimilate, and/or eliminate racialized bodies. These discursive and material circulations maintain racial hierarchies while obscuring the role of racism in criminalizing certain bodies, cultures, and communities as internal threats to "homeland and hometown security."

Despite the utility in mapping these transits, not all technologies are comparable. One incomparable technology of anti-Blackness, for example, "is the production of the Black body as in itself the preeminent site for antiblackness," whereas "settler technologies can focus on space, and technologies of Indigenous erasure can focus on land" (paperson 2017, 12). As these distinct yet co-constitutive technologies mutate and transit, they connect racial hierarchies, corresponding practices of state-sanctioned violence, and struggles for freedom and liberation. These transmutable technologies, however, produce differential forms of state-sanctioned violence. Although Muslim communities live under constant surveillance and intimidation that produce an "internment of the psyche" (Naber 2006), these racialized technologies of control are distinct from the hyperincarceration and police killings of Black people.

In this racialized context, "the state recruits people of color to demand their due recognition as deserving U.S. citizens or law-abiding immigrants" by "disavowing another devalued racial other of U.S. citizenship and American empire" (Cacho 2012, 15). Unfortunately, "there is no way out of this dilemma because recuperating social value *requires* rejecting the other Other" (17). Documented immigrants, for example, sometimes mark themselves as "deserving citizens" by demonizing undocumented immigrants, ultimately reaffirming technologies of statecraft (legal citizenship) that support racial hierarchies. For Muslims "cast out" of U.S. citizenship through racial and religious profiling, participating in CVE initiatives has offered political power, cultural recognition, and community resources (Razack 2008). As Yusuf Elmi warned, the U.S. security state has cultivated this impossible dilemma to fuel an "internal war" that distracts from "challenging the government."

To recuperate their social value in this charged context, some Muslim leaders eagerly accepted opportunities within the U.S. security state to restrain racialized surveillance and institute a more community-driven domestic antiterrorism initiative that "learned from past mistakes." Guided by these commitments, some Muslim leaders engaged the U.S. security state through CVE initiatives while marking those who refused to participate in these collaborations as "ostriches" unwilling to acknowledge the problem of terrorist radicalization in their own homes, community centers, and places of worship. To establish more liberal national security policies that affirmed the social and cultural value of their communities, some Muslim leaders sought inclusion into the U.S. political establishment by contributing to CVE while others rejected such institutional arrangements as additive reforms incapable of transforming oppressive systems.

Unfortunately, the U.S. security state has designed CVE to legitimize and shore up support for the very institutions that historically have criminalized communities of color, while appearing to learn from and attenuate past practices of coercive policing, racial profiling, and political exclusion. This means that struggles to make U.S. security regimes more liberal—"participatory," "democratic," and "community-driven"—have led to the increased surveillance and monitoring of Muslim communities, particularly by calling on racialized populations to serve as terrorist watchdogs and giving law enforcement access to spaces otherwise unavailable to them. Although CVE practitioner Junaid Afeef (2018) encouraged the "cooperation of government with groups like Muslim Advocates and ACLU of Illinois" to ensure the protection of civil liberties and civil rights in pursuit of national security, increasing community collaborations with government organizations has enhanced, rather than destabilized, the U.S. security state while reaffirming CVE's organizing logics that "leech out the political dynamics" of extremist groups by amplifying the atomistic study of individual motivations "with little if any regard to what [people] may be fighting for" (Li 2015, paras. 21–22). This approach reduces political violence to an individual radicalization process defined by cultural, psychological, and theological pathologies.

Informed by radicalization research, the U.S. security state has engaged "moderate Muslims" and social service providers to enhance its daily operations, without abandoning its more coercive practices like FBI stings, intelligence-gathering activities, and war-making. Social service providers therefore have come to view their clients through an antiterrorism lens, sometimes equating common immigrant experiences like homesickness as signs of radicalization. As one component of a multipronged approach to combatting terrorism, CVE has contributed to, and articulated with, more coercive antiterrorism methods by strengthening community-police partnerships, deputizing community members as terrorist watchdogs, and reinforcing dominant radicalization narratives.

Given the operational failures of CVE and its damaging logics, targeted communities have reaffirmed their commitment to building alternative forms of public safety independent of the policing institutions that have oppressed, surveilled, and controlled them across history. In this view, the drive for recognition by, and integration into, the U.S. political establishment has reinforced rather than disrupted contemporary racial hierarchies and national security regimes that harm Muslim communities and articulate with anti-Black, anti-Brown, and anti-immigrant policing. These political struggles therefore have refused liberal reforms like "community-driven" antiterrorism initiatives that do not contest the institutions, practices, and logics that criminalize communities of color. Rather than "remain[] dependent on their oppressors for their freedom and self-worth," anti-CVE organizers have struggled against the "assimilative lure of colonial recognition" by creating alternative forms of self-recognition and developing new methods to ensure community safety without relying on the U.S. security state (Coulthard 2014, 43).

Against Deceptive Solutions: A Struggle for Freedom

Although I was drawn to the unsure and hesitant contradictions CVE actors regularly expressed, the fierce organizing and political imaginations of targeted communities compelled me to reorient my ethnographic gaze. I learned, firsthand, how institutions and policies do not always produce their intended results and often carry subversive beings who refuse to consent to their dehumanization. In the CVE context, community organizers have connected freedom struggles across targeted communities to incubate revolutionary dreams aimed at liberation.

In their analyses and struggles for freedom, community organizers have crafted "scale-jumping" and "geography-crossing" counter-topographies that intentionally connect "disparate places similarly constituted or affected by certain problems" (C. Katz 2001a, 1216, 2008, 25–26). Although topographies explore the social and historical relations through which places are made, counter-topographies examine how expansive social processes link seemingly disparate places and struggles together. Counter-topographies therefore cultivate political imaginations that connect distinct yet co-constitutive systems of oppression and freedom struggles, from anti-Black police brutality in Chicago to anti-Muslim national security policies in Minneapolis to U.S. military operations in Iraq. These political imaginations importantly locate state violence within global systems of dominance like gendered racial capitalism and heteropatriarchal colonialism that disproportionately harm nondominant communities.

By drawing counter-topographical contour lines between anti-Black, anti-Brown, anti-Muslim, and anti-immigrant racisms, community organizers affirmed their commitment to "stand up against any and all programs that work to criminalize our community." In

Minneapolis, two hundred demonstrators took to the streets to protest CVE, call for the end of the global war on terror, and support the Movement for Black Lives and the Indigenous struggle to stop the Dakota Access Pipeline. In Chicago, community organizers collectively have struggled to end state-sanctioned violence by drawing connections between anti-Muslim surveillance, immigrant detention and deportation, the police department's discriminatory gang database, the disappearance of Black girls and women, and the global war on terror. In Los Angeles, community organizers studied the mass incarceration of U.S.-Japanese families during World War II and its resonance in contemporary anti-Muslim surveillance practices. Recognizing these interrelated forms of state violence, communities have developed viable alternatives that reduce our dependence on police interventions, like creating community-based crisis assistance teams that respond to mental health emergencies without law enforcement (Meiners 2016; Berger, Kaba, and Stein 2017; Kaba and Meiners 2014). Through these struggles, community organizers have come to imagine and build alternative futures within oppressive contexts not of their own making.

In our various roles as academics, community members, and political subjects, we must continue to take our cue from community organizers who connect oppressive institutions and refuse security reforms that do not challenge the institutional arrangements that criminalize communities of color, from new community policing paradigms to "ideologically ecumenical" CVE programs. As Angela Davis (2016) instructs, "Our understandings of and resistance to contemporary modes of racist violence should . . . be sufficiently capacious to acknowledge the embeddedness of historical violence—of settler colonial violence against Native Americans and of the violence of slavery inflicted on Africans" (82). These "deep understandings of racist violence arm us against deceptive solutions. When we are told that we simply need better police and better prisons, we counter with what we really need. We need to reimagine security, which will involve the abolition of policing and imprisonment as we know them" (90). Through their intensive study of and experiences with structural racism, colonialism, and state-sponsored violence, Muslim organizers came to view CVE as a "deceptive solution" that encouraged working with, rather than dismantling, the U.S. security state on the premise that "our kids are inherently violent and in need of rehabilitation" (participant observation, April 21, 2017). Instead of calling for better or more community-driven domestic war on terror initiatives, community organizers began developing alternative forms of safety and security independent of "the same institutions" that "we have seen oppress people through various methods" since the creation of slave patrols and Indian constables (participant observation, August 20, 2017).

By imagining a world without CVE and establishing community resources independent of national security funding, community organizers have begun transforming the conditions that have shaped their everyday lives, reaching for freedom, liberation, and self-determination. Rather than rely on oppressive institutions to ensure public safety and grant political recognition, communities have struggled for these ends themselves. With political, intellectual, and moral clarity, one community organizer concluded, "We're going to do it ourselves."

APPENDIX
An Overview of National Security Policies in the United States

Although not exhaustive, this is an overview of U.S. policies that have informed contemporary security regimes.

1798 Sedition Act	This act criminalized the making of "false, scandalous, and malicious writing" intending to "stir up sedition" against the United States government.
1882 Chinese Exclusion Act	This act instituted a ten-year moratorium on Chinese labor migration.
1903 Alien Immigration Act (Anarchist Exclusion Act)	This act regulated immigration into the United States, creating four new inadmissible classes: anarchists, people with intellectual and psychiatric disabilities, "professional beggars," and sex workers and traffickers.
1917 Espionage Act	As the United States entered World War I, this act prohibited protesting the war and criminalized the distribution of information to interfere with the U.S. war effort or aid U.S. enemies.
1917 Literacy Act	This act imposed the first restriction on immigration through a literacy test and excluded immigration from the "Asiatic Barred Zone."

1918 Sedition Act	This act amended the Espionage Act to prohibit antigovernment political speech, including "disloyal, profane, scurrilous, or abusive language about the form of the Government of the United States."
1918 Dillingham-Hardwick Act	This act excluded and expelled noncitizens who were members of anarchist and similar groups.
1921 Emergency Quota Act	This act instituted quotas to limit the number of immigrants from each sending country using the National Origins Formula.
1924 Johnson-Reed Act	This act recalibrated the National Origins Formula to further limit immigration and authorized the exclusion of any immigrant whose race or nationality rendered them ineligible for U.S. citizenship, like the Japanese.
1938–1944 House Un-American Activities Committee	This House of Representatives committee investigated the subversive and communist activities of private citizens.
1939 Hatch Act	This act limited the political activities of federal employees.
1940 Alien Registration Act	This act prohibited advocating the overthrow of the government, authorized the deportation of any noncitizen engaged in subversive activities, and required noncitizens to register and be fingerprinted.
1947 Taft-Hartley Act	By amending the National Labor Relations Act, this legislation restricted the organizing activities and power of labor unions.
1947 National Security Act	This act established the National Security Council and Central Intelligence Agency (CIA).
1950 McCarran Internal Security Act	To protect the United States from "un-American and subversive activities," this act required community organizations to register with the U.S. Attorney General and authorized the investigation of persons suspected of engaging in subversive activities.

1954 Communist Control Act

Since the 1950 Internal Security Act did not criminalize affiliation with the Communist Party, this legislation made membership to the Communist Party a criminal act. Although this act still exists, no administration has enforced it.

1965 Immigration and Naturalization Act

This act abolished the immigration quota system and sought to reunite families and attract skilled labor to the United States.

1969 *Brandenburg v. Ohio*

Appealing the conviction of Ku Klux Klan leader Clarence Brandenburg who called for revenge against people of color at a rally, this case decided that the United States cannot criminalize expressions of extremist ideology.

1972–1975 Operation Boulder

Following the 1972 Munich Olympic massacre, this Nixon-era program authorized the FBI to conduct special screenings of Arab visa applications.

1979 Iranian registry

Following the 1979 Iranian Hostage Crisis, the Carter administration mobilized the Immigration and Naturalization Service (INS) to register the seventy-five thousand Iranian students studying in the United States.

1980 First Joint Terrorism Task Force

The FBI and NYPD initiated the first Joint Terrorism Task Force (JTTF).

1984 Comprehensive Crime Control Act

In addition to revising the U.S. Criminal Code, this act authorized the FBI to conduct investigations.

1987 Los Angeles Eight trial and the "Alien Terrorists and Undesirables: A Contingency Plan" memo

These court proceedings tried eight people speciously charged with providing financial support to the Popular Front for the Liberation of Palestine. This legal process revealed a DOJ "contingency plan" for the mass arrest of thousands of "alien activists" from Algeria, Iran, Jordan, Lebanon, Libya, Morocco, Syria, and Tunisia. Once detained, the DOJ planned to incarcerate these individuals in remote internment camps in Louisiana.

1989 Terrorist Threat Warning System

The FBI developed this system to communicate with other law enforcement agencies about imminent terrorist threats.

1990 Aviation Security Improvement Act	Following the Lockerbie bombing, this act strengthened airport security and subjected airline personnel to stricter screening procedures.
1991 Special Registration Program	This program required the special registration of persons holding Iraqi and Kuwaiti passports and/or travel documents.
1995 FBI made lead agency	President Reagan designated the FBI as the lead agency in responding to terrorist threats and attacks.
1996 Antiterrorism and Effective Death Penalty Act	Following the Oklahoma City bombing, this act criminalized providing material support to foreign (but not domestic) terrorist organizations, among other provisions.
1996 FBI Counterterrorism Center established	The FBI developed a Counterterrorism Center to combat both international and domestic terrorism.
1998 Center for Domestic Preparedness established	In 1998, the FBI Counterterrorism Center began training emergency responders.
2001 Uniting and Strengthening America by Providing Appropriate Tools Required to Intercept and Obstruct Terrorism Act (USA PATRIOT Act)	Passed after the September 11 attacks, this act authorized efforts to deter and punish terrorists and enhanced the investigatory tools of law enforcement, particularly through wiretapping and surveillance.
2001 Twenty-day hold on visa applications	The U.S. State Department issued a classified cable that imposed a twenty-day hold on all nonimmigrant visa applications submitted by men, aged eighteen to forty-five, from twenty-six countries.
2002 Alien Absconder Initiative	This INS initiative sought to find and deport six thousand noncitizen men from Middle Eastern countries with a pending deportation order.
2002 INS selective enforcement of section 265(a) of the Immigration and Naturalization Act	Section 265(a) of the Immigration and Naturalization Act requires people to register their address change within ten days of moving, which has been enforced selectively.
2002 Homeland Security Act	This act created the Department of Homeland Security and the Secretary of Homeland Security.

2002 Enhanced Border Security and Visa Entry Reform Act

Passed after the September 11 attacks, this act made the INS/ICE database interoperable, required that federal law enforcement and intelligence agencies share data with INS/ICE and the State Department, and mandated that all travel documents include a biometric identifier.

2002–2016 National Security Entry-Exit Registration System (NSEERS)

NSEERS facilitated the special registration of certain noncitizens within the United States as well as nonimmigrant men and boys from Arab and Muslim-majority countries. The process included being photographed, interviewed, and fingerprinted.

2006–present NYPD surveillance

In 2006, the NYPD formally began surveilling colleges, including Muslim Student Associations, in the name of national security.

2007–2009 FBI Operation Rhino

As an FBI counterterrorism project, Operation Rhino sought to disrupt al-Shabaab recruitment through counter-messaging, collaborations with local elders, and surveillance in the Twin Cities.

2008 Controlled Application Review and Resolution Program (CARRP)

CARRP is a covert operation that has given extra scrutiny to immigrants and noncitizens arriving in the United States from Arab, Middle Eastern, Muslim, and South Asian countries. The extra scrutiny has caused long delays in the processing of applications.

2008–2014 Secure Communities Initiative

This ICE program facilitated data and biometric sharing and analysis between police departments and immigration agencies to enhance immigration enforcement and deportation.

2010 National launch of If You See Something, Say Something®

Initially a New York City Metropolitan Transportation Authority initiative, this DHS project raised public awareness of the indicators of terrorism and encouraged the reporting of suspicious activities.

2010 National launch of the Nationwide Suspicious Activity Reporting Initiative (NSI)

As a multiagency effort, the NSI has collected and shared "suspicious activity reports" with local, state, and federal law enforcement.

2015 White House Summit on CVE	The Obama administration convened a three-day summit with local, state, federal, and global leaders to discuss CVE.
2015 DHS Office for Community Partnerships instituted	In 2015, DHS created the OCP to enhance its community partnerships to develop programs that counter violent extremism.
2016 CVE Task Force launched	According to DHS, the U.S. government formed this interagency task force to unify the domestic CVE effort by bringing together experts from DHS, DOJ, FBI, and NCTC.
2016 Bureau of Counterterrorism redesigned	In 2016, the Obama administration reorganized the Bureau of Counterterrorism, including rebranding it as the Bureau of Counterterrorism and Countering Violent Extremism.
2017 Executive Order 13769: Protecting the Nation from Foreign Terrorist Entry into the United States	This Trump administration executive order (EO) banned all travelers from Iran, Iraq, Libya, Somalia, Sudan, Syria, and Yemen for at least 90 days, including U.S. permanent residents. It also suspended the United States Refugee Admissions Program and related refugee settlement for 120 days. A temporary restraining order rendered the EO moot.
2017 Executive Order 13780: Protecting the Nation from Foreign Terrorist Entry into the United States	Revising EO 13769, this EO banned the entry of travelers from Iran, Libya, Somalia, Sudan, Syria, and Yemen for at least 90 days, excluding U.S. permanent residents. It also suspended the United States Refugee Admissions Program and related refugee settlement for 120 days. In March 2017, this order expired, after federal court rulings placed a nationwide block on its provisions.
2017 Presidential Proclamation 9645: Enhancing Vetting Capabilities and Processes for Detecting Attempted Entry into the United States by Terrorists or Other Public-Safety Threats	Colloquially known as "Muslim Ban 3.0," this proclamation has banned the entry of travelers from Chad, Iran, Libya, North Korea, Syria, Venezuela, and Yemen until these countries improve their immigration screening and vetting procedures. In April 2018, the Trump administration lifted the restrictions on Chad. In June 2018, the Supreme Court upheld this proclamation.

NOTES

Introduction

1. Nancy Hiemstra (2014) argues that the term *homeland security* has become "the anchor for a powerful normative discourse, scripted and manipulated by authors of statecraft" (572). The concept of the "homeland" denotes and generates fear of the "excludable foreigner" (572). Recognizing how discursive representations of the "homeland" install the ideological undercurrents that drive the global war on terror and the criminalization of Muslim communities, I use the term *national security,* unless referencing a research participant, policy, or program. Recognizing the transnational flows of gendered racial capital, policing, war, and empire, I use the term *U.S. security state* rather than *U.S. national security state.* This follows Grewal (2017), who refers to the current phase of U.S. empire as the "security state" to mark the turn to war as the primary means to maintain its superpower status.

2. See, for example, Los Angeles Interagency Coordination Group in collaboration with community stakeholders 2015; Weine 2012; Weine and Ahmed 2012; Police Foundation 2016; United States Attorney's Office of Minneapolis 2015; Nashville International Center for Empowerment 2016; and Denver Police Department 2016.

3. Pursue works to "stop terrorist attacks" by detecting and prosecuting terrorists. Protect intensifies the United Kingdom's "protection against a terrorist attack" by enhancing the security of its borders, transportation systems, and critical infrastructures. Prepare seeks to "mitigate the impact of a terrorist attack" by establishing emergency management procedures (Her Majesty's Government 2011, 6).

4. U.N. Special Rapporteur Ben Emmerson (2016) explains that despite the primacy of CVE, "there is no generally acceptable definition of violent extremism" and no clear distinction between violent extremism and terrorism (4). In this book, I use these two terms interchangeably.

5. Although most Somalis with whom I spoke referred to themselves as "Somali," they also identified as Muslim and pointed to their intersectional

experiences with CVE as Black Muslim refugees. As Somali organizers taught me, an analysis of CVE in Minneapolis cannot ignore anti-Blackness as a defining feature of this national security approach.

6. In this book, I largely refrain from using the term *American* because "America" refers to two continents. In addition, not all people living in the United States identify as Americans. In educational anthropologist Thea Renda Abu El-Haj's (2015) research, for example, youth sometimes identified as *being* Arab and *having* U.S. citizenship rather than identifying as American. By referring to participants as U.S. Muslims, Arabs, Somalis, or South Asians, I seek to disrupt the primacy of American identity and, instead, privilege the geopolitical location of research participants. In addition, I recognize the multiplicity of U.S. Muslims, noted in the use "Muslim communi*ties*" rather than "Muslim community."

7. These FBI interpretations regarding the permissibility of racial profiling conform to the DOJ's 2014 revision of its 2003 fact sheet (Department of Justice 2014a).

8. The American Civil Liberties Union created a timeline to clarify these bans and their evolution. "Timeline of the Muslim Ban," ACLU Washington, https://www.aclu-wa.org/pages/timeline-muslim-ban.

9. For a historical overview of the policies that have contributed to contemporary national security practices, please see the appendix.

10. A Freedom of Information Act (FOIA) request by Benjamin Wittes revealed that the Department of Justice data Trump cited do not exist (Wittes 2018).

11. For more on this issue, please refer to C. Katz 2001b; Naber 2008; Shryock 2008; Bayoumi 2006; and Rana 2011.

12. These violent actors include Eric Harris and Dylan Klebold (1999, Littleton, Colorado), Jared Loughner (2011, Tucson, Arizona), James Holmes (2012, Aurora, Colorado), and Adam Lanza (2012, Sandy Hook, Connecticut).

13. See, for example, Gallagher 2007; McNeal and Dunbar 2010; Casella 2003; and N. Nguyen 2013.

14. The acronym "pbuh" presumably stands for "peace be upon him," an honorific phrase used after any mention of the prophets.

15. Under the "Technical Merit" section of its grant proposal, the DPD (2016) reported that "Colorado, with a population of 5,456,574, has experienced several instances of high profile violent extremism over the past two decades. The mass shootings at Columbine High School in Littleton, Colorado, on April 20, 1999, touched off a string of domestic and foreign terrorist acts and plots in the state, the most recent being the attacks on the Aurora Movie Theater shooting in July 2012 and the attack at a Colorado Springs Planned Parenthood site in November 2015" (2). All three of these acts of violence were perpetrated by white, U.S.-born young men.

16. Later, the DPD (2016) mentioned that "the Denver Metro airport has seen [ISIS] recruiting in recent years; in 2014 an Arvada resident was caught at Denver International Airport as she attempted to travel to Syria to meet and

marry an ISIS fighter who had recruited her online. Later that same year, three Aurora teenage girls (two Somali sisters and their Sudanese friend) were also intercepted in Europe as they attempted a similar plan" (2). In this discussion, the DPD detailed the national origins of the "three Aurora teenage girls" but not the U.S.-born "Arvada resident."

17. For more on these scientific studies, please see Horgan 2008; Patel 2011; and Patel and Koushik 2017.

18. Although community organizers invited me to attend this event, these quotations come from a publicly available online recording of this public forum and subsequent media posts citing the panelists.

1. Ethnographic Dilemmas

1. To conduct this study, I hired a research assistant, Stacey Krueger, who helped interview participants, observe CVE events, analyze policy documents, transcribe interviews, and contribute to the overall analysis of CVE. We often attended CVE events together, allowing us to debrief, compare notes, and provide different interpretations of the same data. We also transcribed each other's interviews, which allowed us to become familiar with, and talk through, all data together.

2. Throughout this book, I use *CVE actors* as an umbrella term for all individuals directly involved in CVE work. The term therefore includes people in greater and lesser positions of power. Under this umbrella, I refer to street-level bureaucrats whose regular course of work involved constant contact with communities as "CVE practitioners" (Lipsky 1980). I describe individuals as "elite" if they served as powerful actors, like DHS agents or U.S. Attorneys. Given the growing commitment to "community outreach," however, high-level actors often interfaced with local clients as a part of their work while street-level bureaucrats sometimes contributed to policymaking. These conditions blurred the distinctions between these categories. Lastly, in using these terms, I recognize that all CVE actors maintained varying degrees of power, influence, and privilege within their institutions and communities. A term like *CVE practitioners* thus encompasses a range of individuals with different roles and understandings of those roles.

3. The individuals with whom we spoke were young adults, typically college students and recent high school graduates.

4. Because CVE policies have targeted youth, I use pseudonyms for all young adults, even for public statements made in public forums such as local newspapers and events livestreamed online. At one event, a former FBI agent confirmed that the U.S. security state interpreted resistance to CVE as an indicator of terrorist radicalization. Publicly resisting CVE placed youth at risk of additional surveillance, harassment, and arrest. This agent implored the audience to "stand in front of the youth to protect them" from the crosshairs of the U.S. security state as they "speak up and speak out about CVE in their own communities." Maintaining anonymity is one form of protection.

5. Sent and received through state email accounts, this message is a matter of public record and subject to Freedom of Information Act (FOIA) requests.

2. Left of Boom

1. The U.S. government has used the Racketeer Influenced and Corrupt Organizations Act (RICO) against perceived terrorist enterprises.

2. Although Kundnani (2014) uses the term *culturalists*, he notes that Mamdani (2004) uses the term *culture talk* and that Stolcke (1995) uses the term *cultural fundamentalism* to describe the same conceptual terrain (58n4).

3. In this book, I investigate explicitly liberal counterinsurgencies. As Khalili (2015) explains, "illiberal counterinsurgents—Russians in Chechnya, or the Sri Lankan defeat of the Tamil Tigers—use kinetic, or killing force indiscriminately and very often deploy the language of sovereignty as the ultimate justification for their use of force" (1). Liberal counterinsurgencies, however, "calibrate their use of force, co-opt legal and administrative apparatuses in the service of warfare, and increasingly deploy a language of humanitarianism and/or development as both the justification and impetus for war" (Khalili 2015, 1).

4. For more on the counterinsurgency cases that have informed the thinking of contemporary military strategists, please refer to Kilcullen 2010; Gorka and Kilcullen 2011; Sewall 2007; and U.S. Army/Marine Corps 2007.

5. When I asked Baker if CVE functioned as a counterinsurgency tool because "it's kinetic; it's non-kinetic; it's hearts and minds," he said, "No." For him, "Under counterinsurgency, the state oftentimes is the direct provider along all five of these lines of services [engagement, prevention, intervention, interdiction, and rehabilitation/reintegration]. Essentially, insofar as U.S. domestic CVE is concerned, there is a division of labor, at least theoretically that's meant to be there between civil society and private citizens on the one hand and state actors on the other." In other words, Baker defined CVE in opposition to counterinsurgency because CVE was enacted, "at least theoretically," by civil society and private citizens rather than state actors. However, as the Illinois Criminal Justice Information Authority's Targeted Violence Prevention Program (TVPP) demonstrates, state actors, including law enforcement agents, have funded, and contributed to, local "community-led" CVE efforts. Furthermore, CVE has mobilized "civil society and private citizens" to carry out the functions of the police.

3. "The R Word"

1. For a comprehensive summary of the indicators used to identify individuals at risk of or in the process of radicalizing, please refer to Patel, Lindsay, and DenUyl 2018a.

2. For the full study, please see Pyrooz et al. 2018.

4. Patriot Acts

1. Initially used by U.S. Counselor to the President Kellyanne Conway to reframe a false statement as factual, the term "alternative fact" is a pejorative colloquialism that describes a lie.

2. CIE stands for Countering Islamic Extremism.

3. According to its website, "The Redirect Method uses Adwords targeting tools and curated YouTube videos uploaded by people all around the world to confront online radicalization. It focuses on the slice of ISIS' audience that is most susceptible to its messaging, and redirects them towards curated YouTube videos debunking ISIS recruiting themes" (for more, please see https://redirectmethod.org/).

4. These rebranding strategies followed the DHS Homeland Security Academic Advisory Council's recommendation to use terminology that "positively resonates with intended audiences," rather than CVE (2017, 5).

5. Following these community organizations, Los Angeles mayor Eric Garcetti turned down the city's $425,000 CVE grant in 2018, after a year of community protests and public forums.

6. In fact, Aysha Khoury reported that when Muslim youth "define *their own* problem space," only 20 percent of the responses "are around anything to do with violent extremism. It's just not a major issue for anyone's life" (interview, January 25, 2017, emphasis in original).

7. Evoking Malcolm X's 1964 "Ballot or Bullet" speech, Average Mo implored Muslim youth to turn to democratic practices like voting, rather than terrorist violence, to express their political, social, and economic grievances. The choices Average Mo listed, however, constrained political expression to conventional democratic exercises rather than more radical forms of political power, including protesting in the streets and reimagining the social structures that organize everyday life in the United States. In fact, Malcom X declared in his "Ballot or Bullet" speech that "if it's necessary to form a black nationalist army, we'll form a black nationalist army. It'll be the ballot or the bullet. It'll be liberty or it'll be death." Contravening Average Mo's choice between democratic inclusion and terrorism, Malcolm X envisioned a Black nationalist movement that struggled for political independence, community control, and self-determination. Malcolm X never sought inclusion into mainstream politics; he viewed the political machine as inherently anti-Black and therefore demanded Black sovereignty, not recognition.

5. The Generational Threat

1. In addition to implementing global citizenship education, Kovac stressed the importance of using the Intercultural Development Inventory's assessment tool "to measure progress on the creation of the global citizen, from ethnocentric to ethno-relative."

2. Kovac drew from the field of international education, which has examined the relationship between conflict and education (Novelli 2010a, 2010b; Burde 2005, 2007, 2014; Bush and Saltarelli 2000).

3. https://www.operation250.org/.

4. For more on this issue, please refer to M. W. Morris 2016; Fenning and Rose 2007; Nolan 2011; Reyes 2006; Fuentes 2011; McNeal and Dunbar 2010; Verdugo 2002; Noguera 2003; Sojoyner 2016; and Vaught 2017.

5. In 2009, the FBI also launched an intelligence-gathering community engagement program called Specialized Community Outreach Teams (SCOT). The SCOT program's mission was "to strategically expand outreach to the Somali community to address counterterrorism-related issues" (Federal Bureau of Investigation 2009, 2–3). The SCOT program leveraged "FBI outreach to support operational programs" in Minneapolis, Cincinnati, Seattle, San Diego, Denver, and Washington, D.C. (7). To "establish a more focused outreach effort" with the assistance of FBI community outreach specialists, intelligence analysts, supervisory special agents, and linguists, the SCOT program developed a "baseline profile of individuals that are vulnerable to being radicalized or participating in extremist activities in order to establish a more focused outreach effort" (5). Community outreach programs like SCOT have served as "the FBI's initial conduit into the diverse communities in which we serve" and have facilitated the reporting of suspicious individuals (2).

BIBLIOGRAPHY

Aaronson, Trevor. 2013. *The Terror Factory: Inside the FBI's Manufactured War on Terrorism*. New York: Ig Publishing.

Abdi, Ali A. 2015. "Decolonizing Global Citizenship Education: Critical Reflections on the Epistemic Intersections of Location, Knowledge, and Learning." In *Decolonizing Global Citizenship Education*, edited by Ali A. Abdi, Lynette Shultz, and Thashika Pillay, 11–26. Rotterdam, Netherlands: Sense Publishers.

Abdi, Ali A., Lynette Shultz, and Thashika Pillay. 2015. "Decolonizing Global Citizenship: An Introduction." In *Decolonizing Global Citizenship Education*, edited by Ali A. Abdi, Lynette Shultz, and Thashika Pillay, 1–10. Rotterdam, Netherlands: Sense Publishers.

Abdollah, Tami. 2017. "Fourth Muslim Group Rejects Federal Grant to Fight Extremism." *Associated Press*, February 11, 2017. https://apnews.com/094bda0413674c59bdda412b3fe43749/fourth-muslim-group-rejects-federal-grant-fight-extremism.

Abu El-Haj, Thea Renda. 2015. *Unsettled Belonging: Educating Palestinian American Youth after 9/11*. Chicago: University of Chicago Press.

Abu El-Haj, Thea Renda, and Sally Wesley Bonet. 2011. "Education, Citizenship, and the Politics of Belonging: Youth from Muslim Transnational Communities and the 'War on Terror.'" *Review of Research in Education* 35 (1): 29–59. https://doi.org/10.3102/0091732X10383209.

Afeef, Junaid. 2014. "How Muslims Can Halt Extremism." *Chicago Tribune*, October 9, 2014. http://www.chicagotribune.com/news/opinion/commentary/ct-muslim-leaders-stop-radical-perspec-1009-20141008-story.html.

Afeef, Junaid. 2015. "CVE in the Illinois Muslim Community: Presentation at Community Builders Council." JunaidAfeef.net. Accessed February 2, 2018. https://junaidafeef.net/category/targeted-violence-prevention/.

Afeef, Junaid. 2018. "Preventing targeted violence & safeguarding civil liberties: Not a zero sum game." LinkedIn, July 26, 2018. https://www.linkedin.com/pulse/preventing-targeted-violence-safeguarding-civil-liberties-afeef/?published=t.

Afeef, Junaid, and Alejandro J. Beutel. 2015. "CVE Critics Are Right, and CVE Is Still Necessary." *Patheos,* July 27, 2015. http://www.patheos.com/blogs/altmuslim/2015/07/cve-critics-are-right-and-cve-is-still-necessary/#disqus_thread.

Ahmed, Leila. 1992. *Women and Gender in Islam: Historical Roots of a Modern Debate.* New Haven, Conn.: Yale University Press.

Ahmed, Sara. 2000. *Strange Encounters: Embodied Others in Post-Coloniality.* London: Routledge.

Ahmed, Sara. 2004a. *The Cultural Politics of Emotion.* Edinburgh: Edinburgh University Press.

Ahmed, Sara. 2004b. "Declarations of Whiteness: The Non-performativity of Anti-racism." *Borderlands E-Journal* 3 (2).

Ahmed, Sara. 2012. *On Being Included: Racism and Diversity in Institutional Life.* Durham, N.C.: Duke University Press.

Ainsley, Julia Edwards, Dustin Volz, and Kristina Cooke. 2017. "Exclusive: Trump to Focus Counter-Extremism Program Solely on Islam—Sources." *Reuters,* February 2, 2017. http://www.reuters.com/article/us-usa-trump-extremists-program-exclusiv-idUSKBN15G5VO.

Al-Arian, Abdullah, and Hafsa Kanjwal. 2014. "The Perils of American Muslim Politics." *Jadaliyya,* July 10, 2014. http://www.jadaliyya.com/pages/index/18475/the-perils-of-american-muslim-politics.

Alexander, Audrey. 2017. "Women and Violent Extremism." In Linking Security of Women & Security of States. Policymaker Blueprint, May 2017. https://www.futureswithoutviolence.org/wp-content/uploads/FWV_blueprint_5-Women-and-VE.pdf.

Alexander, M. Jacqui. 2005. *Pedagogies of Crossing: Mediations of Feminism, Sexual Politics, Memory, and the Sacred.* Durham, N.C.: Duke University Press.

Alfred, Taiaiake. 2008. *Peace, Power, Righteousness: An Indigenous Manifesto.* 2nd ed. Don Mills, Ontario: Oxford University Press.

Ali, Ayaan Hirsi. 2017. "Ideology and Terror: Understanding the Tools, Tactics, and Techniques of Violent Extremism." https://www.hsgac.sentate.gov/imo/media/doc/Testimony-Hirsi%20Ali-2017-06-14.pdf.

Ali, Safia Samee. 2017. "Islamic School Walked Away from Nearly $1M in Federal Funding Because of Trump." *NBC News,* March 6, 2017. http://www.nbcnews.com/news/us-news/islamic-school-walked-away-nearly-1m-federal-funding-because-trump-n727746.

Aly, Anne. 2014. "Moral Disengagement and Building Resilience to Violent Extremism: An Education Intervention." *Studies in Conflict & Terrorism* 37: 369–85.

American Civil Liberties Union. 2014. "The Problem with 'Countering Violent Extremism' Programs." ACLU.org. Accessed April 15, 2019. https://www.aclu.org/problem-countering-violent-extremism-programs.

American Civil Liberties Union. n.d. "Factsheet: The NYPD Muslim Surveillance Program." ACLU.org. Accessed April 15, 2019. https://www.aclu.org/other/factsheet-nypd-muslim-surveillance-program.

American Civil Liberties Union. n.d. "Surveillance under the Patriot Act." ACLU.org. Accessed March 22, 2019. https://www.aclu.org/issues/national-security/privacy-and-surveillance/surveillance-under-patriot-act.

Amoore, Louise, and Marieke de Goede. 2008. "Introduction: Governing by Risk in the War on Terror." In *Risk and the War on Terror,* edited by Louise Amoore and Marieke de Goede, 1–20. Abingdon, U.K.: Routledge.

Anderson, Jessica. 2013. "Accused School Shooter Had Troubled Childhood, Witnesses Say." *Baltimore Sun,* January 30, 2013. http://articles.baltimoresun.com/2013-01-30/news/bs-md-co-gladden-hearing-20130130_1_gladden-sandy-hook-elementary-school-shooter.

Anderson-Levy, Lisa. 2010. "An (Other) Ethnographic Dilemma: Subjectivity and the Predicament of Studying Up." *Transforming Anthropology* 18 (2): 181–92. https://doi.org/10.1111/j.1548-7466.2010.01095.x.181.

Arab American Action Network. 2017. "AAAN Warns Community: Beware of Countering Violent Extremism (CVE) Program." Mailing list archive, January 13, 2017. http://myemail.constantcontact.com/AAAN-Warns-Community—Beware-of-Countering-Violent-Extremism—CVE—program.html?soid=1101996057236&aid=Szk24Et6m_A.

Atkinson, Paul, and Amanda Coffey. 1997. "Analyzing Documentary Realities." In *Qualitative Research: Theory, Method, and Practice,* edited by David Silverman, 45–62. London: Sage.

Average Mohamed. "The Bullet or the Ballot." YouTube video, 00:01:20. Posted October 2015. https://youtu.be/MDJJFn0-9ek.

Ayat, Femi. 2017. "Ambiguities of CVE Theory & Practice." *Horn of Africa Bulletin.* http://life-peace.org/hab/ambiguities-cve-theory-practice/.

Aziz, Sahar. 2012. "From the Oppressed to the Terrorist: Muslim-American Women in the Crosshairs of Intersectionality." *Hastings Race & Poverty Law Journal* 9 (1): 191–264.

Aziz, Sahar. 2015. "The Islamic Monthly Debate—CVE." *Islamic Monthly,* June 27, 2015. https://www.theislamicmonthly.com/tim-debate-cve/.

Baird, Theodore. 2017. "Knowledge of Practice: A Multi-sited Even Ethnography of Border Security Fairs in Europe and North America." *Security Dialogue* 48 (3): 187–205.

Bakali, Naved. 2016. *Islamophobia: Understanding Anti-Muslim Racism through the Lived Experiences of Muslim Youth.* Rotterdam, Netherlands: Sense Publishers.

Balibar, Etienne. 1991. "Is There 'Neo-racism'?" In *Race, Nation, Class: Ambiguous Identities,* edited by Etienne Balibar and Immanuel Wallerstein, 17–28. London: Verso Press.

Bartlett, Lesley, and Catherine Lutz. 1998. "Disciplining Social Difference: Some Cultural Politics of Military Training in Public High Schools." *Urban Review* 30 (2): 119–37.

Bayoumi, Moustafa. 2006. "Racing Religion." *CR: The New Centennial Review* 6 (2): 267–93.

Beck, Ulrich. 2011. "Cosmopolitanism as Imagined Communities of Global Risk." *American Behavioral Scientist* 55 (10): 1346–61.

Becker, Sarah, and Brittnie Aiello. 2013. "The Continuum of Complicity: 'Studying up'/Studying Power as a Feminist, Anti-racist, or Social Justice Venture." *Women's Studies International Forum* 38: 63–74.

Bell, Colleen. 2011. "Civilianising Warfare: Ways of War and Peace in Modern Counterinsurgency." *Journal of International Relations and Development* 14: 309–32.

Berger, Dan, Mariame Kaba, and David Stein. 2017. "What Abolitionists Do." *Jacobin,* August 2017. https://www.jacobinmag.com/2017/08/prison-abolition-reform-mass-incarceration.

Berger, J. M., and Jonathon Morgan. 2015. *The ISIS Twitter Census: Defining and Describing the Population of ISIS Supporters on Twitter.* Brookings Project on U.S. Relations with the Islamic World analysis paper, no. 20, March 2015. https://www.brookings.edu/wp-content/uploads/2016/06/isis_twitter_census_berger_morgan.pdf.

Berlant, Lauren. 1997. *The Queen of America Goes to Washington City: Essays on Sex and Citizenship.* Durham, N.C.: Duke University Press.

Berman, Mark. 2016. "Prosecutors Say Dylann Roof 'Self-Radicalized' Online, Wrote Another Manifesto in Jail." *Washington Post,* August 22, 2016. https://www.washingtonpost.com/news/post-nation/wp/2016/08/22/prosecutors-say-accused-charleston-church-gunman-self-radicalized-online/?utm_term=.1a1428c41887.

Beutel, Alejandro J., Asma Shah, and Mimi Yu. 2016. "Advancing the Conversation on CVE." Al-Madina Institute. November 29, 2016. http://almadinainstitute.org/blog/advancing-the-conversation-on-countering-violent-extremism-cve/.

Bever, Lindsey. 2015. "Dzhokhar Tsarnaev's Scrawled Message: 'We Muslims Are One Body, You Hurt One You Hurt Us All.'" *Washington Post,* March 11, 2015. https://www.washingtonpost.com/news/morning-mix/wp/2015/03/11/dzhokhar-tsarnaevs-scrawled-message-we-muslims-are-one-body-you-hurt-one-you-hurt-us-all/?utm_term=.8e196a653a9f.

Bharath, Deepa. 2018. "LA Mayor Turns Down $425K in Federal Funding to Counter Violent Extremism after Opposition from Civil Rights Groups Stalls Process." *Daily News,* August 16, 2018. https://www.dailynews.com/2018/08/16la-mayor-turns-down-425k-in-federal-funding-to-counter-violent-extremism-after-opposition-from-civil-rights-groups-stalls-process/amp/.

Bhungalia, Lisa. 2015. "Managing Violence: Aid, Counterinsurgency, and the Humanitarian Present in Palestine." *Environment and Planning A* 47: 2308–23.

Bienkov, Adam. 2012. "Astroturfing: What Is It and Why Does It Matter?" *Guardian,* February 8, 2012. https://www.theguardian.com/commentisfree/2012/feb/08/what-is-astroturfing.

Bjørgo, Tore. 2011. "Dreams and Disillusionment: Engagement in and Disengagement from Militant Extremist Groups." *Crime, Law, and Social Change* 55 (4): 277–85.

Borum, Randy. 2011. "Radicalization into Violent Extremism I: A Review of Social Science Theories." *Journal of Strategic Security* 4 (4): 7–36.

Brennan Center for Justice at New York University School of Law. 2015. "Countering Violent Extremism: Myths and Fact." Brennan Center for Justice. https://www.brennancenter.org/sites/default/files/analysis/102915%20Final%20CVE%20Fact%20Sheet.pdf.

Browne, Simone. 2015. *Dark Matters: On the Surveillance of Blackness.* Durham, N.C.: Duke University Press.

Burde, Dana. 2005. "Education in Crisis Situations: Mapping the Field." Washington, D.C.: United States Agency for International Development. http://www.beps.net/publications/EdCrisisFinal.pdf.

Burde, Dana. 2007. "Empower or Control? Education in Emergencies and Global Governance." *Comparative and General Pharmacology* 9 (2): 55–64.

Burde, Dana. 2014. *Schools for Conflict or for Peace in Afghanistan.* New York: Columbia University Press.

Burgess, Matt. 2015. "Schools Monitoring Web Use 'Unlikely to Stop Radicalisation.'" *Wired,* December 2015. http://www.wired.co.uk/article/schools-monitor-children-internet-use.

Bush, George W. 2001a. "Address to a Joint Session of Congress and the American People." The White House, September 20, 2001. https://2001-2009.state.gov/coalition/cr/rm/2001/5025.htm.

Bush, George W. 2001b. "Bush Welcomes Muslim Americans to White House." The White House, September 26, 2001. https://2001-2009.state.gov/coalition/cr/rm/2001/5077.htm.

Bush, George W. 2001c. "International Campaign against Terror Grows." The White House, September 25, 2001. https://georgewbush-whitehouse.archives.gov/news/releases/2001/09/20010925-1.html.

Bush, George W. 2001d. "Presidential Address to the Nation." The White House, October 7, 2001. https://georgewbush-whitehouse.archives.gov/news/releases/2001/10/20011007-8.html.

Bush, George W. 2002. "President Delivers State of the Union Address." The White House, January 29, 2002. https://georgewbush-whitehouse.archives.gov/news/releases/2002/01/20020129-11.html.

Bush, Kenneth D., and Saltarelli, Diana. 2000. *The Two Faces of Education in Ethnic Conflict: Towards a Peacebuilding Education.* Florence, Italy: UNICEF.

Bush, Laura. 2001. "Radio Address by Laura Bush to the Nation." Crawford, Tex., November 17, 2001. https://2001-2009.state.gov/g/wi/7192.htm.

Byrd, Jodi A. 2011. *The Transit of Empire: Indigenous Critiques of Colonialism.* Minneapolis: University of Minnesota Press.

Cacho, Lisa Marie. 2012. *Social Death: Racialized Rightlessness and the Criminalization of the Unprotected.* New York: New York University Press.

Cahill, Kevin M. 2010. Introduction to *Even in Chaos: Education in Times of Emergency,* edited by Kevin M. Cahill, 1–6. New York: Fordham University Press and the Center for International Humanitarian Cooperation.

Cainkar, Louise A. 2008. "Thinking Outside the Box: Arabs and Race in the United States." In *Race and Arab Americans before and after 9/11: From Invisible Citizens to Visible Subjects,* edited by Amaney Jamal and Nadine Naber, 46–80. Syracuse, N.Y.: Syracuse University Press.

Cainkar, Louise A., and Saher Selod. 2018. "Review of Race Scholarship and the War on Terror." *American Sociological Association* 4 (2): 165–77.

Campbell, David. 1992. *Writing Security: United States Foreign Policy and the Politics of Identity.* Minneapolis: University of Minnesota Press.

Casella, Ronnie. 2003. "Zero Tolerance Policy in Schools: Rationale, Consequences, and Alternatives." *Teachers College Record* 105 (5): 872–92. https://doi.org/10.1111/1467–9620.00271.

Center on Global Counterterrorism Cooperation, and Hedayah Center. 2013. "The Role of Education in Countering Violent Extremism." Meeting note, December 2013. http://www.hedayahcenter.org/Admin/Content/File-34 201675349.pdf.

Central Intelligence Agency. 2012. "On the Front Lines: CIA in Afghanistan." Last updated November 21, 2012. https://www.cia.gov/about-cia/ cia-museum/experience-the-collection/text-version/stories/on-the-front -lines-cia-in-afghanistan.html.

Chalfin, Brenda. 2010. *Neoliberal Frontiers: An Ethnography of Sovereignty in West Africa.* Chicago: University of Chicago Press.

Chang, Cindy, and Victoria Kim. 2016. "For Law Enforcement, There Is No Single Profile of a Self-Radicalized Jihadist." *LA Times,* March 22, 2016. http:// www.latimes.com/local/california/la-me-terrorist-profile-20160322-story .html.

Chishti, Maliha, and Cheshmak Farhoumand-Sims. 2011. "Transnational Feminism and the Women's Rights Agenda in Afghanistan." In *Globalizing Afghanistan: Terrorism, War, and the Rhetoric of Nation Building,* edited by Zubeda Jalalzai and David Jefferess, 117–43. Durham, N.C.: Duke University Press.

City of Houston. 2016. "Houston Countering Violent Extremism (CVE) Training and Engagement Initiative." Department of Homeland Security grant application. https://www.dhs.gov/sites/default/files/publications/EMW -2016-CA-APP-00158 Full Application.pdf.

City of Los Angeles Mayor's Office of Public Safety. 2016. "Building Healthy Communities in Los Angeles: Managing Intervention Activities." Department of Homeland Security grant application. https://www.dhs.gov/sites/ default/files/publications/EMW-2016-CA-APP-00294 Full Application.pdf.

Clinton, Hillary. 2016. "Second Presidential Debate." October 9, 2016, Washington University, St. Louis, Missouri.

Code, Lorraine. 1995. *Rhetorical Spaces: Essays on Gendered Locations*. New York: Routledge.

Coe, George. 1927. "What Do Professors of Secondary Education Think of Military Training in High Schools?" *School and Society* 26: 147–78.

Cohn, Carol. 1987. "Sex and Death in the Rational World of Defense Intellectuals." *Signs* 12 (4): 687–718.

Cohn, Carol. 2006. "Motives and Methods: Using Multi-sited Ethnography to Study National Security Discourses." In *Feminist Methodologies for International Relations*, edited by Brooke Ackerly and Jacqui True, 91–107. Cambridge: Cambridge University Press.

Community Policing Consortium. 1994. "Understanding Community Policing: A Framework for Action." National Criminal Justice Reference Service, August 1994. https://www.ncjrs.gov/pdffiles/commp.pdf.

Conti, Joseph A., and Moira O'Neil. 2007. "Studying Power: Qualitative Methods and the Global Elite." *Qualitative Research* 7 (1): 63–82. https://doi .org/10.1177/1468794107071421.

Cosgrave, John. 2004. "The Impact of the War on Terror on Aid Flows." Action Aid. https://www.actionaid.org.uk/sites/default/files/doc_lib/114_1_war _terror_aid.pdf.

Coulthard, Glen Sean. 2014. *Red Skin, White Masks: Rejecting the Colonial Politics of Recognition*. Minneapolis: University of Minnesota Press.

Council on American-Islamic Relations. 2015. "About Us: Vision, Mission, Core Principles." https://www.cair.com/about_us.

Craven, Julia. 2015a. "Dylann Roof Wasn't Charged with Terrorism Because He's White." *Huffington Post,* July 23, 2015. http://www.huffingtonpost .com/entry/dylann-roof-terrorism_us_55b107c9e4b07af29d57a5fc.

Craven, Julia. 2015b. "White Supremacists More Dangerous to America than Foreign Terrorists, Study Says." *Huffington Post,* June 24, 2015. http:// www.huffingtonpost.com/2015/06/24/domestic-terrorism-charleston_n _7654720.html.

Currier, Cora. 2015. "Spies among Us: How Community Outreach Programs to Muslims Blur the Lines between Outreach and Intelligence." *Intercept,* January 21, 2015. https://theintercept.com/2015/01/21/spies-among-us -community-outreach-programs-muslims-blur-lines-outreach-intelligence/.

Currier, Cora, and Murtaza Hussain. 2016. "Letter Details FBI Plan for Secretive Anti-radicalization Committees." *Intercept,* April 28, 2016. https:// theintercept.com/2016/04/28/letter-details-fbi-plan-for-secretive-anti -radicalization-committees/.

Das, Jishnu. 2010. "The Black Hole of Pakistan: Are Billions of Dollars of U.S. Aid Going to Waste?" *Foreign Policy,* October 7, 2010. http://www.foreignpol icy.com/articles/2010/10/07/the_black_hole_of_pakistan.

Davis, Angela Y. 2016. *Freedom Is a Constant Struggle: Ferguson, Palestine, and the Foundations of a Movement*. Chicago: Haymarket Books.

Davis, Matthew. 2005. "New Name for 'War on Terror.'" *BBC News,* July 27, 2005. http://news.bbc.co.uk/2/hi/americas/4719169.stm.

Dearborn Police Department. 2016. "Community Training and Awareness Briefs (CTAB) to Counter Violent Extremism." Department of Homeland Security grant application. https://www.dhs.gov/sites/default/files/publications/EMW-2016-CA-APP-00184 Full Application.pdf.

de Leeuw, Sarah. 2007. "Intimate Colonialisms: The Material and Experienced Places of British Columbia's Residential Schools." *Canadian Geographer* 51 (3): 339–59. https://doi.org/10.1111/j.1541–0064.2007.00183.x.

de Leeuw, Sarah. 2016. "Tender Grounds: Intimate Visceral Violence and British Columbia's Colonial Geographies." *Political Geography* 52 (1): 14–23.

Denoeux, Guilain, and Lynn Carter. 2009. *Guide to the Drivers of Violent Extremism.* Management Systems International, for USAID. https://pdf.usaid.gov/pdf_docs/Pnadt978.pdf.

Denver Police Department. 2016. "Countering Violent Extremism Collaborative Grant Program." Department of Homeland Security grant application. https://www.dhs.gov/sites/default/files/publications/EMW-2016-CA-APP-00381 Full Application.pdf.

Department of Homeland Security. 2014. "CBP Explorer Program." U.S. Customs and Border Protection. http://www.cbp.gov/border-security/along-us-borders/explorer-program.

Department of Homeland Security. 2015. "Factsheet: A Comprehensive U.S. Government Approach to Countering Violent Extremism." https://www.dhs.gov/sites/default/files/publications/US Government Approach to CVE-Fact Sheet.pdf.

Department of Homeland Security. 2016. "Community Engagement." https://www.dhs.gov/community-engagement.

Department of Homeland Security. 2017. "DHS Countering Violent Extremism Grants." https://www.dhs.gov/cvegrants.

Department of Homeland Security. 2019. "Acting Secretary McAleenan Announces Establishment of DHS Office for Targeted Violence and Terrorism Prevention." https://www.dhs.gov/news/2019/04/19/acting-secretary-mcaleenan-announces-establishment-dhs-office-targeted-violence-and.

Department of Homeland Security. n.d. "If You See Something, Say Something™." Accessed February 18, 2017. https://www.dhs.gov/see-something-say-something.

Department of Homeland Security, and Federal Bureau of Investigation. 2016. "Indicators of Violent Extremist Radicalization." *Joint Intelligence Bulletin,* July.

Department of Homeland Security CVE Curriculum Working Group. 2011. "Community Policing and Countering Violent Extremism: Draft of Curriculum Components." Washington, D.C.

Department of Homeland Security Homeland Security Academic Advisory

Council. 2017. "Academic Subcommittee on Countering Violent Extremism: Report and Recommendations." Washington, D.C.

Department of Justice. 2003. "Fact Sheet: Racial Profiling." June 17, 2003. https://www.justice.gov/archive/opa/pr/2003/June/racial_profiling_fact_sheet.pdf.

Department of Justice. 2014a. "Guidance for Federal Law Enforcement Agencies Regarding the Use of Race, Ethnicity, Gender, National Origin, Religion, Sexual Orientation, or Gender Identity." Washington, D.C.

Department of Justice. 2014b. "Weed and Seed." United States Department of Justice, the United States Attorney's Office Northern District of California. https://www.justice.gov/usao-ndca/weed-and-seed.

Depue, Roger. n.d. "Red Flags, Warning Signs, and Indicators." University of New Orleans Counseling Services. https://www.uno.edu/counseling-services/documents/redflags.pdf.

DeVault, Marjorie. 1999. *Liberating Method: Feminism and Social Research*. Philadelphia: Temple University Press.

DiIulio, John J. 1995. "The Coming of the Super-Predators." *Weekly Standard* 1 (11): 23–28.

Dower, Nigel, and John Williams. 2002. Introduction to *Global Citizenship: A Critical Introduction*, edited by Nigel Dower and John Williams, 1–10. New York: Routledge.

Edwards, Elise. 2007. "An Ethics for Working Up?: Japanese Corporate Scandals and Rethinking Lessons about Fieldwork." *Critical Asian Studies* 39 (4): 561–82. https://doi.org/10.1080/14672710701686042.

Emmerson, Ben. 2016. "Report of the Special Rapporteur on the Promotion and Protection of Human Rights and Fundamental Freedoms While Countering Terrorism." Advance unedited version. *Just Security*, February 22, 2016. https://www.justsecurity.org/wp-content/uploads/2016/04/Emmerson-UNHRC-Report-A-HRC-31-65_UneditedVersion.pdf.

England, Kim V. L. 1994. "Getting Personal: Reflexivity, Positionality, and Feminist Research." *Professional Geographer* 46 (1): 80–89.

Erevelles, Nirmala. 2014. "Crippin' Jim Crow: Disability, Dis-location, and the School-to-Prison Pipeline." In *Disability Incarcerated: Imprisonment and Disability in the United States and Canada*, edited by Liat Ben-Moshe, Chris Chapman, and Allison C. Carey, 81–99. New York: Palgrave.

Erickson, Erick. 2013. "Boston Bombing Just the Beginning of Homegrown Terror Threats." *Fox News*, April 25, 2013. http://www.foxnews.com/opinion/2013/04/25/america-has-gone-from-melting-pot-to-pressure-cooker.html.

Estes, Nick. 2017. "Born on the Fourth of July: Counterinsurgency, Indigenous Resistance, and Black Revolt." *Red Nation*, July 2017. https://therednation.org/2017/07/04/born-on-the-fourth-of-july-counterinsurgency-indigenous-resistance-and-black-revolt/.

Federal Bureau of Investigation. 2009. "Implementation of Specialized Community Outreach Team (SCOT)." Washington, D.C. http://bit.ly/1yrQGae.

Federal Bureau of Investigation. 2015a. "FBI Strategic Plan to Curb Violent Extremism." Washington, D.C. https://www.brennancenter.org/sites/default/files/16-cv-00672%20-%20FBI%20Strategic%20Plan%20to%20Curb%20Violent%20Extremism.PDF.

Federal Bureau of Investigation. 2015b. "White House CVE Summit Memorandum." Washington, D.C. https://www.brennancenter.org/sites/default/files/16-cv-00672%20-%20White%20House%20CVE%20Summit%20Press%20Points.PDF.

Federal Bureau of Investigation. 2016a. "Domestic Investigations Operations Guide." Washington, D.C. FBIDomesticInvestigationsandOperationsGuideDIOG2016VersionPart01of02.pdf.

Federal Bureau of Investigation. 2016b. "Don't Be a Puppet." https://cve.fbi.gov/home.html.

Federal Bureau of Investigation. 2016c. "Don't Be a Puppet: Pull Back the Curtain on Violent Extremism Flyer." https://www.fbi.gov/cve508/dont-be-a-puppet-website-flyer.

Federal Bureau of Investigation. 2017a. "Black Identity Extremists Likely Motivated to Target Law Enforcement Officers." Intelligence assessment, August 3, 2017. Document uploaded to Document Cloud by Sharon Weinberger, Foreign Policy. https://www.documentcloud.org/documents/4067711-BIE-Redacted.html.

Federal Bureau of Investigation. 2017b. "Making Prevention a Reality: Identifying, Assessing, and Managing the Threat of Targeted Attacks." Washington, D.C. https://www.fbi.gov/file-repository/making-prevention-a-reality.pdf/view.

Federal Bureau of Investigation. 2018. "What We Investigate: Terrorism." https://www.fbi.gov/investigate/terrorism.

Federal Bureau of Investigation. n.d. "Letter to SRC Members." https://assets.documentcloud.org/documents/2815794/FBI-SRC-Letter.pdf.

Federal Bureau of Investigation: Office of Partner Engagement. 2015. "ASAC Conference—Countering Violent Extremism Conference." Washington, DC. https://www.brennancenter.org/sites/default/files/9D189AFA9E878DF18145FA7D70DE4A5B36CFB1E.pdf.

Federal Bureau of Investigation. 2016. "Preventing Violent Extremism in Schools." Public Intelligence. https://info.publicintelligence.net/FBI-PreventingExtremismSchools.pdf.

Fenning, Pamela, and Jennifer Rose. 2007. "Overrepresentation of African American Students in Exclusionary Discipline: The Role of School Policy." *Urban Education* 42 (6): 536–59.

Forsythe, Diane E., and David J. Hess. 2001. *Studying Those Who Study Us: An Anthropologist in the World of Artificial Intelligence.* Palo Alto, Calif.: Stanford University Press.

Foucault, Michel. 1976. *The History of Sexuality.* Vol. 1, *An Introduction.* New York: Vintage Books.

Foucault, Michel. 1999. *Abnormal: Lectures at the Collège de France, 1974–1975*. New York: Picador.

Foucault, Michel. 2003. *"Society Must Be Defended": Lectures at College de France, 1975–1976*. New York: Picador.

Fuentes, Annette. 2011. *Lockdown High: When the Schoolhouse Becomes a Jailhouse*. London: Verso Press.

Gallagher, Kathleen. 2007. *The Theatre of Urban: Youth and Schooling in Dangerous Times*. Toronto: University of Toronto Press.

Gartenstein-Ross, Daveed, and Laura Grossman. 2009. *Homegrown Terrorists in the US and UK: An Empirical Examination of the Radicalization Process*. Washington, D.C.: FDD Press.

Gazit, Nir, and Yael Maoz-Shai. 2010. "Studying-Up and Studying-Across: At-Home Research of Governmental Violence Organizations." *Qualitative Sociology* 33 (3): 275–95. https://doi.org/10.1007/s11133-010-9156-y.

German, Michael. 2016. "Is Your Kid a Threat? The Feds Want to Know." *USA Today*, June 17, 2016. https://www.usatoday.com/story/opinion/2016/06/17/fbi-program-countering-violent-extremism-speech-terrorism-theories-column/85650404/.

Gilson, Dave, Alex Park, and A. J. Vicens. 2013. "How We Got from 9/11 to Massive NSA Spying on Americans: A Timeline." *Mother Jones*, September 11, 2013. https://www.motherjones.com/politics/2013/09/nsa-timeline-surveillance/.

Glebbeek, Marie-Louise. 2003. *In the Crossfire of Democracy: Police Reform and Police Practice in Post-Civil War Guatemala*. Amsterdam: Rosenberg Publishers.

Global Peace Foundation. 2016. "CVE Train-the-Trainer and Cross Community Engagement Program." Department of Homeland Security grant application. https://www.dhs.gov/sites/default/files/publications/EMW-2016-CA-APP-00104 Full Application.pdf.

Goffman, Erving. 1959. *The Presentation of Self in Everyday Life*. New York: Doubleday.

Gonzalez, Roberto J. 2010. *Militarizing Culture: Essays on the Warfare State*. Walnut Creek, Calif.: Left Coast Press.

Gordon, Avery. 1997. *Ghostly Matters: Haunting and the Sociological Imagination*. Minneapolis: University of Minnesota Press.

Gorka, Sebastian, and David J. Kilcullen. 2011. "An Actor-Centric Theory of War: Understanding the Difference between COIN and Counterinsurgency." *Joint Forces Quarterly* 60 (1): 14–18.

Gorz, Andre. 1967. *Strategy for Labor: A Radical Proposal*. Boston: Beacon Press.

Gossett, Stephen. 2017. "2 Arrested at UIC after Disrupting Panel That 'Supports Targeting Muslims,' Protesters Say." *Chicagoist*, October 28, 2017. http://chicagoist.com/2017/10/28/2_arrested_at_uic_after_disrupting.php.

Government Accountability Office. 2018. "K-12 Education: Discipline Disparities for Black Students, Boys, and Students with Disabilities." Report to Congressional Requesters. March 2018. https://www.gao.gov/assets/700/690828.pdf.

Graham, David A. 2015. "Deadly American Extremism: More White than Muslim." *Atlantic,* June 25, 2015. http://www.theatlantic.com/politics/archive/2015/06/terrorism-threat/396749/.

Graham, Stephen. 2010. *Cities under Siege: The New Military Urbanism.* London: Verso Press.

Green, Shannon, and Keith Proctor. 2016. "Turning Point: A New Comprehensive Strategy for Countering Violent Extremism." https://csis-ilab.github.io/cve/report/Turning_Point.pdf.

Greenwald, Glenn. 2013. "Why Is Boston 'Terrorism' but Not Aurora, Sandy Hook, Tucson, and Columbine?" *Guardian,* April 22, 2013. https://www.theguardian.com/commentisfree/2013/apr/22/boston-marathon-terrorism-aurora-sandy-hook.

Gregory, Derek. 2004. *The Colonial Present: Afghanistan, Palestine, Iraq.* Hoboken, N.J.: Wiley & Sons.

Gregory, Derek. 2008. "The Rush to the Intimate: Counterinsurgency and the Cultural Turn in Late Modern War." *Radical Philosophy* 150: 8–23.

Grewal, Inderpal. 2017. *Saving the Security State: Exceptional Citizens in Twenty-First Century America.* Durham, N.C.: Duke University Press.

Griffin, Drew, David Fitzpatrick, and Curt Devine. 2016. "Was Dallas Cop Killer Micah Johnson Radicalized Online?" *CNN,* July 10, 2016. http://www.cnn.com/2016/07/10/us/micah-johnson-dallas-radicalized-online/.

Guardian. 2018. "The Counted: People Killed by Police in the US." https://www.theguardian.com/us-news/ng-interactive/2015/jun/01/the-counted-police-killings-us-database.

Gusterson, Hugh. 1996. *Nuclear Rites: A Weapons Laboratory at the End of the Cold War.* Berkeley: University of California Press.

Gusterson, Hugh. 1997. "Studying Up Revisited." *Political and Legal Anthropology Review* 20 (1): 114–19.

Gusterson, Hugh. 2008. "The US Military's Quest to Weaponize Culture." *Bulletin of the Atomic Scientist,* June 2008. http://thebulletin.org/us-militarys-quest-weaponize-culture.

Haney, Lynne Allison. 2010. *Offending Women: Power, Punishment, and the Regulation of Desire.* Berkeley: University of California Press.

Haraway, Donna. 1988. "Situated Knowledges: The Science Question in Feminism and the Privilege of Partial Perspective." *Feminist Studies* 14 (3): 575–99.

Harding, Sandra. 1993. "Rethinking Standpoint Epistemology: What Is 'Strong Objectivity'?" In *Feminist Epistemologies,* edited by Linda Alcoff and Elizabeth Potter, 49–82. New York: Routledge.

Hennepin County Sheriff's Office. 2016. "Focus Area 2 - Community Engagement: A Frontline Strategy for Countering Violent Extremism." Department of Homeland Security grant application. https://www.dhs.gov/sites/

default/files/publications/EMW-2016-CA-APP-00081 Full Application .pdf.

Her Highness Sheikha Mozah Bint Nasser Al Missned. 2010. "Ensuring the Right to Education." In *Even in Chaos: Education in Times of Emergency,* edited by Kevin M. Cahill, 7–8. New York: Fordham University Press and the Center for International Humanitarian Cooperation.

Her Majesty's Government. 2011. "CONTEST: The United Kingdom's Strategy for Countering Terrorism." July 2011. https://www.gov.uk/government/ uploads/system/uploads/attachment_data/file/97994/contest-summary .pdf.

Her Majesty's Government. 2015. "Prevent Duty Guidance." http://www .legislation.gov.uk/ukdsi/2015/9780111133309/pdfs/ukdsiod_97801111 33309_en.pdf.

Hiemstra, Nancy. 2014. "Performing Homeland Security within the US Immigrant Detention System." *Environment and Planning D: Society and Space* 32 (4): 571–88.

Hirsi, Ibrahim. 2017. "Why Many in the Twin Cities' Somali Community Have Such Mixed Feelings about Former U.S. Attorney Andy Luger." *MinnPost,* March 31, 2017. https://www.minnpost.com/new-americans/2017/03/ why-many-twin-cities-somali-community-have-such-mixed-feelings-about -former-us.

Ho, Karen. 2009. *Liquidated: An Ethnography of Wall Street.* Durham, N.C.: Duke University Press.

Homeland Security Advisory Council. 2016. "Countering Violent Extremism (CVE) Subcommittee Interim Report and Recommendations." Department of Homeland Security, June 2016. https://www.dhs.gov/sites/default/ files/publications/HSAC/HSAC CVE Final Interim Report June 9 2016 508 compliant.pdf.

Hoover, J. Edgar. 1967. "Counterintelligence Program." Washington, D.C. https: //vault.fbi.gov/cointel-pro/cointel-pro-black-extremists/cointelpro-black -extremists-part-01-of/view.

Hoover, J. Edgar. 1968. "Counterintelligence Program: Black Nationalist Hate Groups, Racial Intelligence." Washington, D.C. https://archive.org/stream/ FBI-COINTELPRO-BLACK/100-HQ-448006-01#page/n67/mode/2up.

Horgan, John. 2008. "From Profiles to Pathways and Roots to Routes: Perspectives from Psychology on Radicalization into Terrorism." *Annals of the American Academy of Political and Social Science* 618 (1): 80–94.

Huggins, Martha K. 1998. *Political Policing: The United States and Latin America.* Durham, N.C.: Duke University Press.

Huggins, Martha K., and Marie-Louise Glebbeek. 2003. "Women Studying Violent Male Institutions: Cross-Gendered Dynamics in Police Research on Secrecy and Danger." *Theoretical Criminology* 7 (3): 363–87.

Huntington, Samuel P. 1996. *The Clash of Civilizations and the Remaking of World Order.* New York: Touchstone.

Hussain, Murtaza. 2016. "18-Year-Old Arrested on Terrorism Charges Is Mentally 'Like a Child.'" *Intercept,* August 3, 2016. https://theintercept .com/2016/08/03/18-year-old-arrested-on-terrorism-charges-is-mentally -like-a-child/.

Illinois Criminal Justice Information Authority. 2016. "Engaged Bystander-Gatekeeper Training for Ideologically Inspired Targeted Violence." Department of Homeland Security grant application. https://www.dhs.gov/ sites/default/files/publications/EMW-2016-CA-APP-00169%20Full%20 Application.pdf.

Impero Software. 2016. "Impero Software's Keyword Library for US Schools Addresses Online Safety Concerns Such as Self-Harm and Radicalization." https://www.imperosoftware.com/us/resources/press-releases/impero -softwares-keyword-library-us-schools-addresses-online-safety-concerns -self-harm-radicalization/.

Insolacion, Fatima. 2013. "The Insurgent Southwest: Death, Criminality, and Militarization on the US-Mexican Border." In *Life during Wartime: Resisting Counterinsurgency,* edited by Kristian Williams, Will Munger, and Lara Messersmith-Glavin, 187–209. Oakland, Calif.: AK Press.

International Association of Chiefs of Police. 2014. "Using Community Policing to Counter Violent Extremism: Five Key Principles for Law Enforcement." Washington, D.C.: Office of Community Oriented Policing Services. https://ric-zai-inc.com/Publications/cops-p299-pub.pdf.

Jama, Mohamed, Sarfaroz Niyozov, and Mahad Yusuf. 2015. "Youth Radicalization: Policy and Education Response Conference Final Report." February 12–13, 2015. https://www.oise.utoronto.ca/oise/UserFiles/File/Youth_ Radicalization_Policy_Education_Response_Conference_Final_ Report_June_2015_.pdf.

Jamieson, Alastair. 2013. "Two Muslim Converts Guilty of Killing UK Soldier Lee Rigby on London Street." *NBC News,* December 19, 2013. https://www .nbcnews.com/news/world/two-muslim-converts-guilty-killing-uk-soldier -lee-rigby-london-flna2D11775017.

Jenkins, Brian Michael. 2007. "Outside Expert's View." In *Radicalization in the West: The Homegrown Threat,* 11–12. New York: New York City Police Department.

Jensen, Dennis L. 2006. "Enhancing Homeland Security Efforts by Building Strong Relationships between the Muslim Community and Local Law Enforcement." Thesis, Naval Postgraduate School, Monterey, Calif.

Johnson, Jenna, and Abigail Hauslohner. 2017. "'I Think Islam Hates Us': A Timeline of Trump's Comments about Islam and Muslims." *Washington Post,* May 20, 2017. https://www.washingtonpost.com/news/post-politics/ wp/2017/05/20/i-think-islam-hates-us-a-timeline-of-trumps-comments -about-islam-and-muslims/?noredirect=on&utm_term=.4c64242 b577d.

Kaba, Mariame, and Erica Meiners. 2014. "Arresting the Carceral State." *Ja-*

cobin, February 2014. https://www.jacobinmag.com/2014/02/arresting-the-carceral-state/.

Kanigher, Steve. 1996. "New Life Breathed into ACLU." *Las Vegas Sun*, November 25, 1996. https://lasvegassun.com/news/1996/nov/25/new-life-breathed-into-aclu/.

Katz, Cindi. 2001a. "On the Grounds of Globalization: A Topography for Feminist Political Engagement." *Signs* 26 (4): 1213–34. http://www.ncbi.nlm.nih.gov/pubmed/17615660.

Katz, Cindi. 2001b. "Vagabond Capitalism and the Necessity of Social Reproduction." *Antipode* 33 (4): 709–28. https://doi.org/10.1111/1467-8330.00 207.

Katz, Cindi. 2008. "Bad Elements: Katrina and the Scoured Landscape of Social Reproduction." *Gender, Place & Culture: A Journal of Feminist Geography* 15 (1): 15–29.

Katz, Rita. 2014. "The State Department's Twitter War with ISIS Is Embarrassing." *Time*, September 2014. http://time.com/3387065/isis-twitter-war-state-department/.

Kazi, Nazia. 2017. "Against a Muslim Misleadership Class." *Jacobin*, June 2, 2017. https://www.jacobinmag.com/2017/06/islamophobia-countering-violent-extremism-muslim-leaders.

Keddie, Amanda. 2014. "The Politics of Britishness: Multiculturalism, Schooling, and Social Cohesion." *British Educational Research Journal* 40 (3): 539–54.

Khaleeli, Homa. 2015. "'You Worry They Could Take Your Kids': Is the Prevent Strategy Demonising Muslim Schoolchildren?" *Guardian*, September 23, 2015. https://www.theguardian.com/uk-news/2015/sep/23/prevent-counter-terrorism-strategy-schools-demonising-muslim-children.

Khalili, Laleh. 2013. *Time in the Shadows: Confinement in Counterinsurgencies.* Palo Alto, Calif.: Stanford University Press.

Khalili, Laleh. 2015. "Counterterrorism and Counterinsurgency in the Neoliberal Age." In *The Oxford Handbook of Contemporary Middle-Eastern and North African History*, edited by Amal Ghazal and Jens Hanssen, 1–17. Oxford: Oxford University Press.

Khan, Humera. 2015. "Why Countering Extremism Fails: Washington's Top-Down Approach to Prevention Is Flawed." *Foreign Affairs*, February 2015. https://www.foreignaffairs.com/articles/united-states/2015-02-18/why-countering-extremism-fails.

Kiernat, Kourtney. 2015. "Minneapolis Public Schools CVE Program." Filmed February 18, 2015. C-SPAN video, 1:12. Posted March 9, 2015. https://www.c-span.org/video/?c4530677/minneapolis-public-school-cve-program.

Kilcullen, David J. 2007. "Religion and Insurgency." Small Wars Journal Blog. http://smallwarsjournal.com/blog/religion-and-insurgency.

Kilcullen, David J. 2010. *Counterinsurgency.* Oxford: Oxford University Press.

Ki-moon, Ban. 2016. "UN Secretary-General's Remarks at General Assembly

Presentation of the Plan of Action to Prevent Violent Extremism [as Delivered]." United Nations Secretary-General, January 15, 2016. http://www.un.org/sg/statements/index.asp?nid=9388.

Knoll, James L., IV, and George D. Annas. 2016. "Mass Shootings and Mental Illness." In *Gun Violence and Mental Illness,* edited by Liza H. Gold and Robert I. Simon, 81–104. Arlington, Va.: American Psychiatric Association Publishing.

Krebs, Ronald R. 2015. *Narrative and the Making of US National Security.* Cambridge: Cambridge University Press.

Kumar, Deepa. 2012. *Islamophobia and the Politics of Empire.* Chicago: Haymarket Books.

Kundnani, Arun. 2014. *The Muslims Are Coming! Islamophobia, Extremism, and the Domestic War on Terror.* London: Verso Press.

Lacy, Karyn R. 2007. *Blue-Chip Black: Race, Class, and Status in the New Black Middle Class.* Berkeley: University of California Press.

Laqueur, Walter. 1999. *The New Terrorism: Fanaticism and the Arms of Mass Destruction.* London: Oxford University Press.

Laqueur, Walter. 2004. "The Terrorism to Come." *Policy Review,* August 1, 2004.

Laqueur, Walter. 2006. "Terror's New Face." *Harvard International Review* 20 (4): 48.

Lather, Patti. 1993. "Fertile Obsession: Validity after Poststructuralism." *Sociological Quarterly* 34 (4): 673–93.

Lenczowski, John. 2017. "How to Fight the War of Ideas against Radical Islamism." https://www.hsgac.senate.gov/imo/media/doc/Testimony-Lenczowski-2017-06-14-REVISED.pdf.

Li, Darryl. 2015. "A Jihadism Anti-primer." *Middle East Research and Information Project* 276. http://www.merip.org/mer/mer276/jihadism-anti-primer.

Life After Hate. 2016. "Preventing Violent Radicalization and Supporting the De-radicalization Process via Targeted Online and Offline Individualized Interventions." Department of Homeland Security grant application. Chicago, Ill.

Lincoln, Yvonna S., and Egon G. Guba. 1985. *Naturalistic Inquiry.* Newbury Park, Calif.: Sage.

Lipsky, Michael. 1980. *Street-Level Bureaucracy: Dilemmas of the Individual in Public Service.* New York: Russell Sage Foundation.

LoCicero, Alice, and J. Wesley Boyd. 2016. "The Dangers of Countering Violent Extremism (CVE) Programs." *Psychology Today,* July 19, 2016. https://www.psychologytoday.com/blog/almost-addicted/201607/the-dangers-countering-violent-extremism-cve-programs.

Los Angeles Interagency Coordination Group in collaboration with community stakeholders. 2015. "The Los Angeles Framework for Countering Violent Extremism." Department of Homeland Security, February 2015. https://www.dhs.gov/sites/default/files/publications/Los Angeles Framework for CVE-Full Report.pdf.

Love, Erik. 2017. *Islamophobia and Racism in America*. New York: New York University Press.

Lowe, Lisa. 2015. *The Intimacies of Four Continents*. Durham, N.C.: Duke University Press.

Lutz, Catherine. 2002. *Homefront: A Military City and the American 20th Century*. Boston: Beacon Press.

Lyon, David. 2003. "Surveillance as Social Sorting: Computer Codes and Mobile Bodies." In *Surveillance as Social Sorting: Privacy, Risk, and Digital Discrimination*, edited by David Lyon, 1–10. London: Routledge.

Maira, Sunaina. 2016. *The 9/11 Generation: Youth, Rights, and Solidarity in the War on Terror*. New York: New York University Press.

Mamdani, Mahmood. 2004. *Good Muslim, Bad Muslim: America, the Cold War, and the Roots of Terror*. New York: Three Leaves Press.

Manning, Chelsea. 2013. "Chelsea Manning's Personal Statement to Court Martial: Full Text." *Guardian*, March 1, 2013. https://www.theguardian.com/world/2013/mar/01/bradley-manning-wikileaks-statement-full-text.

Martin, Kathryn. 2013. "The USA Patriot Act's Application to Library Patron Records." *Journal of Legislation* 29 (2): 283–306.

Mason, Melanie, and David Zucchino. 2013. "Bullying May Have Motivated Nevada School Shooter." *LA Times*, October 22, 2013. http://articles.latimes.com/2013/oct/22/nation/la-na-middle-school-shooting-20131023.

Mazzei, Patricia. 2018. "Noor Salman Acquitted in Pulse Nightclub Shooting." *New York Times*, March 30, 2018. https://www.nytimes.com/2018/03/30/us/noor-salman-pulse-trial-verdict.html.

McCarthy, Kristin. 2016. "Is the FBI's Flawed Terrorist Intervention Program Really Cancelled? There's Reason to Believe 'Shared Responsibility Committees' Are Still Alive." Arab American Institute blog. November 3, 2016. http://www.aaiusa.org/is_the_fbi_s_terrorist_intervention_program_really_cancelled.

McCaskill, Claire. 2017. "Ideology and Terror: Understanding the Tools, Tactics, and Techniques of Violent Extremism." https://www.hsgac.senate.gov/imo/media/doc/Opening%20Statement-McCaskill-2017-06-14.pdf.

McCormack, David. 2016. "FBI Director Criticized for Saying Charleston Church Shooting Is NOT an Act of Terrorism." *Daily Mail*, June 22, 2016. http://www.dailymail.co.uk/news/article-3133472/FBI-director-criticized-saying-Charleston-church-shooting-NOT-act-terrorism.html.

McNeal, Laura, and Christopher Dunbar Jr. 2010. "In the Eyes of the Beholder: Urban Student Perceptions of Zero Tolerance Policy." *Urban Education* 45 (3): 293–311. https://doi.org/10.1177/0042085910364475.

Meiners, Erica R. 2016. *For the Children? Protecting Innocence in a Carceral State*. Minneapolis: University of Minnesota Press.

Melamed, Jodi. 2011. *Represent and Destroy: Rationalizing Violence in the New Racial Capitalism*. Minneapolis: University of Minnesota Press.

Mercer, Morgan. 2016. "An Investment in the Future." Youthprise.org. Ac-

cessed April 15, 2019. https://youthprise.org/blog/an-investment-in-the
-future/.

Metzl, Jonathan M. 2009. *The Protest Psychosis: How Schizophrenia Became a Black Disease.* Boston: Beacon Press.

Milbank, Dana. 2004. "Reprising a War with Words." *Washington Post,* August 17, 2004. http://www.washingtonpost.com/wp-dyn/articles/A6375-2004 Aug16.html.

Miller, Todd. 2014. *Border Patrol Nation: Dispatches from the Front Lines of Homeland Security.* San Francisco: City Lights Books.

Mirza, Waqas. 2016. "Montgomery County's Flawed Model for Nationwide Counterterror Programs." *MuckRock,* September 28, 2016. https://www .muckrock.com/news/archives/2016/sep/28/cve-community-resistence/.

Moffett, Katie, and Tony Sgro. 2016. "School-Based CVE Strategies." *Annals of the American Academy of Political and Social Science* 668 (1): 145–64.

Morgan, Kelly. 2018. "Pathologizing 'Radicalization' and the Erosion of Patient Privacy Rights." *Boston College Law Review* 59 (2): 791–820.

Morris, Edward W. 2007. "'Ladies' or 'Loudies'?: Perceptions and Experiences of Black Girls in Classrooms." *Youth & Society* 38 (4): 490–515.

Morris, Monique W. 2016. *Pushout: The Criminalization of Black Girls in Schools.* New York: New Press.

Morsi, Yassir. 2017. *Radical Skin, Moderate Masks: De-radicalising the Muslim and Racism in Post-Racial Societies.* London: Rowman and Littlefield Publishers.

Mountz, Alison. 2004. "Embodying the Nation-State: Canada's Response to Human Smuggling." *Political Geography* 23: 323–45.

Mountz, Alison. 2010. *Seeking Asylum: Human Smuggling and Bureaucracy at the Border.* Minneapolis: University of Minnesota Press.

Murdocca, Carmela. 2002. "Foreign Bodies: Race, Canadian Nationalism, and the Trope of Disease." Master's thesis, Ontario Institute for Studies in Education, University of Toronto.

Muslim Matters. 2016. "The Muslim Lords of CVE." *Muslim Matters,* October 2016. http://muslimmatters.org/2016/10/19/the-muslim-lords-of-cve/.

Muslim Matters. 2017. "The Trouble with CVE Cash for Muslim Groups: Navigating the Murky Waters of CVE Funding and Establishing Transparency in the American Muslim Community." *Muslim Matters,* February 2017. http://muslimmatters.org/2017/02/12/the-trouble-with-cve-cash-for -muslim-groups/.

Muslim Public Affairs Council. 2014. "Safe Spaces Initiative: Tools for Developing Healthy Communities." Washington, D.C. https://www.mpac.org/ safespaces/files/MPAC-Safe-Spaces.pdf.

Muslim Public Affairs Council. 2017. "MPAC Responds to Revised List of DHS Grant Awardees." MPAC.org. Accessed April 15, 2019. https://www.mpac .org/blog/statements-press/mpac-responds-to-revised-list-of-dhs-grant -awardees.php.

Muslim Student Association-West. 2015. "Muslim Student Associations across

CA against Federal Government's Countering Violent Extremist Programs." Mailing list archive, February 21, 2015. https://us4.campaign-archive.com /?u=30d739eaae2442c8d20aad278&id=25a5c44b43&e=%5BUNIQID.

Naber, Nadine. 2006. "The Rules of Forced Engagement: Race, Gender, and the Culture of Fear among Arab Immigrants in San Francisco Post-9/11." *Cultural Dynamics* 18 (3): 235–67.

Naber, Nadine. 2008. "Introduction: Arab American and US Racial Formations." In *Race and Arab Americans before and after 9/11: From Invisible Citizens to Visible Subjects,* edited by Amaney Jamal and Nadine Naber, 1–45. Syracuse, N.Y.: Syracuse University Press.

Nader, Laura. 1972. "Up the Anthropologist: Perspectives Gained from Studying Up." In *Reinventing Anthropology,* edited by Dell H. Hymes, 284–311. New York: Random House.

Nader, Laura. 1997. "Controlling Processes: Tracing the Dynamic Components of Power." *Current Anthropology* 38 (5): 711–37.

Nagar, Richa, and Susan Geiger. 2007. "Reflexivity and Positionality in Feminist Fieldwork Revisited." In *Politics and Practice in Economic Geography,* edited by Adam Tickell, Jamie Sheppard, Jamie Peck, and Trevor Barnes, 267–78. London: Sage.

Nan, Madalina Elena. 2010. "New Humanitarianism with Old Problems: The Forgotten Lesson of Rwanda." *Journal of Humanitarian Assistance,* October 4, 2010. https://sites.tufts.edu/jha/archives/780.

Nashville International Center for Empowerment. 2016. "Proactive Engagement to Achieve Community Empowerment (PEACE)." Department of Homeland Security grant application. https://www.dhs.gov/sites/default/ files/publications/EMW-2016-CA-APP-00066 Full Application.pdf.

National Academies of Sciences, Engineering, and Medicine. 2017. *Countering Violent Extremism through Public Health Practice: Proceedings of a Workshop.* Washington, D.C.: National Academies Press.

National Consortium for the Study of Terrorism and Responses to Terrorism. 2017a. "Gang Members, Domestic Extremists Vastly Different, Says First Study to Compare the Two." START. June 9, 2017. http://start.umd.edu/ news/gang-members-domestic-extremists-vastly-different-says-first-study -compare-two.

National Consortium for the Study of Terrorism and Responses to Terrorism. 2017b. "Profiles of Individual Radicalization in the United States— PIRUS." START. http://www.start.umd.edu/profiles-individual-radical ization-united-states-pirus-keshif.

National Counterterrorism Center. 2014. "Countering Violent Extremism: A Guide for Practitioners and Analysts." Washington, DC. https://www .documentcloud.org/documents/1657824-cve-guide.html.

New York City Police Department. n.d. "Sports Venue Report." New York.

Nguyen, Mimi Thi. 2015. "The Hoodie as Sign, Screen, Expectation, and Force." *Signs: Journal of Women in Culture and Society* 40 (4): 791–816.

Nguyen, Nicole. 2013. "Scripting 'Safe' Schools: Mapping Urban Education and Zero Tolerance during the Long War." *Review of Education, Pedagogy, and Cultural Studies* 35 (4): 277–97. https://doi.org/10.1080/10714413.2013.8 19725.

Nguyen, Nicole. 2014. "Education as Warfare?: Mapping Securitised Education Interventions as War on Terror Strategy." *Geopolitics* 19 (1): 109–39. https://doi.org/10.1080/14650045.2013.789866.

Nguyen, Nicole. 2016. *A Curriculum of Fear: Homeland Security in US Public Schools.* Minneapolis: University of Minnesota Press.

Nixon, Robert. 2011. *Slow Violence and the Environmentalism of the Poor.* Cambridge, Mass.: Harvard University Press.

Nixon, Ron. 2017. "Students Are the Newest US Weapon against Terrorist Recruitment." *New York Times,* July 18, 2017. https://www.nytimes.com/2017/07/18/us/politics/students-are-the-newest-us-weapon-against-terrorist-recruitment.html.

Noguera, Pedro A. 2003. "Schools, Prisons, and Social Implications of Punishment: Rethinking Disciplinary Practices." *Theory into Practice* 42 (4): 341–51.

Nolan, Kathleen. 2011. *Police in the Hallways: Discipline in an Urban High School.* Minneapolis: University of Minnesota Press.

Nomani, Asra. 2017. "'This is for Allah': Preventing Islamic Extremism." https://www.hsgac.senate.gov/imo/media/doc/Testimony-Nomani-2017-06-14-REVISED.pdf.

Nordstrom, Carolyn. 2004. *Shadows of War: Violence, Power, and International Profiteering in the Twenty-First Century.* Berkeley: University of California Press.

Novelli, Mario. 2010a. "Education, Conflict, and Social (In)Justice: Insights from Colombia." *Educational Review* 62 (3): 271–85.

Novelli, Mario. 2010b. "The New Geopolitics of Educational Aid: From Cold Wars to Holy Wars?" *International Journal of Educational Development* 30 (5): 453–59. https://doi.org/10.1016/j.ijedudev.2010.03.012.

Nye, Joseph S., Jr. 2009. "Get Smart: Combining Hard and Soft Power." *Foreign Affairs* 88 (4): 160–63.

Obama, Barack. 2010. "Remarks at the Millennium Development Goals Summit in New York City." United Nations, September 22, 2010. https://obamawhitehouse.archives.gov/the-press-office/2010/09/22/remarks-president-millennium-development-goals-summit-new-york-new-york.

Obama, Barack. 2015a. "Our Fight against Violent Extremism." *LA Times,* February 17, 2015. http://www.latimes.com/nation/la-oe-obama-terrorism-conference-20150218-story.html.

Obama, Barack. 2015b. "Remarks at the Summit on Countering Violent Extremism." United Nations, September 29, 2015. https://obamawhitehouse.archives.gov/the-press-office/2015/09/29/remarks-president-obama-leaders-summit-countering-isil-and-violent.

Obama, Barack. 2015c. "State of the Union Address." United States Capi-
tol, January 20, 2015. https://obamawhitehouse.archives.gov/the-press
-office/2015/01/20/remarks-president-state-union-address-January-20
-2015.

Office of the Press Secretary. 2006. "Fact Sheet: Strategy for Victory in Iraq:
Clear, Hold, and Build." Washington, D.C. https://2001-2009.state.gov/p/
nea/rls/63423.htm.

Office of the Press Secretary. 2015. "Fact Sheet: The White House Summit on
Countering Violent Extremism." The White House, February 18, 2015.
https://www.whitehouse.gov/the-press-office/2015/02/18/fact-sheet
-white-house-summit-countering-violent-extremism.

O'Hara, Kieron. 2016. "The Limits of Redirection: The Problem with This
Google Plan to Divert Would-Be Jihadis Searching for ISIS Information Online." *Slate*, September 2016. http://www.slate.com/articles/technology/
future_tense/2016/09/the_problem_with_google_jigsaw_s_anti_
extremism_plan_redirect.html.

Omar, Manal. 2015. "The United States Will Never Win the Propaganda War
against the Islamic State." *Foreign Policy*, January 2015. http://foreignpolicy
.com/2015/01/09/the-united-states-will-never-win-the-propaganda-war
-against-the-islamic-state/.

paperson, la. 2017. *A Third University Is Possible*. Minneapolis: University of Minnesota Press.

Patel, Faiza. 2011. "Rethinking Radicalization." New York: Brennan Center
for Justice. https://www.brennancenter.org/sites/default/files/legacy/Re
thinkingRadicalization.pdf.

Patel, Faiza, and Meghan Koushik. 2017. "Countering Violent Extremism."
Brennan Center for Justice. https://www.brennancenter.org/sites/default/
files/publications/Brennan Center CVE Report.pdf.

Patel, Faiza, Andrew Lindsay, and Sophia DenUyl. 2018a. "Chart: Terrorism
Indicators." Brennan Center for Justice. https://www.brennancenter.org/
sites/default/files/CVE Chart Terrorism Indicators_final.pdf.

Patel, Faiza, Andrew Lindsay, and Sophia DenUyl. 2018b. "Countering Violent
Extremism in the Trump Era." Brennan Center for Justice. https://www
.brennancenter.org/analysis/countering-violent-extremism-trump-era.

Patel, Faiza, Andrew Lindsay, and Sophia DenUyl. 2018c. "Countering Violent Extremism Programs in the Trump Era." Brennan Center for Justice.
https://www.brennancenter.org/blog/countering-violent-extremism
-programs-trump-era.

Patel, Faiza, Andrew Lindsay, and Sophia DenUyl. 2018d. "CVE Lexicon." Brennan Center for Justice. https://www.brennancenter.org/sites/default/files/
CVE%20Chart%20Lexicon_final.pdf.

Patel, Faiza, and Amrit Singh. 2016. "The Human Rights Risks of Countering
Violent Extremism Programs." *Just Security*, April 7, 2016. https://www

.justsecurity.org/30459/human-rights-risks-countering-violent-extrem
ism-programs/.

Patterson, Orlando. 1985. *Slavery and Social Death: A Comparative Study*. Cambridge, Mass.: Harvard University Press.

Peck, Jamie, and Nik Theodore. 2012. "Follow the Policy: A Distended Case Approach." *Environment and Planning A* 44: 21–30.

Police Foundation. 2016. "Developing Resilience to Violent Extremism in the Boston Somali Community." Department of Homeland Security grant application. https://www.dhs.gov/sites/default/files/publications/EMW -2016-CA-APP-00112%20Full%20Application.pdf.

Prevent Watch. 2016. "The Cucumber Case." London. https://www.prevent watch.org/the-cucumber-case/.

Price, Michael. 2015. "Community Outreach or Intelligence Gathering? A Closer Look at 'Countering Violent Extremism' Programs." Brennan Center for Justice. https://www.brennancenter.org/sites/default/files/analysis/ Community_Outreach_or_Intelligence_Gathering.pdf.

Price, Rob. 2016. "When My School Received Prevent Counter-Terrorism Training, the Only Objectors Were White. That Says It All." *Independent,* March 29, 2016. http://www.independent.co.uk/voices/when-my-school -received-counter-terrorism-prevent-training-the-only-objectors-were -white-that-says-a6957916.html.

Puar, Jasbir K., and Amit S. Rai. 2002. "Monster, Terrorist, Fag: The War on Terrorism and the Production of Docile Patriots." *Social Text* 72 20 (3): 118–48.

Pupavac, Vanessa. 2001. "Therapeutic Governance: Psycho-Social Intervention and Trauma Risk Management." *Disasters* 25 (4): 358–72.

Pupavac, Vanessa. 2005. "Human Security and Rise of Global Therapeutic Governance." *Conflict, Security and Development* 5 (2): 161–81.

Pylypa, Jen. 1998. "Power and Bodily Practice: Applying the Work of Foucault to an Anthropology of the Body." *Arizona Anthropologist* 13: 21–36.

Pyrooz, David C., Gary LaFree, Scott H. Decker, and Patrick A. James. 2018. "Cut from the Same Cloth? A Comparative Study of Domestic Extremists and Gang Members in the United States." *Justice Quarterly* 35 (1): 1–32.

Quinn, Ben. 2016. "Nursery 'Raised Fears of Radicalisation over Boy's Cucumber Drawing.'" *Guardian,* March 11, 2016. https://www.theguardian .com/uk-news/2016/mar/11/nursery-radicalisation-fears-boys-cucumber -drawing-cooker-bomb.

Rabasa, Angel, Cheryl Benard, Lowell H. Schwartz, and Peter Sickle. 2007. "Building Moderate Muslim Networks." Rand Center for Middle East Public Policy. http://www.rand.org/content/dam/rand/pubs/monographs/2007/ RAND_MG574.pdf.

Rana, Junaid. 2011. *Terrifying Muslims: Race and Labor in the South Asian Diaspora*. Durham, N.C.: Duke University Press.

Razack, Sherene H. 2008. *Casting Out: The Eviction of Muslims from Western Law and Politics*. Toronto: University of Toronto Press.

Rehberg, Katherine. 2014. "Revisiting Therapeutic Governance: The Politics of Mental Health and Psychosocial Programmes in Humanitarian Settings." Refugee Studies Centre, working paper series no. 98. https://www.rsc.ox.ac .uk/files/files-1/wp98-revisiting-therapeutic-governance-2014.pdf.

Reinhold, Susan. 1994. "Local Conflict and Ideological Struggle: Positive Images and Section 28." PhD diss., University of Sussex, Falmer, U.K.

Reyes, Augustina H. 2006. *Discipline, Achievement, Race: Is Zero Tolerance the Answer?* Lanham, Md.: Rowman and Littlefield Education.

Ritchie, Andrea J. 2017. *Invisible No More: Police Violence against Black Women and Women of Color.* Boston, Mass.: Beacon Press.

Rochester Institute of Technology. 2016. "It's Time to #ExOut through Education." Department of Homeland Security grant application. https://www .dhs.gov/sites/default/files/publications/EMW-2016-CA-APP-00246 Full Application.pdf.

Rose, Gillian. 1997. "Situating Knowledge: Positionality, Reflexivities and Other Tactics." *Progress in Human Geography* 21 (3): 305–20. https://doi .org/10.1191/030913297673302122.

Rubenstein, Richard L. 1978. *The Cunning of History: The Holocaust and the American Future.* New York: Torchbooks.

Rumsfeld, Donald H. 2006. "Remarks by Secretary Rumsfeld at the Landon Lecture at Kansas State University, Manhattan, Kan." U.S. Department of Defense, November 9, 2006. http://archive.defense.gov/Transcripts/ Transcript.aspx?TranscriptID=3781.

Ruppenthal, Alex. 2017. "Illinois Agency Awarded Controversial Counter-Extremism Grant." *Chicago Tonight,* May 23, 2017. http://chicagotonight .wttw.com/2017/05/23/illinois-agency-awarded-controversial-counter -extremism-grant.

Ryan, Evan. 2016. "Challenge Extremism Together." *Huffington Post,* March 1, 2016. http://www.huffingtonpost.com/evan-ryan/challengeextremism -togeth_b_9357156.html.

Sageman, Marc. 2008. *Leaderless Jihad: Terror Networks in the Twenty-First Century.* Philadelphia: University of Pennsylvania Press.

Sageman, Marc. 2014. "The Stagnation in Terrorism Research." *Terrorism and Political Violence* 26 (4): 565–80.

Sageman, Marc. 2015. "Declaration of Marc Sageman in Opposition to Defendants' Cross-Motion for Summary Judgment, Latif v. U.S. Department of Justice et al., No. 3:10-cv-00750-BR." Filed August 7, 2015. https://www .aclu.org/sites/default/files/field_document/268._declaration_of_marc_ sageman_8.7.15.pdf.

Sageman, Marc. 2016. *Misunderstanding Terrorism.* Philadelphia: University of Pennsylvania Press.

Said, Edward. 1997. *Covering Islam: How the Media and the Experts Determine How We See the Rest of the World.* New York: Vintage Books.

Saint Paul Police Department. 2009. "Project Abstract: African Immigrant

Muslim Coordinated Outreach Program." Recovery Act grant application. Saint Paul, Minn. https://www.brennancenter.org/sites/default/files/analysis/FN%20120%20%28Saint%20Paul%20Police%20Dep%27t,%20Program%20Narrative--African%20Immigrant%20Muslim%20Coordinated%20Outreach%20Program%29.pdf.

Saint Paul Police Department. 2015. "Project Application." State Homeland Security Grant Program application. Saint Paul, Minn.

Salaita, Steven. 2006. *Anti-Arab Racism in the USA: Where It Comes from and What It Means for Politics Today*. Ann Arbor, Mich.: Pluto Press.

Salter, Mark. 2008. "Risk and Imagination in the War on Terror." In *Risk and the War on Terror*, edited by Louise Amoore and Marieke de Goede, 233–46. Abingdon, U.K.: Routledge.

Scales, Robert. 2004. "Army Transformation: Implications for the Future." Washington, D.C. http://www.au.af.mil/au/awc/awcgate/congress/04-07-15scales.pdf.

Schanzer, David H. 2012. "The Way Forward on Combating Al-Qa'ida-Inspired Violent Extremism in the United States: Suggestions for the next Administration." Institute for Social Policy and Understanding, Duke Islamic Studies Center, ISLAMiCommentary, and the Triangle Center on Terrorism and Homeland Security.

Schirch, Lisa. 2015. "Policy Brief: Theories of Change on Counterterrorism, Counterinsurgency, and Preventing Violent Extremism." Washington, D.C.: Alliance for Peacebuilding.

Schirch, Lisa, ed. 2016. *Handbook on Human Security: A Civil-Military-Police Curriculum*. The Hague, Netherlands: Alliance for Peacebuilding, GPPAC, Kroc Institute.

Schmitt, Eric. 2013. "A US Reply, in English, to Terrorists' Online Lure." *New York Times*, December 4, 2013. http://www.nytimes.com/2013/12/05/world/middleeast/us-aims-to-blunt-terrorist-recruiting-of-english-speakers.html.

Schmitt, Eric, and Thom Shanker. 2005. "US Officials Retool Slogan for Terror War." *New York Times*, July 26, 2005. http://www.nytimes.com/2005/07/26/politics/us-officials-retool-slogan-for-terror-war.html.

Scott, James C. 1998. *Seeing like a State: How Certain Schemes to Improve the Human Condition Have Failed*. New Haven, Conn.: Yale University Press.

Select Committee to Study Governmental Operations with Respect to Intelligence Activities. 1976. "Final Report." Washington, D.C.

Selk, Avi. 2015. "Ahmed Mohamed Swept up, 'Hoax Bomb' Charges Swept Away as Irving Teen's Story Floods Social Media." *Dallas News*, September 15, 2015. http://www.dallasnews.com/news/dallas-county/2015/09/15/ahmed-mohamed-swept-up-hoax-bomb-charges-swept-away-as-irving-teen-s-story-floods-social-media.

Sewall, Sarah. 2007. "Introduction to the University of Chicago Press Edition:

A Radical Field Manual." In *The US Army/Marine Corps Counterinsurgency Manual,* xxi–xliii. Chicago: University of Chicago Press.

Shah, Naureen. 2014a. "The FBI's Counterterrorism Sting Operations Are Counterproductive." *Al Jazeera America,* July 21, 2014. http://america .aljazeera.com/opinions/2014/7/fbi-sting-operationscounterterrorismade ldaoud.html.

Shah, Naureen. 2014b. "Terrorist or . . . Teenager?" *Slate,* November 12, 2014. http://www.slate.com/articles/news_and_politics/politics/2014/11/ justice_department_s_countering_violent_extremism_program_ripe_ for_abuse.html.

Shane, Scott. 2015. "Homegrown Extremists Tied to Deadlier Toll than Jihadists in U.S. since 9/11." *New York Times,* June 24, 2015. http://www.nytimes .com/2015/06/25/us/tally-of-attacks-in-us-challenges-perceptions-of-top -terror-threat.html?_r=0.

Shaw, Devin Zane, and Veldon Coburn. 2017. "The Colonial Politics of Recognition in Trudeau's Relationship with Indigenous Nations." *E-International Relations,* September 7, 2017. http://www.e-ir.info/2017/09/07/the-colonial -politics-of-recognition-in-trudeaus-relationship-with-indigenous-nations/.

Shore, Cris, and Susan Wright. 1997. "Policy: A New Field of Anthropology." In *Anthropology of Policy: Critical Perspectives on Governance and Power,* edited by Cris Shore and Susan Wright, 3–30. London: Routledge.

Shryock, Andrew. 2008. "The Moral Analogies of Race: Arab American Identity, Color Politics, and the Limits of Racialized Citizenship." In *Race and Arab Americans before and after 9/11: From Invisible Citizens to Visible Subjects,* edited by Amaney Jamal and Nadine Naber, 81–113. Syracuse, N.Y.: Syracuse University Press.

Sian, Katy Pal. 2012. "Gurdwaras, Guns, and Grudges in 'Post-Racial' America." *Sikh Formations* 8 (3): 293–97.

Silber, Mitchell D. 2009. "Statement of Clarification." In *Radicalization in the West: The Homegrown Threat,* 11–12. New York: New York City Police Department.

Silber, Mitchell D., and Arvin Bhatt. 2007. "Radicalization in the West: The Homegrown Threat." New York: New York City Police Department. https:// www.brennancenter.org/sites/default/files/legacy/Justice/20070816 .NYPD.Radicalization.in.the.West.pdf.

Silva, Kumarini. 2016. *Brown Threat: Identification in the Security State.* Minneapolis: University of Minnesota Press.

Silver, James, Andre Simons, and Sarah Craun. 2018. "A Study of the Pre-attack Behaviors of Active Shooters in the United States between 2002 and 2013." Washington, D.C.: Federal Bureau of Investigation, U.S. Department of Justice. https://www.fbi.gov/file-repository/pre-attack-behaviors-of-active -shooters-in-us-2000-2013.pdf.

Simpson, Leanne Betasamosake. 2011. *Dancing on Our Turtle's Back: Stories of*

Nishnaabeg Re-creation, Resurgence, and a New Emergence. Winnipeg, Canada: Arbeiter Ring Publishing.

Slutkin, Gary. 2016. "Voice of an Infectious Disease Control Specialist." Center for Strategic and International Studies, *On Violent Extremism* (podcast). http://podbay.fm/show/1117542794/e/1469720700?autostart=1.

Slutzker, Jillian. 2016. "Applying Lessons from Gang Violence to Preventing Extremism Explained at Conference." Creative Associates International, October 6, 2016. https://www.creativeassociatesinternational.com/news/applying-lessons-from-gang-violence-to-preventing-extremism-explained-at-conference/.

Sobe, Noah W. 2007. "An Historical Perspective on Coordinating Education Post-Conflict: Biopolitics, Governing at a Distance, and States of Exception." *Current Issues in Comparative Education* 9 (2): 45–54.

Sojoyner, Damien M. 2016. *First Strike: Educational Enclosures in Black Los Angeles.* Minneapolis: University of Minnesota Press.

Southorn, Debbie. 2017. "We Can't Fight Trump-Style Hate with the Surveillance State." *In These Times*, September 19, 2017. http://inthesetimes.com/article/20531/CVE-surveillance-donald-trump-life-after-hate-islamophobia.

Spencer, Alexander. 2006. "Questioning the Concept of 'New Terrorism.'" *Peace, Conflict and Development* 8: 1–33.

Springer, Simon. 2012. "Neoliberalizing Violence: Of the Exceptional and the Exemplary in Coalescing Moments." *Area* 44 (2): 136–43.

Stampnitzky, Lisa. 2013. *Disciplining Terror: How Experts Invented "Terrorism."* Cambridge: Cambridge University Press.

"Statement: AMEMSA Groups Oppose Expansion of the Countering Violent Extremism Program." 2017. Muslim Justice League. https://www.muslimjusticeleague.org/wp-content/uploads/2017/09/Statement-AMEMSA-Groups-Oppose-Expansion-of-the-Countering-Violent-Extremism-Program.pdf.

Stolcke, Verna. 1995. "Talking Culture: New Boundaries, New Rhetorics of Exclusion in Europe." *Cultural Anthropology* 36 (1): 1–24.

Stoler, Ann Laura. 2016. *Duress: Imperial Durabilities in Our Times.* Durham, N.C.: Duke University Press.

Sturken, Marita. 2002. "Memorializing Absence." In *Understanding September 11,* edited by Craig Calhoun, Paul Price, and Ashley Timmer, 374–85. New York: New Press.

Taylor, Diane. 2015. "Schools Monitoring Pupils' Web Use with 'Anti-radicalization Software.'" *Guardian,* June 10, 2015. https://www.theguardian.com/uk-news/2015/jun/10/schools-trial-anti-radicalisation-software-pupils-internet.

Taylor, Keeanga-Yamahtta. 2016. *From #BlackLivesMatter to Black Liberation.* Chicago: Haymarket Books.

Telhami, Shibley. 2015. "What Americans Really Think about Muslims and

Islam." Brookings Institution, *Markaz* (blog), December 6, 2015. https://www.brookings.edu/blog/markaz/2015/12/09/what-americans-really-think-about-muslims-and-islam/.

Tett, Gillian. 2009. *Fool's Gold: The Inside Story of J. P. Morgan and How Wall St. Greed Corrupted Its Bold Dream and Created a Financial Catastrophe.* New York: Free Press.

Tharoor, Kanishk. 2013. "NYPD Youth Cricket League Marred by Spying Scandal." *Al Jazeera America,* October 4, 2013. http://america.aljazeera.com/articles/2013/10/4/nypda-s-youth-cricketleaguemarredbyspyingscandal.html.

Theoharis, Athan G., ed. 2000. *The FBI: A Comprehensive Reference Guide from J. Edgar Hoover to the X-Files.* New York: Checkmark Books.

Thomas, Paul. 2010. "Failed and Friendless: The UK's 'Preventing Violent Extremism' Programme." *British Journal of Politics and International Relations* 12 (3): 442–58.

Thrasher, Steven W. 2015. "The Nine People Killed in Charleston Are Victims of America's Racist Present." *Guardian,* June 18, 2015. https://www.theguardian.com/commentisfree/2015/jun/18/people-killed-charleston-america-racist-present.

Truelsen, Mike. 2016. "Parents of Tucson Terrorism Suspect Mahin Khan Release Statement." *News4Tucson,* August 4, 2016. http://www.kvoa.com/story/32501286/parents-of-tucson-terrorism-suspect-mahin-khan-release-statement-ask-for-understanding.

Trump, Donald J. 2017. "Remarks by President Trump in Joint Address of Congress." The White House, February 28, 2017. https://www.whitehouse.gov/briefings-statements/remarks-president-trump-joint-address-congress/.

Tuck, Eve. 2009. "Suspending Damage: A Letter to Communities." *Harvard Educational Review* 79 (3): 409–28.

U.K. Department for Communities and Local Government. 2007. "Preventing Violent Extremism: Winning Hearts and Minds." London. https://webarchive.nationalarchives.gov.uk/20070701080545/http://www.communities.gov.uk/embedded_object.asp?id=1509401.

U.K.'s Joint Intelligence Committee. 2003. "International Terrorism: War with Iraq." London. https://webarchive.nationalarchives.gov.uk/20171123123130/http://www.iraqinquiry.org.uk/media/230918/2003-02-10-jic-assessment-international-terrorism-war-with-iraq.pdf.

UNESCO. 2016. "Teacher's Guide on the Prevention of Violent Extremism." Paris, France. https://unesdoc.unesco.org/ark:/48223/pf0000244676.

United States Attorney's Office of Minneapolis. 2015. "Building Community Resilience: Minneapolis-St. Paul Pilot Program: A Community-Led Local Framework." United States Department of Justice. https://www.justice.gov/usao-mn/file/642121/download.

United States Institute of Peace. 2014. "Inclusive Approaches to Community Policing and CVE." Special Report 352, September 2014. https://www

.usip.org/sites/default/files/SR352_Inclusive-Approaches-to-Community-Policing-and-CVE.pdf.

U.S. Army. 2013. "Welcome to the Human Terrain System." Accessed August 16, 2016. http://humanterrainsystem.army.mil/.

U.S. Army/Marine Corps. 2007. *Field Manual 3–24: Counterinsurgency.* Chicago: University of Chicago Press.

U.S.-Muslim Engagement Project. 2008. "Changing Course: A New Direction for U.S. Relations with the Muslim World." Report of the Leadership Group on U.S.-Muslim Engagement. http://pa.cair.com/files/Changing_Course.pdf.

Varadarajan, Tunku. 2009. "Going Muslim." *Forbes,* November 2009. https://www.forbes.com/2009/11/08/fort-hood-nidal-malik-hasan-muslims-opinions-columnists-tunku-varadarajan.html.

Vaught, Sabina E. 2017. *Compulsory: Education and the Dispossession of Youth in a Prison School.* Minneapolis: University of Minnesota Press.

Verdugo, Richard R. 2002. "Race-Ethnicity, Social Class, and Zero-Tolerance Policies: The Cultural and Structural Wars." *Education and Urban Society* 35 (1): 50–75. https://doi.org/10.1177/001312402237214.

Vine, David. 2011. *Island of Shame: The Secret History of the US Military Base on Diego Garcia.* Princeton, N.J.: Princeton University Press.

Volpp, Leti. 2002. "The Citizen and the Terrorist." *UCLA Law Review* 49: 1575–1600.

Wallace, Randy. 2017. "Muslim Special Needs Student's Father Says Teacher Called Police on Boy." *Fox26Houston,* November 30, 2017. http://www.fox26houston.com/news/muslim-special-needs-students-father-says-teacher-called-police-on-boy.

Webster, Katharine. 2017. "Students Create Winning Counterterrorism Website." UMass-Lowell. February 16, 2017. https://www.uml.edu/News/stories/2017/P2PWinners.aspx.

Wedel, Janine R., Cris Shore, Gregory Feldman, and Stacy Lathrop. 2005. "Toward an Anthropology of Public Policy." *American Academy of Political and Social Science* 600: 30–51.

Weine, Stevan. 2012. "Family and Community Capacities among US Minorities: A Key to Preventing Violent Extremism." START. http://www.start.umd.edu/research-projects/family-and-community-capacities-among-us-minorities-key-preventing-violent.

Weine, Stevan. 2017. "Giving CVE a Chance." *Just Security,* July 5, 2017. https://www.justsecurity.org/42823/giving-cve-chance/#more-42823.

Weine, Stevan, and Osman Ahmed. 2012. "Building Resilience to Violent Extremism among Somali-Americans in Minneapolis-St. Paul." START, August 2012. https://www.start.umd.edu/sites/default/files/files/publications/Weine_BuildingResiliencetoViolentExtremism_SomaliAmericans.pdf.

Weine, Stevan, and David Eisenman. 2016. "How Public Health Can Improve

Initiatives to Counter Violent Extremism." START, April 5, 2016. http://www.start.umd.edu/news/how-public-health-can-improve-initiatives-counter-violent-extremism.

Weine, Stevan, David P. Eisenman, La Tina Jackson, Janni Kinsler, and Chloe Polutnik. 2017. "Utilizing Mental Health Professionals to Help Prevent the Next Attacks." *International Review of Psychiatry* 29 (4): 334–40.

Weine, Stevan, David P. Eisenman, Janni Kinsler, Deborah C. Glik, and Chloe Polutnik. 2017. "Addressing Violent Extremism as Public Health Policy and Practice." *Behavioral Sciences of Terrorism and Political Aggression* 9 (3): 208–21.

Weine, Stevan, Ahmed Younis, and Chloe Polutnik. 2017. "Community Policing to Counter Violent Extremism: A Process Evaluation in Los Angeles." START, July 2017. https://www.start.umd.edu/pubs/START_CSTAB_CommunityPolicingtoCounterViolentExtremism_July2017.pdf.

Weizman, Eyal. 2011. *The Least of All Possible Evils: Humanitarian Violence from Arendt to Gaza*. London: Verso Press.

White House. 2011. "Empowering Local Partners to Prevent Violent Extremism in the United States." Department of Homeland Security, August 2011. https://www.dhs.gov/sites/default/files/publications/empowering_local_partners.pdf.

White House. 2016. "Strategic Implementation Plan for Empowering Local Partners to Prevent Violent Extremism in the United States." Brennan Center for Justice, October 2016. https://www.brennancenter.org/sites/default/files/2016_strategic_implementation_plan_empowering_local_partners_prev%20(2).pdf.

Wiktorowicz, Quintan. 2005. *Radical Islam Rising: Muslim Extremism in the West*. Lanham, Md.: Rowman and Littlefield Publishers.

Williams, Kristian. 2004. *Our Enemies in Blue: Police and Power in America*. New York: Soft Skull Press.

Williams, Michael J., John G. Horgan, and William P. Evans. 2016. "Evaluation of a Multi-faceted, U.S. Community-Based, Muslim-Led CVE Program." National Criminal Justice Reference Service, June 2016. https://www.ncjrs.gov/App/Publications/abstract.aspx?ID=272096.

Wilson, James Q., and George L. Kelling. 1989. "Making Neighborhoods Safe." *Atlantic*, February 1989. https://www.theatlantic.com/past/docs/politics/crime/safehood.htm.

Winter, Jana, and Sharon Weinberger. 2017. "The FBI's New U.S. Terrorist Threat: 'Black Identity Extremists.'" *Foreign Policy*, October 6, 2017. http://foreignpolicy.com/2017/10/06/the-fbi-has-identified-a-new-domestic-terrorist-threat-and-its-black-identity-extremists/.

Winton, Richard, Teresa Watanable, and Greg Krikorian. 2007. "LAPD Defends Muslim Mapping Effort." *LA Times*, November 10, 2007. http://www.latimes.com/local/la-me-lapd10nov10-story.html.

Wise, Tim. 2001. "School Shootings and White Denial." *AlterNet*, March 5,

2001. http://www.alternet.org/story/10560/school_shootings_and_white _denial.

Wittes, Benjamin. 2018. "The Justice Department Finds 'No Responsive Records' to Support a Trump Speech." *Lawfare* (blog), July 31, 2018. https:// www.lawfareblog.com/justice-department-finds-no-responsive-records -support-trump-speech.

Wooffitt, Robin. 2005. *Conversation Analysis and Discourse Analysis: A Comparative and Critical Introduction.* London: Sage.

World Organization for Resource Development and Education. 2014. "COPS Application." Office of Community Oriented Policing grant application. Montgomery Village, MD.

World Organization for Resource Development and Education. 2016. "Developing a Community-Led Approach to Countering Violent Extremism (CVE): An Instructor's Manual." Montgomery Village, MD. WORDE. org. Accessed September 15, 2016. http://www.worde.org/wp-content/ uploads/2016/08/WORDE-Developing-a-Community-Led-Approach-to -CVE.pdf.

World Organization for Resource Development and Education. 2017a. "Global Citizen's Forum (GCF)." 2017. WORDE.org Accessed March 5, 2018. http://www.worde.org/programs/global-citizens-forum-gcf/.

World Organization for Resource Development and Education. 2017b. "The Montgomery County BRAVE Model." 2017. WORDE.org. Accessed March 5, 2018. http://www.worde.org/programs/the-montgomery-county -model/.

Zaloom, Caitlin. 2006. *Out of the Pits: Traders and Technology from Chicago to London.* Chicago: University of Chicago Press.

Zirin, Dave. 2013. "Not a Game: How the NYPD Uses Sports for Surveillance." *Nation,* September 10, 2013. https://www.thenation.com/article/ not-game-how-nypd-uses-sports-surveillance/.

INDEX

AAAN. *See* Arab American Action Network

Adams, Elliott, 35, 50

Afeef, Junaid, 86, 130–31, 132, 181, 250; CVE and, 238; TVPP and, 85

African Immigrant Muslim Coordinated Outreach Program (AIMCOP), 234, 235, 236

afterschool programs, 171, 209, 228

Ahmad, Fatema, 152

Ahmed, Mohammed (Average Mo), 265n7; videos by, 183, 184, 185, 185 (fig.)

Ahmed, Munira: portrait of, 127 (fig.)

Ahmed, Yasir, 142, 177, 178, 180

Aiello, Brittnie, 40

AIMCOP. *See* African Immigrant Muslim Coordinated Outreach Program

Al-Arian, Abdullah, 163

Ali, Ayaan Hirsi, 149, 152

Ali, Bassem, 86, 108, 151–52, 164

al-Qaeda, 56, 61, 93, 106, 147, 148

Al-Shabaab, 148, 234, 237, 241

anti-knowledge, politics of, 26, 27

antiterrorism, 34, 70, 72, 83, 112, 168, 169, 177, 201, 223, 250, 251; agenda, 32, 91, 175, 197; domestic, 84, 231, 249; government-led,

182; law enforcement–centric, 59; programs, 6, 7, 32, 77, 90, 100; theory of change, 89–90

Arab American Action Network (AAAN), 238, 239

assassinations, targeted, 61–68, 70, 71, 72, 90, 121

assimilation, 126, 151, 182, 183, 195, 196, 219, 245, 248, 251

astroturfing, 155–64, 174

at-risk youth, 203, 211, 218, 220

Aurora Movie Theater, 262n15

Average Mo. *See* Ahmed, Mohammed

Ayloush, Hussam, 126, 127, 223–24

Aziz, Sahar, 10

Bailey, Susan, 129, 168

Baker, Adrian, 48, 50, 82, 100, 135, 147, 165–66, 172, 179, 218; CVE and, 17, 134, 176, 264n5; methodological concerns and, 99; on Trump, 175–76

Ban Ki-Moon, 6

Beck, Ulrich, 191

Becker, Sarah, 40

behavior, 35, 101, 102, 211, 214, 220; changes in, 212, 216; criminal, 113; deviant, 108, 123, 213; law enforcement and, 172; non-criminal, 117, 118; pre-criminal, 114–19; profiles and, 212, 218;

generational threats, 31, 190, 197, 221, 231
geopolitics, 56, 75, 123, 126, 190, 195, 231, 233, 262
Glickman, Daniel, 59, 147, 167, 221
Global Citizen Forum, 193
Global Citizenship Education (GCED), 192
Global Peace Foundation, 116
global struggle against violent extremism (G-SAVE), 60
Goffman, Erving, 44–45
"going Muslim" thesis, 151–52, 154
Goodwill Industries, 116
governance, 226, 227; colonial system of, 183; global, 191; programs, 82, 145
Greene, David, 87, 155, 166, 220; civil liberties and, 142; community resources and, 221; on criminal justice system, 141; CVE and, 142, 146, 165, 232–33; national security workers and, 141; profiling and, 142; Somali community and, 42, 143; storytelling by, 88
Greenwald, Glenn, 19, 65
Grossman, David, 120; police training module of, 120 (fig.)
Gusterson, Hugh, 46, 47
gut instincts, 209–10, 217

Hadley, Steven, 60
Hampton, Fred, 66
Harris, Eric, 262n12
Hasan, Nidal, 150–51
Hassan, Hodan, 34, 88, 89, 182, 239
Hawari, Mustafa, 240
Hennepin County Sheriff's Office, 112, 115, 116
hijabs, 18, 35, 126, 218
history: cultural, 16, 30, 216; political, 16, 217; social, 6, 16, 217
Hitchens, Christopher, 109
Hofstad Group, 95

Holmes, James, 262n12
homeland security, 2, 12, 248
Homeland Security Academic Advisory Council (HSAAC) (DHS), 147, 148, 158, 265n4
Homeland Security Act (2002), 128
Homeland Security Civil Rights and Civil Liberties Protection Act (2004), 128
Hoover, J. Edgar, 66
House Bill 2344 (2013) (Virginia), 211
Howard, Teddy, 112
HSAAC. See Homeland Security Academic Advisory Council
Hughes, Sarah, 204, 205, 206
humanitarian aid, 229; securitization of, 73–77, 190, 233
humanitarianism, 72, 75, 76–77, 233, 239
human rights, 76, 129, 141, 145
Huntington, Samuel P., 70
Hussein, Saddam, 109
hyperincarceration, 15, 154

ICE. See Immigration and Customs Enforcement
ICJIA. See Illinois Criminal Justice Information Authority
identity, 55, 56, 122, 196, 232; cultural, 10; ethnic, 93; global, 192; groups, 215; integrated, 192; national, 191, 194; racial, 54, 245; religious, 54, 93, 245; social, 51; transnational, 184–85; traumatized, 242
ideology, 106, 147, 150, 201, 203; colonial, 195; cultural, 40; extremist, 1, 2, 99, 111, 144, 153, 192; jihadi-Salafi, 96; radical, 1, 69; Salafi, 96, 97; terrorist, 103
Illinois Criminal Justice Information Authority (ICJIA), 82, 101, 122, 137, 139; TVPP and, 264n5
Illinois Department of Human Ser-

NICOLE NGUYEN is associate professor of social foundations of education at the University of Illinois–Chicago. She is author of *A Curriculum of Fear: Homeland Security in U.S. Public Schools* (Minnesota, 2016).